The
Simon and Schuster
SHORT
PROSE
READER

Second Edition

ROBERT FUNK
Eastern Illinois University

SUSAN X DAY
Iowa State University

ELIZABETH McMAHAN
Illinois State University

D0222089

Prentice Hall, Upper Saddle River, New Jersey 07458

Library of Congress Cataloging-in-Publication Data

The Simon & Schuster short prose reader / [compiled by] Robert Funk,
  Susan X Day, Elizabeth McMahan.—2nd ed.
     p.   cm.
  Includes index.
  ISBN 0-13-095995-2
  1. College readers. 2. English language—Rhetoric—Problems,
exercises, etc.   I. Funk, Robert.   II. Day, Susan.   III. McMahan,
Elizabeth.   IV. Title: Simon and Schuster short prose reader.
V. Title: Short prose reader.
PE1417.S453 2000
808'.0427—dc21   99-13465
                                                  CIP

Editor-in-Chief: Charlyce Jones Owen
Acquisition Editor: Maggie Barbieri
Editorial Assistant: Joan Polk
AVP, Director of Production and Manufacturing: Barbara Kittle
Senior Managing Editor: Bonnie Biller
Production Liaison: Fran Russello
Project Manager: Linda B. Pawelchak
Manufacturing Manager: Nick Sklitsis
Prepress and Manufacturing Buyer: Mary Ann Gloriande
Cover Director: Jayne Conte
Cover Design: Bruce Kenselaar
Marketing Manager: Sue Brekka
Copy Editing: Nancy Menges
Proofreading: Maine Proofreading Services

This book was set in 11/13 Bembo by Lori Clinton
and was printed and bound by Courier Companies, Inc.
The cover was printed by Phoenix Color Corp.

Credits appear on pages 351–354, which constitute a continuation
of this copyright page.

Printed in the United States of America
10 9 8 7 6 5 4 3 2

ISBN 0-13-095995-2

Prentice-Hall International (UK) Limited, *London*
Prentice-Hall of Australia Pty. Limited, *Sydney*
Prentice-Hall Canada Inc., *Toronto*
Prentice-Hall Hispanoamericana, S.A., *Mexico*
Prentice-Hall of India Private Limited, *New Delhi*
Prentice-Hall of Japan, Inc., *Tokyo*
Pearson Education Asia Pte. Ltd., *Singapore*
Editora Prentice-Hall do Brasil, Ltda., *Rio de Janeiro*

To our friend and editor

Maggie Barbieri

*for her expert guidance
and enthusiastic support*

CONTENTS

"I did my best to avoid showing pleasure, but what I was feeling was pure ecstasy at this startling demonstration that my words had the power to make people laugh."

"The wind got louder, then the windows blew out, and we realized we were in trouble when the heat stove went around the corner and out a wall that had just come down."

"When Robinson stepped into the batter's box, it was as if someone had flicked a switch. The place went silent."

"Getting no worse than garbage thrown at you is the prison equivalent of everything going smoothly."

"Every time a child was due, she would demand, *More space, more space.*"

"My sister and Scott had been dating a couple of years, despite the disapproval of my family."

THEMATIC CONTENTS

GENDER

HUMAN BEHAVIOR

SOCIAL ISSUES

EDITING SKILLS CONTENTS

PREFACE

Good readers are usually good writers, and good writers are always good readers. Researchers tell us that reading and writing are complementary processes that involve the use of language to create meaning. This text is designed to reinforce this relationship and to encourage reading by students who want to improve their writing. The selections are short and lively, not too difficult but rich enough to provide ideas for thought and discussion. The instructional apparatus accompanying each reading has two main goals:

1. to encourage students to use writing as a means of exploring the readings, and
2. to point out strategies used in the essays that students can employ in their own compositions.

The Simon & Schuster Short Prose Reader is a flexible resource. The numerous readings and activities and writing topics give instructors the freedom to select from a broad range of assignments and approaches.

THE READING SELECTIONS

The readings are brief, accessible, and easy to teach. They cover a wide range of topics and viewpoints to involve students with ideas and issues that relate to their own experience. A special effort has been made to appeal to a cross-section of students by including a number of works by women and writers from various cultures. Many of the selections are standard pieces that have been used successfully in writing classes; the rest are new readings that have never been anthologized before. We also include several examples of humorous writing by such well-known authors as Dave Barry, Russell Baker, Garrison Keillor, and Suzanne Britt.

The readings are grouped according to their major pattern of organization. These patterns are presented as strategies for approaching a given writing task—as organizational guides frequently used in combination and always subject to variation and revision. The introduction to each strategy explains the point, the principles, and the pitfalls of using this particular pattern for shaping and developing an essay. The "Further Readings" (Chapter 11) provide additional examples of essays that combine strategies in a variety of ways.

For the second edition, we have updated the readings by replacing ten selections with new essays that we think are more relevant and engaging. These additions include a cluster of three articles about the controversial issue of cloning. We have also added eight student essays to this edition, each one illustrating a different writing strategy. Students will be able to see how writers at their own level use the patterns presented in this book. The student samples can also be used for discussion of various writing strategies and for practice in peer editing and revision.

INSTRUCTIONAL FEATURES

Two *introductory chapters* present a concise explanation of the interrelated processes of reading and writing. Chapter 1 gives specific directions for learning how to become active readers, including a sample reading that has been annotated by an active reader. Chapter 2 describes the process of writing in response to reading. This second chapter also includes a sample student essay (with commentary by the writer) and a brief reading to respond to and write about.

The *pre-reading apparatus* includes three instructional aids. First, a brief thinking/writing activity ("Preparing to Read") gets students ready to read by evoking their own thoughts and feelings on the subject of the reading. Then, a short biographical headnote provides background, and finally, a list of "Terms to Recognize" defines in context potentially unfamiliar words that the students will encounter in the selection.

The *post-reading apparatus* includes a selection of activities that instructors can assign, as needed, to help students increase their skills in reading and writing:

1. *Responding to Reading*—a journal writing assignment that asks students to record their reactions to an issue or idea in the selection they have just read. This brief expressive-writing activity promotes fluency and may be used as the basis for the essay assignments that follow.

2. *Gaining Word Power*—an exercise that draws words from the reading and helps students add them to their active vocabulary. These exercises employ a variety of creative strategies for enabling students to develop verbal proficiency.

3. *Considering Content*—a series of questions that assist students in becoming focused, attentive readers. Answering these questions assures basic comprehension.

4. *Considering Method*—several questions that help students to identify successful strategies in the reading and to examine rhetorical choices that the author made.

5. *Writing Step by Step*—a sequence of specific directions that guide students in writing a short essay imitating the reading's structure and purpose. This directed writing can be used to provide inexperienced writers with a successful composing experience.

6. *Other Writing Ideas*—two or three additional writing assignments that relate to the rhetorical mode or subject matter of the reading. These assignments include a mixture of personal and academic topics, giving the students several options for writing. At least one of the assignments calls for collaborative learning or investigation.

7. *Editing Skills*—an exercise that helps students to check and improve the essay they have just written. Each editing section focuses on a different skill, one that pertains to some grammatical, mechanical, or rhetorical feature of the reading selection. These skills are frequently omitted from textbooks that focus on reading.

This extensive apparatus gives teachers and students a wide variety of choices for exploring the reading-writing connection.

OTHER FEATURES

To help instructors who want to correlate reading assignments or who prefer to organize their courses according to issue-centered units, the *alternative table of contents* groups the reading selections according to several common themes. The text also includes a *glossary* of useful rhetorical terms and an *editing skills table of contents*.

ACKNOWLEDGMENTS

We want to extend warm thanks to the many people who have helped us in producing this book, especially our editors and the editorial and production staff at Prentice Hall: Maggie Barbieri, Joan Polk, and Linda Pawelchak. We are also grateful for the excellent ideas and suggestions provided by our reviewers: Margo L. Eden-Camann, DeKalb College; Vicki Holmsten, San Juan College; Marjorie A. Oliver, Wayne Community College; Lillian Polak, Nassau Community College; William J. Scarpaci, Rock Valley College; and Barbara L. Siek, Washington College.

Robert Funk
Susan X Day
Elizabeth McMahan

ACTIVE READING

Most people who write well also read well—and vice versa. The two skills are so intertwined that they are often taught together, as we do in this textbook. Reading gives you not only information and amusement but also a sense of how sentences and paragraphs work. Most of the time, you get this sense without really paying attention: it just seeps into your mind with the rest of the material. When you use this textbook, we ask you to make the reading-writing connection more consciously than you may have done before. By looking carefully at good writing, you will better understand the content as well as the techniques the writers use.

LEARNING TO BE AN ACTIVE READER

Did you ever finish reading something, look up from the page, and realize that you didn't take in anything at all? That you passed your eyes over the print, but you might as well have stared out the window? At such times, you know that you have been an extremely passive reader. On the opposite end of the spectrum, you've probably had the experience of being swept away from reality while reading, so involved in the printed word that the rest of your world fades. Much of your college reading won't be able to carry you off that completely. By learning to be an active reader, though, you will be able to handle your reading assignments competently. The main idea is to stay involved with the reading through interaction— bringing mental and emotional energy to the task.

KEEPING A JOURNAL

One good way to become an interactive reader is to keep a journal about what you read. In a journal, you can experiment with ideas and express your responses with greater freedom than you can in formal writing assignments. Before each reading selection in most chapters of this book, we ask you a "Preparing to Read" question that you may answer in your journal as well as in class discussions. This activity starts you thinking about the ideas you will find in the essay that follows. After each selection, we give you a "Responding to Reading" suggestion to consider in your journal, encouraging you to write about your personal reactions. As this chapter goes along, you will see how your two journal entries fit into your role as an active reader.

PREVIEWING THE READING

If you are the type that just plunges right into a reading assignment, you're missing something. Study skills experts emphasize the value of previewing the reading, getting your mind ready for full comprehension. Previewing involves more than merely counting the number of pages you have to go: no one needs to remind you to do that! The trick is to develop a mental set that makes your brain most receptive to the material.

Title

Try stopping after you read the title and asking yourself what it suggests to you. The sample essay we use in this chapter is titled "Burned Out and Bored." What does that phrase mean? What image does it bring to your mind? The title often gives you a clue about what's ahead.

Author and Other Publication Facts

With some assignments, you will recognize the author's name, but probably not in this chapter. This essay is one of the series of "My Turn" columns published in *Newsweek* magazine, usually written by unknown authors commenting on some contemporary social issue. In this case the writer is Dr. Ronald Dahl, a professor of psychiatry and pediatrics at the University of Pittsburgh Medical Center, and the article appeared in December of 1997.

Sometimes the author's name provides clues about the essay that follows. You know something about when it was written (as you would if the byline read "Mark Twain"). If the byline read "Dave Barry," you'd expect a humorous column about modern life. If the byline read "John Madden," you'd expect something about sports, probably football.

Even when you don't recognize the author, you can take note of other publication facts. The date of publication, if you have it, gives you an idea of how current the information is. If the reading is reprinted, as the ones in this textbook are, consider where it originally appeared and whether that means anything to you. If an essay first appeared in *U.S. News & World Report,* you can assume it will have a conservative political slant; if it came from the *Nation,* it will probably have a liberal slant. If it came from a city newspaper, like the *Chicago Tribune,* you can't be so sure about the political slant, since most big newspapers attempt to cover a range of views.

Visual Features and Supplements

Page through the reading looking at parts that stand out from the ordinary print, like headnotes, headings, photos, diagrams, boxed material, summaries, and questions after the reading. Your textbooks are specially designed to include lots of these helpful materials. Unfortunately, many students skip them, thinking they're not as important as the rest. Actually, they are there to focus attention on what *is* important in the reading. Or they may give you information that assists you in understanding the reading; for example, the headnote paragraphs before essays in this textbook give some biographical information about the writer. The "Terms to Recognize" section lists some difficult words from the essay and their definitions, so you won't have to look them up in the dictionary right away. In this list, we provide only the definition that fits the way the term is used in the reading; the term probably has other meanings as well.

Some reading material doesn't include any obvious helps. It's just straight print. But you can benefit from the only visual clue: paragraph indentations. Read the first sentence of each paragraph. This survey will probably give you ideas about the content and organization of the reading.

Responses and Predictions

"This preview stuff just slows me down," you may be thinking. "I don't have time for it." Let us assure you, the first stage does seem slow, but it makes later stages faster and more efficient. It also markedly increases your memory for what you read.

The main thing you're doing as you preview is responding to clues and making predictions about what the reading contains. It may just seem like a guessing game, but actually you are clearing the brush from pathways in your brain, opening the way for the information to get through. By anticipating what to expect, you are directing your attention, focusing on the material so that it won't be fighting through a tangle of thoughts about why you squabble with your roommate and what you'll have for lunch.

Instead, let your mind wander through the associations and experiences you already have with the material suggested by your preview. What people, events, and feelings in your own life did you stumble across in your preview? If you've ever been "burned out and bored," the title may spark memories of past or present hassles. If you're a teenager or the parent of a teenager, the essay may hold the promise of help with one of your most pressing problems.

A FIRST READING

Now it's time to plunge in. Try to place yourself in a setting that aids concentration. This setting varies from person to person, and you probably know your ideal situation. You can't always get it, but at least don't undermine yourself by choosing a spot where you know you'll be distracted or lulled to sleep. Sitting up at a table or desk is a good idea because the position suggests that you are going to work.

You'll need a pencil or pen to read interactively. Make it a habit. Mark words and terms that you need to look up later. Write questions—or just question marks—in the margins near material you don't quite understand. Write your spontaneous responses (Yes! No! Reminds me of Aunt Selma! What!? Prejudiced crap!) in the margins. Underline sentences that you think may contain the main ideas and phrases that impress you with the way they are worded. We will provide one reader's markings of "Burned Out and Bored" in this chapter.

STAYING AWARE OF CONVENTIONS

Conventions are the traditional ways of doing things; for example, we have conventional ways of beginning and ending telephone conversations, and we expect everyone to follow them. The same thing goes for writing conventions, some of which we will outline here. Stories and poems don't have to follow these conventions, but nonfiction works like essays, textbooks, and manuals do. You can enhance your reading by looking for conventional features as you go along.

Subject

Each piece of writing is expected to deal with one subject or topic. This should be fairly clear to you near the beginning, perhaps even from the title ("Flea Facts," in Chapter 8, provides exactly that). Once you identify the subject, you can be pretty sure the whole reading will stay on that topic.

Main Idea or Thesis

We expect a reading not only to have a subject but also to say something *about* the subject. That is the **thesis** or main idea. Frequently, the main idea comes up early in the reading, clearly expressed in one sentence. At other times, you must put together the main point piece by piece as you read. It may finally be stated in a sentence at the end, or it may not be stated directly at all. As you read, underline sentences that seem to add to your understanding of the author's main point.

Supporting Material

Writers must prove their main points by providing convincing supporting material. This can be in the form of logical reasoning, emotional appeal, examples, evidence from experts, specific details, facts, and statistics. Different main points lend themselves to different types of supporting material; for example, your math textbook uses mostly logical reasoning and examples, while an essay about capital punishment might use all the forms we listed. As you read an assignment, ask yourself, "What forms of supporting material does this author use?"

Patterns of Organization

The conventions of subject, thesis, and supporting material deal with the content of the reading. You also need to look at *how* the content is presented. After each selection in the following chapters, you will find questions called "Considering Content" and "Considering Method." The method questions ask you to consider the techniques the author used to present material, including organization.

We arranged the chapters in this book according to the patterns of development that are the most conventional ways to organize writing: patterns like comparison and contrast, cause and effect, and narration. Each chapter will explain one basic pattern. As you read an essay, notice how the writer uses a pattern (or a combination of patterns) to arrange ideas.

Paragraphs

As a reader, you will also notice how writers package their meaning in units of thought called **paragraphs.** Paragraph indention usually signals the introduction of a new topic or a new aspect of a current topic. In other words, writers start new paragraphs to show that they are moving on to another topic or subtopic. When reading articles from newspapers and magazines, however, you need to be aware that these publications are printed in narrow columns and that journalists break their paragraphs frequently to make these columns easier to read. Many of the readings in this book, including the one in this chapter, originally appeared in newspapers and magazines.

Transitions

Another element of a writer's method involves how he or she makes connections between ideas. These connections are called **transitions.** A common place for a transition is between two paragraphs (at the end of one and/or at the beginning of the next one), where the author shows the logical relationship between them. Recognizing transitions helps you to direct your thought process in the way the author wants you to. For example, a paragraph that begins "Furthermore" lets you know that you should expect material that adds to and agrees with the material preceding it. A paragraph that begins "On the other hand" lets you know that you should expect material that contradicts or shows the opposite of the material preceding it. By noticing transitions, you prepare yourself for understanding what comes next.

MARKING THE TEXT

Here is an example of an essay showing the pencil markings of a student reader.

Burned Out and Bored

Ronald Dahl

Each summer, no matter how pressing my work schedule, I take off one day exclusively for my son. We call it dad-son day. This year our third stop was the amusement park, where he discovered (at the age of 9) that he was tall enough to ride one of the fastest roller coasters in the world. We blasted through face-stretching turns and loops for 90 seconds. Then, as we stepped off the ride, he shrugged and, in a distressingly calm voice, remarked that it was not as exciting as other rides he'd been on. As I listened, I began to sense something seriously out of balance. *catches interest*

1

One day a year??

good details

Throughout the season, I noticed similar events all around me. Parents seemed hard pressed to find new thrills for nonchalant kids. I saw this pattern in my family, in the sons

2

look up

and daughters of friends and neighbors and in many of my patients with behavioral and emotional problems. Surrounded by ever-greater stimulation, their young faces were looking disappointed and bored.

thesis?

3

By August, neighborhood parents were comparing their children's complaints of "nothing to do" to the sound of fingernails on a chalkboard. They were also shelling out large numbers of dollars for movies, amusement parks, video arcades, camps and visits to the mall. In many cases the money seemed to do little more than buy transient relief from the terrible moans of their bored children. This set me pondering the obvious question: "How can it be so hard for kids to find something to do when there's never been such a range of stimulating entertainment available to them?"

sharp comparison

What really worries me is the intensity of the stimulation. I watch my 11-year-old daughter's face as she absorbs the powerful onslaught of arousing visuals and gory special effects in movies. Although my son is prohibited from playing violent video games, I have seen some of his third-grade friends at an arcade inflicting blood-splattering, dismembering blows upon on-screen opponents in

why? —— distressingly realistic games. My 4-year-old boy's high-tech toys have consumed enough batteries to power a small village for a year.

main idea again? 4

exaggeration?

Why do children immersed in this much excitement seem starved for more? That was, I realized, the point. I discovered during my own reckless adolescence that what creates

Thesis, for sure! 5

true | exhilaration is not going fast, but going faster. Accelerating from 0 to 60 mph in a few seconds slams the body backward with powerful sensations, but

convincing examples here going 60 for hours on the interstate causes so little feeling of speed that we fight to stay awake. At a steady velocity of 600 mph we can calmly sip coffee on an airplane. Thrills have less to do with speed than changes in speed.

right!

Since returning to school, the kids have been navigating ever more densely packed schedules. The morning rush to make the school bus is matched by a rapid shuttle through after-school sports, piano, foreign-language programs and social activities. Dinner is, too often, a series of snacks eaten on the run. Then, if they manage to get their homework done, the kids want to "relax" in front of highly arousing images on the television or computer screen.

neat word choice

6

good evidence

I'm concerned about the cumulative effect of years at these levels of feverish activity. It is no mystery to me why many teenagers appear apathetic and burned out, with a "been there, done that" air of indifference toward much of life. As increasing numbers of friends' children are prescribed medications--stimulants to deal with inattentiveness at school or antidepressants to help with the loss of interest and joy in their lives—I question the role of kids' boredom in some of the diagnoses.

Back to thesis

7

I've heard about this!

My own work--behavioral pediatrics and child psychiatry--is focused on the chemical imbalances and biological underpinnings to behavioral and

his credentials

8

8

emotional disorders. These are complex problems. Some of the most important research concentrates on (genetic) (vulnerabilities) and the effects of stress on the developing brain. Yet I've been reflecting more and more on how the pace of life and the intensity of stimulation may be contributing to the rising rates of psychiatric problems among children and adolescents in our society.

??-ask about this

echo transition

9

The problem of overstimulation arises frequently in my work on children's sleep. Although I diagnose and treat many unusual (neurologically) based sleep disorders, the most common is deceptively simple--many kids and adolescents don't get enough sleep. There are (myriad) factors in delaying bedtime despite the need to get up early for school. Even when tired, children often find stimulation through exciting activities. Fighting off tiredness by going faster can turn into a habit—and habits can be very hard to change. Most important, as thrills displace needed rest, sleep-deprived kids have trouble with irritability, inattention and moodiness. Ironically, stimulants can seem to help children with these symptoms.

Does anybody?

for sure

Why?

Our research also suggests that difficulties in turning down one's emotions after a stressful event may be a major factor leading to adolescent mood disorders. Constant access to high stimulation may also create patterns of emotional imbalance. An adolescent moving too fast emotionally for too long can experience the same sense of stillness as the

transition

10

such as?

good example—could be true

9

airline passenger traveling at
breakneck speed.

My wait at the airport for a flight   11
home from a scientific meeting gave me
time to think more about this fast-
track phenomenon. I fleetingly
considered my own need to slow down
and the disturbing truth in the cliché
that each year goes by more quickly. I
realized with sadness how soon my
children will be grown, and I sensed
the fear that I may miss chapters of   *interesting*
their childhood amid my hectic,   *word choice*
overfilled life. In these images, I
saw clearly the need to help our
children find alternatives to the
thrill-seeking fast lane by leading a
slower version of life ourselves.
I became convinced that nothing could   *suggests*
be so important as finding a more   *solution*
balanced path, rediscovering slower,
simpler pleasures before we all become   *-yes-*
burned out and bored to death.   *but how?*

CLARIFYING MEANING

After you have finished reading and marking the text, go back to work on gaining a complete understanding of what you've just read. If the selection is challenging, you may need to go through all of the following steps.

Using the Dictionary

First, look up terms and words you marked as unfamiliar on the first reading. In this textbook, some will be defined right before the selection. Sometimes you may have to puzzle out the meaning. Take the term *genetic vulnerabilities* in paragraph 8. "Some of the most important research," says Dr. Dahl, "concentrates on genetic vulnerabilities and the effects of stress on the developing brain." You know that genes are those mysterious substances that control heredity. And *vulnerable* means "capable of being injured." So, doctors studying *genetic vulnerabilities* are probably looking for gene patterns that could account for those "behavioral and emotional disorders."

With some readings you may want to use specialized dictionaries to look up unfamiliar references. For example, if an author's name is mentioned in an essay or if there is a quotation from an author's work, you may find helpful information in a biographical or literary dictionary. Often writers refer to names from mythology, philosophy, and literature. The reference librarian will show you where the specialized dictionaries on all those subjects are kept.

Reading Aloud

Return to any unclear spots where you drew a question mark, and read those passages slowly aloud. Hearing your voice find the proper way to read a sentence may shed the necessary light on its meaning.

Discussing

Having a conversation about your reading will often help you understand it better. Another person who has read the same selection will have different reactions and may be able to clarify points that stumped you. Even someone who has not read the selection may be a good sounding board to discuss the ideas with.

Rereading

At some point, you will need to go back and reread the whole assignment, especially if you are going to be tested on it. With difficult material, the second run-through will be easier and will allow you to notice things you missed the first time.

MAKING INFERENCES AND ASSOCIATIONS

Sometimes, especially in narrative essays, the meaning is not clearly spelled out, and no thesis is stated. Then you have to make judgments and inferences in order to draw conclusions about what the writer means.

Reading between the Lines

You can train yourself to infer knowledge that lies below the surface meaning of words. To infer means to arrive at an idea or a conclusion through reasoning. When you infer, you balance what the writer says with your own ideas and hunches about what is left unsaid. This process may sound difficult, but making **inferences** is a skill that can be learned.

Developing Inference Skills

Here are some suggestions for improving your ability to read between the lines:

Read beyond the words. Fill in details and information to complete the writer's suggestions. Use the writer's hints to discover the meanings that often lie beneath the surface. But don't go too far: you should be able to point to words and phrases that support what you have inferred.

Question yourself as you read and after you finish. You might use questions like these: Why did the author include these details? What does this example mean? How am I supposed to react to this sentence?

Draw conclusions and speculate on outcomes. You won't have to do too much of this after reading Dr. Dahl's essay, since it is fairly straightforward. At the end of the first paragraph, if you wondered what "was seriously out of balance," you found out in the next few paragraphs. But if a selection is difficult and you're not entirely sure what every sentence means, you need to ask yourself questions. The "Considering Content" sections following each reading in this book are designed to lead you to a complete understanding. As you study this text, you'll eventually learn the kinds of questions you need to ask yourself in order to grasp the full meaning of an essay.

Consider the tone. The tone refers to the author's attitude toward the subject he or she is writing about. For example, you might say that Lincoln maintains a "solemn" tone throughout the Gettysburg Address, that Mark Twain writes "longingly" of his boyhood, or that Ronald Dahl's essay is "serious" but "lively." Identifying the tone requires paying close attention to the words. When you read that "The City Council surpassed its usual high standard of idiocy," you should detect an emotional message that is quite different from the one you read in "The City Council may have shown poor judgment," even though the point is roughly the same in both sentences.

Make associations between the reading and your own experience. Relating the reading to your own experience can add richness to the meaning of a work. How did you respond to Dr. Dahl's essay? Did you see yourself as caught up in the "fast-track phenomenon" like him? Or perhaps you've been racing for years along "the thrill-seeking fast lane," like the kids. Do you agree with him that we all need to slow down? And if so, how? In this text, the "Responding to Reading" exercises at the end of each selection will assist you in developing your personal reactions.

WRITING TO UNDERSTAND AND RESPOND

If you write out your "Responding to Reading" assignment, you have already begun the interactive process that will set the selection firmly in your memory. Study skills experts point out that we have four modes of verbal communication: we listen, we read, we speak, and we write. Different people learn best through different modes, but college learning often emphasizes just the first two: listening to course lectures and reading text-books. When you add the other two modes to your study habits, you more than double your learning potential. Speaking in class and discussing the material with friends and classmates are important. Writing about what you have heard and read is equally important. Here are some ways to write about a reading assignment:

1. Without looking at the reading, write a summary, 100 to 200 words long, of the selection. While you write, you will feel which parts of the selection are blurry in your mind. These will be the parts you find it hard to express. Compare your summary to the original, and revise it to make it as accurate as possible. This summary will be a fine study aid if you are going to be tested.

2. You can make another study aid by constructing an outline of the important points. This outline can be a simple list of key thoughts in the order they appeared in the essay, like this:

A. Kids these days seem bored even when doing lots of exciting activities.
B. It's not just going fast but a change in speed that brings excitement.
C. So all these constant activities eventually just get old and boring.
D. Some kids get medication to cure what may simply be boredom.
E. Being overstimulated interferes with sleep, and lack of sleep may be the cause of behavior problems for lots of kids and adolescents.
F. Everybody needs to slow down—including the author.

3. In your journal, write a letter to the author of your selection. What would you say to him or her if you could? Do you have any questions? These might be brought up in class discussion if you have them on hand.

4. You will also benefit from writing out answers to the "Considering Content" and "Considering Method" questions, which are designed to help you focus on meaning and technique.

The writing you have done so far will be of great help to you when you need to draft an assigned essay of your own based on your reading. This process is the subject of the next chapter.

C h a p t e r

THE READING-WRITING CONNECTION

The connections between reading and writing are strong: in both activities you use language to create meaning. In Chapter 1 you learned how writing can help you to understand and remember what you read; in this chapter you will learn how reading and responding to essays can help you to improve your writing.

WRITING IN RESPONSE TO READING

The basic principle of this book is that reading and writing go together. Each chapter follows a four-part pattern that you will discover works well in many of your college classes: (1) read a selection, (2) examine the content, (3) analyze the techniques, and (4) write something of your own that relates to the reading.

When you read, you get ideas for your own writing. Reading can supply you with topics to write about and show you how to write about them. Even when you already have a topic, reading can help you to come up with material to develop that topic. Reading will also provide you with models to follow. By studying the strategies and techniques that professional writers use, you can learn methods and procedures for writing effectively on many different subjects and in many different writing situations.

BUILDING AN ESSAY

Writing an essay is a lot like building a house. A writer fits separate pieces of meaning together to make an understandable statement. If you want to write well, you need to learn the basic skills of constructing an essay.

Despite differences in education and personality, most writers follow a remarkably similar process of *prewriting, planning, writing, revising,* and *editing.* Whether building a single paragraph or a ten-page article, successful writers usually follow a series of steps that go roughly like this:

1. Find a subject; gather information. (Prewriting)
2. Focus on a main idea; map out an approach. (Planning)
3. Prepare a rough draft. (Writing)
4. Rework and improve the draft. (Revising)
5. Correct errors. (Editing)

If you follow these steps, you will learn to write more productively and more easily. But keep in mind that this sequence is only a general guide. The steps often overlap and loop around. The important point to remember is that writing is done in stages; successful writers take the time to build their essays step by step and to polish and finish their work the way a good carpenter sands rough surfaces.

Finding Ideas

One of the most difficult challenges of writing is coming up with a topic. Even when you are responding to a reading, you still have to decide what to say about it. In this textbook and in most classes, you will be given some direction toward a topic; the job from there is up to you. Rather than wait for inspiration to strike, you can go after the ideas you need by doing some prewriting. Here are three methods that experienced writers use to generate material for writing.

1. **Freewriting.** Write without stopping for five or ten minutes. Don't pause to consider whether your ideas are any good or not; just get down as many thoughts as you can within the time limit. After the time is up, read through your freewriting and underline anything that strikes you as interesting or important. Then do some more freewriting on one or two of these points.

Here are two examples of freewriting done by student Ann Moroney in response to "Burned Out and Bored," the article by Ronald Dahl in Chapter 1. In the first one, Ann explores her personal reactions to some of the ideas in the article.

```
    I think it's true that the young generation does
seek higher thrills and set higher goals. That's the
story of my life. I have often found myself trying to
```

reach goals that are nowhere near possible. And some
of these goals don't even make sense. Like this
morning. In the shower listening to music I said to
myself that I had to be done shampooing my hair
before the end of the song. And there was only a few
seconds of the song left, but I told myself that
anyway. And I tried to reach it. Why did I do that?
Why did I even try? Of course I couldn't, but I felt
bad anyway. That's just one example of what I do to
myself. There are lots of other examples and times
when I put myself to the test, just to see what I can
do. I always fail. And I always feel bad--that's the
worst part. But why should that be? Why should I feel
bad about something that was completely impossible to
begin with? I don't know. I wish I did. I really do.
Then I could stop setting unrealistic goals for
myself.

At this point, Ann stopped and looked at what she had written. She
decided that she wasn't getting anywhere with this freewriting, so she
returned to Dahl's article and reviewed the comments she had made in the
margin and the notes she had jotted down when reading it the first time.
Then she did another freewriting, focusing on a more specific idea.

I don't know what it is about Great America that
I like so much. I've been there so many times before.
I should be sick of it by now. But that initial rush
that I get when I hit the first drop on the roller
coasters really gets me, it makes me want to come
back for more. But really the first drop is the only
real thrill that I get anymore when I ride the rides,
I guess I've been there so many times I'm starting to
memorize what each ride does, I don't know. But every
time I go, something seems to be missing. Like the
whole reason behind going just isn't as important as
it used to be anymore and I think I know what the
reason is. Danger. There's one ride called "Batman:
The Ride" and it's the world's first outside looping
roller coaster, meaning you sit in a car that hangs
on runners and your legs hang free. It's so scary,
because you think your legs are going to get slammed
into something that the ride goes past, including

itself because it loops around itself. But I
eventually figured out that after the first few
seconds that my legs are not going to hit something.
At first though I was really worried but now I've
become immune to this fear. There are a few other
rides that I still haven't gone on yet because I'm
just too scared to try them. But maybe they're the
something new I need to get out of my no-danger slump
that I seem to be in. Maybe I should try to write
about my relationship with Great America and why the
danger is gone.

With this second freewriting, Ann felt she had a topic that she could develop into an essay. She put this freewriting aside for a while—to let the ideas work around in her mind before she moved on to the next stage in the process.

2. **Brainstorming.** As an alternative to freewriting, you can ask yourself a question and list as many answers as you can. For example: *Are today's young people really burned out and indifferent?* or *Do I feel overstimulated?* Challenge yourself to make the list as long as you can. If necessary, ask yourself a new question: *Are video games too violent and intense?* In making this list you have already started writing. Think of it as a bank of raw material on which you can draw.

3. **Questioning.** Write a broad topic—like *The Problem of Overstimulation*—at the top of a sheet of paper. Then write the headings *Who? What? When? Where? Why? How?* down the page. Fill in any thoughts about the topic that occur to you under these headings. If you can't think of anything for one heading, go to the next, but try to write something under each heading. The goal is to think creatively about the topic as you try to come up with material to use in writing.

Devising a Working Thesis

At this stage you need to collect the ideas that you came up with in prewriting and organize them. One way to focus your material is to ask yourself, "What point do I want to make?" The answer to that question will lead you to your main idea, or working thesis. If you decide what point you want to make, then you can go through your prewriting material and decide which details to use and which ones to toss.

As you learned in Chapter 1, a thesis says something *about* the subject of a reading. As a reader, your job is to discover the writer's thesis; as a writer, your job is to provide a clear thesis for your readers. Look at the difference between a subject and a thesis in these examples:

Subject: Video game violence
Thesis: I think the intense violence of video games is harmful to the young people who play them.

Subject: Teenage boredom
Thesis: Young people who say they have "nothing to do" are reacting normally to the adult world that they are about to enter.

Here is an example of the thesis statement that Ann Moroney devised from her second freewriting in response to "Burned Out and Bored":

```
Danger has been taken out of the equation in most chancy
situations, leaving the thrill-seekers looking for some-
thing more stimulating and treacherous.
```

You can, of course, change or refine your thesis as the paper develops, but having an idea of what you want to say makes the actual writing considerably easier.

Making a Plan

Having a plan to follow makes you less likely to wander from your main point. An outline of your major points will provide you with a framework for your first draft; it can help you shape and arrange your thoughts and keep you from making organizational blunders. There is no need for complete sentences or balanced headings in your outline. Just make a list of your main points in the order that you plan to cover them. The following brief plan is based on the thesis you just read:

ADVENTURE AT SIX FLAGS

```
1. Opening
   Going again tomorrow
   Past trips: remember the thrill of the "Batman" ride
2. The feeling is gone
   Rides really not dangerous
   Tested and equipped with safety devices
   Main point: no real thrill with the danger removed
   Makes me look for something new
```

3. The appeal of adventures
   Fear, especially of the unexpected
   Uncertainty, not knowing—like being in the dark
   Fear contributes to the rush
4. Past trips
   Made in hopes of finding the thrill again
   But came up short
   Stopped feeling the thrill; know what's going to happen
5. Closing
   Still looking for something new and exciting
   The new ride—maybe it will do

Composing a Draft

If you have an outline or plan to work from, you shouldn't have any trouble producing the first draft of your paper. Don't fret over trying to write a brilliant introduction. Skip it if you can't come up with anything inspired, and start right in on the first main point. You can always come back and add an introduction when you revise.

Some people write the first draft from start to finish without bothering to search for the best word or the right phrase. If that's your method, fine. But many successful writers stop frequently to reread what they have written; they consider such rereading an important part of the drafting process. The main goal is to get your ideas down on paper in a reasonably complete form. Then you are ready for the important next step: revising.

Improving the Draft

Set your first draft aside, at least overnight, so you can look at it in a new light. This process of looking at your draft *again* is called **revising,** and it literally means "re-seeing." In fact, you want to try to see your work now with different eyes—the eyes of a reader.

When revising your draft, concentrate on making major improvements in content and organization. Save the smaller changes for the editing stage. Ask yourself these questions:

Have I made my thesis clear to the reader?

Does the introduction get the reader's attention?

Are there any points that the reader might not understand?

Do I need to give the reader more reasons and examples?

Have I shown the reader how every point relates to the thesis?

Does the conclusion tie everything together for the reader?

When you are satisfied with the changes you've made to improve content and organization, you can move on to matters of spelling, word choice, punctuation, capitalization, and mechanics. This is the **editing** stage, and you cannot skip it. Readers quickly become annoyed by writing that is full of errors.

Source: Copyright © 1995 by Lynn Johnston. Reprinted with the permission of Universal Press Syndicate.

Here are some additional tips that will help you revise and edit your first draft:

1. Let your work sit for a day to clear your head and increase your chances of spotting problems.
2. Read your draft out loud, listening for anything that sounds unclear or incomplete or awkward.
3. Ask some reliable readers to look over your draft and suggest changes.
4. Don't try to do everything at once: deal with big problems first, and save time to take a break when you need one.
5. Slow down when you edit: look at each word and punctuation mark individually, and watch for mistakes that you know you usually make.

SAMPLE STUDENT ESSAY WITH AUTHOR'S COMMENTS

The essay that follows was written by Ann Moroney, a first-year student at Eastern Illinois University. She was responding to some of the ideas expressed in "Burned Out and Bored" by Ronald Dahl. The author's comments in the margin call your attention to some of the points made in this chapter.

A New Adventure at Six Flags Great America

In the opening ¶ I wanted to arouse interest by describing the thrill of going on the "Batman" ride.

Tomorrow, I am going to Six Flags Great America. I have been there many times before, and yet I still feel the need to experience the rides again. I remember the way the "Batman: The Ride" throws me back into my seat, making it impossible to move my legs, as it twists and loops around its tangled web of metal supports at sixty miles per hour. It's thrilling to move at such high speeds, whipping around dangerous turns, upside down, in and out of a metal jungle, and all the while I've got my feet dangling free in the air. It almost makes me want to go out there and conquer the world. 1

In this ¶ I explain why the thrill is gone.

Almost. The problem is that I know it really isn't dangerous. It is, after all, a tested and re-tested roller coaster in a theme park that's visited by thousands of people each day. There's a safety harness and a seat belt, hydraulic brakes and special rollers for a smoother ride, and reinforced steel runners that protect me from any harm. And so, the real thrill, the danger, is basically gone-- taken away by modern technology and the need for safety in risky machines such as those frequented by human beings. So I don't actually feel like I'm having the thrill of my life. Why? Because genuine danger, which is the ultimate rush, has been taken away. 2

Danger is the one thing that creates that "high on life" feeling, and it's the one thing that has been removed from the equation in most chancy situations. The absence of danger leaves thrill-seekers like me looking for something more stimulating and treacherous that could possibly furnish that ever-elusive kick we get when we brush against true danger.

Here I state my main point.

This ¶ explains why I think people like adventures.

Why is an adventure so inviting? Maybe it's because there is a certain amount of danger involved in the journey, of course, but also because unexpected surprises lie just around the corner. Thrill-seekers thrive on fear; it's the fear of what may happen that gives us the rush. Not knowing what lies ahead adds to the feeling of danger of the whole expedition. It's that uncertainty that makes the adventure worthwhile to a thrill-seeker. Take me, for example. I'm afraid of the dark because I don't know what may be out there coming to get me. But I still go charging out into the blackness even if I'm scared because there's nothing like the kick I get out of going into something that's potentially dangerous. My fear contributes to the rush.

3

This next ¶ explains why the trips to Six Flags have lost their appeal.

Each one of my previous excursions to Great America was made in hopes of satisfying my cravings for excitement and danger. But each time, I came up short. Eventually I just stopped feeling the thrills of the rides because I've been on them so many times before. There is no excitement in knowing that nothing new and stimulating, other than the usual ride, is going to happen to me.

4

In the
closing
I point
out why
I'm going
back to
Six Flags
anyway.

My predicament has forced me to go   5
out and find new and exciting ways to
put myself in danger in order to spend
a fleeting moment feeling like I'm
standing on top of the world. The
Giant Drop, a ninety foot free-fall
ride, has just opened within the last
year at Great America. Maybe this time
I will feel the danger once again.

RESPONDING TO A READING

Now that you have seen samples of close reading and of writing in response to reading, it's time to try these skills yourself. Use the advice in Chapters 1 and 2 as you practice.

PREPARING TO READ

Are you a good writer? Do you like to write? Did you have any experiences in English class that affected your attitude toward writing? What were they?

Learning to Write

RUSSELL BAKER

The winner of a Pulitzer Prize for journalism, Russell Baker began his career as a writer for the *Baltimore Sun* and moved to the *New York Times* in the 1950s, where he still writes a regular column. Baker is known for his humorous observations of everyday life, but in this excerpt from his autobiography *Growing Up* (1982), his lighthearted tone gives way to a serious description of an important personal event.

TERMS TO RECOGNIZE

notorious *(para. 1)*	known widely and usually unfavorably, disreputable
prim *(para. 1)*	formal and neat, lacking humor
listless *(para. 2)*	without energy, boring
ferocity *(para. 2)*	fierce intensity, savagery
irrepressible *(para. 2)*	impossible to control or hold back
essence *(para. 3)*	the most important ingredient or element, fundamental nature
antecedent *(para. 4)*	the word that a pronoun refers to
exotic *(para. 6)*	rare and unusual
reminiscence *(para. 8)*	a thing remembered, memory
contempt *(para. 10)*	scorn, disrespect
ridicule *(para. 10)*	mockery, teasing
ecstasy *(para. 11)*	bliss, delight, joy

When our class was assigned to Mr. Fleagle for third-year English, I anticipated another grim year in that dreariest of subjects. Mr. Fleagle was notorious among City students for dullness and inability to inspire. He was said to be stuffy, dull, and hopelessly out of date. To me he looked to be sixty or seventy and prim to a fault. He wore primly severe eyeglasses, his wavy hair was primly cut and primly combed. He wore prim vested suits with neckties blocked primly against the collar buttons of his primly starched white shirts. He had a primly pointed jaw, primly straight nose, and a prim manner of speaking that was so correct, so gentlemanly, that he seemed a comic antique.

I anticipated a listless, unfruitful year with Mr. Fleagle and for a long time   2
was not disappointed. We read *Macbeth*. Mr. Fleagle loved *Macbeth* and wanted us to love it too, but he lacked the gift of infecting others with his own passion. He tried to convey the murderous ferocity of Lady Macbeth one day by reading aloud the passage that concludes

. . . I have given suck, and know
How tender 'tis to love the babe that milks me.
I would have, while it was smiling in my face,
Have plucked my nipple from his boneless gums. . . .

The idea of prim Mr. Fleagle plucking his nipple from boneless gums was too much for the class. We burst into gasps of irrepressible snickering. Mr. Fleagle stopped.

"There is nothing funny, boys, about giving suck to a babe. It is the—   3
the very essence of motherhood, don't you see."

He constantly sprinkled his sentences with "don't you see." It wasn't a   4
question but an exclamation of mild surprise at our ignorance. "Your pronoun needs an antecedent, don't you see," he would say, very primly. "The purpose of the Porter's scene, boys, is to provide comic relief from the horror, don't you see."

Later in the year we tackled the informal essay. "The essay, don't you   5
see, is the . . ." My mind went numb. Of all forms of writing, none seemed so boring as the essay. Naturally we would have to write informal essays. Mr. Fleagle distributed a homework sheet offering us a choice of topics. None was quite so simpleminded as "What I Did on My Summer Vacation," but most seemed to be almost as dull. I took the list home and dawdled until the night before the essay was due. Sprawled on the sofa, I finally faced up to the grim task, took the list out of my notebook, and scanned it. The topic on which my eye stopped was "The Art of Eating Spaghetti."

This title produced an extraordinary sequence of mental images. Surg-   6
ing up out of the depths of memory came a vivid recollection of a night in Belleville when all of us were seated around the supper table—Uncle Allen, my mother, Uncle Charlie, Doris, Uncle Hal—and Aunt Pat served spaghetti for supper. Spaghetti was an exotic treat in those days. Neither Doris nor I had ever eaten spaghetti, and none of the adults had enough experience to be good at it. All the good humor of Uncle Allen's

house reawoke in my mind as I recalled the laughing arguments we had that night about the socially respectable method for moving spaghetti from plate to mouth.

Suddenly I wanted to write about that, about the warmth and good 7 feeling of it, but I wanted to put it down simply for my own joy, not for Mr. Fleagle. It was a moment I wanted to recapture and hold for myself. I wanted to relive the pleasure of an evening at New Street. To write it as I wanted, however, would violate all the rules of formal composition I'd learned in school, and Mr. Fleagle would surely give it a failing grade. Never mind. I would write something else for Mr. Fleagle after I had written this thing for myself.

When I finished it the night was half gone, and there was no time left 8 to compose a proper, respectable essay for Mr. Fleagle. There was no choice next morning but to turn in my private reminiscence of Belleville. Two days passed before Mr. Fleagle returned the graded papers, and he returned everyone's but mine. I was bracing myself for a command to report to Mr. Fleagle immediately after school for discipline when I saw him lift my paper from his desk and rap for the class's attention.

"Now, boys," he said, "I want to read you an essay. This is titled 'The 9 Art of Eating Spaghetti.'"

And he started to read. My words! He was reading *my words* out loud 10 to the entire class. What's more, the entire class was listening. Listening attentively. Then somebody laughed, then the entire class was laughing, and not in contempt and ridicule, but with openhearted enjoyment. Even Mr. Fleagle stopped two or three times to repress a small prim smile.

I did my best to avoid showing pleasure, but what I was feeling was 11 pure ecstasy at this startling demonstration that my words had the power to make people laugh. In the eleventh grade, at the eleventh hour as it were, I had discovered a calling. It was the happiest moment of my entire school career. When Mr. Fleagle finished he put the final seal on my happiness by saying, "Now that, boys, is an essay, don't you see. It's—don't you see—it's of the very essence of the essay, don't you see. Congratulations, Mr. Baker."

SUGGESTIONS FOR WRITING

1. Baker's experience in eleventh-grade English changed the way he thought about himself. Have you ever had such an eye-opening experience—some event you really want to write about, some incident you want to "recapture and hold" for yourself? Write an essay in which you describe what happened.

2. Write an essay about the most important thing that happened to you in school. It could be either a positive or negative experience— one that taught you something about yourself or about school or about the subject you were studying.

3. Get together with a small group of classmates and talk about how each of you feels about writing. Compare notes on what you like and don't like about writing. Discuss the kinds of writing that you have done, and tell each other about previous writing experiences. Then write an essay explaining your thoughts and feelings about writing. If you changed your attitude (as Baker did), tell about that change.

4. Write an essay describing your writing process: how you get started, how you go about getting ideas, what you like to write about, where you like to write, whether you like background music or need quiet, whether you make an outline or plunge right in, how long it takes to complete an assignment, whether you work in stages or not, how many drafts you make, whether you write by hand or on a computer, how much correcting and recopying you do, and so on. Think carefully about the way you write, and describe it in as much detail as you can. Conclude your essay by explaining what you think you could do to make your writing process more efficient.

C h a p t e r

STRATEGIES FOR CONVEYING IDEAS

Narration and Description

He falls back upon the bed awkwardly. His stumps, unweighted by legs and feet, rise in the air, presenting themselves. I unwrap the bandages from the stumps, and begin to cut away the black scabs and the dead, glazed fat with scissors and forceps. A shard of white bone comes loose. I pick it away. I wash the wounds with disinfectant and redress the stumps.

—Richard Selzer, "The Discus Thrower"

That powerful paragraph, written by a surgeon good with words as well as with scalpels, combines description and narration. Dr. Selzer, narrating an experience in treating a terminally ill patient, uses description to make his account of this brief event vividly, compellingly real. Simply put, a **narrative** is a story; **narration** is the telling of a story. The previous passage is taken from a longer narrative (with beginning, middle, and end) that makes a point. As you can see, the strength of narrative and descriptive writing lies in the use of vivid language and in the selection of precise details.

THE POINT OF NARRATION AND DESCRIPTION

Most of the selections in this chapter are complete narratives that make a point using descriptive details to add clarity, zest, and interest. But as is true of most of the readings in this text, the writers use both narration and description to help them develop all kinds of essays.

Using Narratives

Consider how often we use narrative in everyday speech. If you want to convince your daughter to avoid becoming pregnant as a teenager, you'll probably tell her the story of your high school friend who made that mistake and missed her chance to become the architect she always wanted to be. We tell stories because they are convincing—they have the ring of truth to them—and most people are able to learn from the experience of others. So, narrative is a good strategy to consider if you are writing to persuade, to make a point.

If you are going to write a narrative essay, be sure your story has a point. You wouldn't tell a joke without a punchline, and only mothers and close friends will hold still for stories without a purpose.

Much more frequently, you will use short narratives as part of a longer essay. Notice in your reading how often writers begin essays with a brief narrative to catch our interest and lead us into the topic. Once the writers have our attention, they may move to other methods to develop their ideas and present the material, but a good story makes an effective lure.

Using Description

Essays of pure description are rare, but descriptive details provide one of the most common ways of adding interest and clarity to your writing. Description can put a picture in the minds of readers, helping them to see what you mean. Most writing would seem dull and lifeless without descriptive details, like this sentence:

The firefighter rescued a child.

Although the action referred to is exciting, the sentence is blah. But add some descriptive details, and the sentence gains meaning and interest:

The exhausted firefighter, a rookie on the force, staggered from the flames with the limp body of an unconscious child cradled in his arms.

You can, of course, use too much description. But use any details that come to you while writing your first draft. Then, when you revise, decide whether you've gone too far, and eliminate any that seem overdone or unnecessary. Of course, add more if you think you have too few.

THE PRINCIPLES OF NARRATION AND DESCRIPTION

Good narrative and descriptive writing depends, as does most writing, on making choices. In narratives, the main choices involve deciding which events to include and which ones to leave out. In descriptions, the choices involve selecting words that appeal to the senses—usually to sight, but also to touch, taste, hearing, and smell.

Organizing the Events

If you've ever listened to a boring storyteller, you know how important a concise and effective framework is to a narrative. Organizing a narrative seems easy because the story almost always proceeds **chronologically** (according to the time in which events happened). But a poor storyteller (or a writer who fails to revise) will get things out of order and interrupt the tale with "Oh, I forgot to mention that Marvin got fired just before his cat got lost and his dog was run over." Or the storyteller will get hung up on a totally unimportant detail: "The moment I saw him—I think it was at the senior prom—or was it at the homecoming dance—or it could have been the party at Yolanda's—oh, wait, I don't think it was at a party at all, it was at a football game—or no, a basketball game. . . ." when the point of the story has nothing to do with where or when it happened.

Get your story straight in your mind before you begin, or else straighten it out when you revise. Eliminate any dull or unnecessary material, and then go to work on making it interesting.

Including Specific Details

All good writing is full of specific details, but a narrative will simply fall flat without them. Recall the paragraph we quoted before written by Dr. Richard Selzer. We could summarize that paragraph in a single sentence:

> After the patient fell back awkwardly in bed, I removed the bandages and cleaned, disinfected, and rebandaged the ends of his amputated legs.

What did we leave out? The details—in this case mostly descriptive details—and what a difference they make in allowing us to visualize the doctor's performance.

Selecting Descriptive Words

Effective description depends heavily on the use of specific details, but also crucial are the words you choose in presenting those details. Consider this sentence quoted from Dr. Selzer's paragraph:

> I unwrap the bandages from the stumps, and begin to cut away the black scabs and the dead, glazed fat with scissors and forceps.

Look at what happens when we substitute less specific, less descriptive words in that same sentence:

I take the bandages off the amputated legs, and begin to remove the dead tissue with my instruments.

The meaning is the same, and most of us would probably have written it that way, but it's clear that the force of Dr. Selzer's sentence lies in his word choice: *unwrap, stumps, cut away, black scabs, glazed fat, scissors, forceps.*

Good description stems from close observation, by paying close attention to the sights, sounds, textures, tastes, or smells around you. Then you must search for exactly the right words to convey what you experience to your readers. Try to think of words that go beyond the general to the specific:

General ⬅——————➡ Specific

a drink	a soft drink	a diet cola	a cold diet Coke
move	run	run hard	race headlong
weather	rain	cold rain	cold, blowing rain

You get the idea. As you read, be alert for words that convey images, that let you know how something looks or feels or moves or tastes or smells or sounds.

When you revise, try to replace the following useful but run-of-the-mill verbs with words that are more specific and more interesting:

is (are, was, were, etc.)	go	get	has
come	move	do	make

See the difference a livelier word choice makes:

O'Malley moved on to second base.
O'Malley slid into second base.

I'm going to do my homework.
I'm going to wrestle with my homework.

Jessie made a luscious chocolate mousse.
Jessie whipped up a luscious chocolate mousse.

Keep a vocabulary list and try to use the new words in speaking and writing. The theory is that if you use a word three times, it enters your vocabulary. Part of becoming a good writer (as well as a good speaker) depends on increasing the number of words you have at your command, so get to work on it.

THE PITFALLS OF NARRATION AND DESCRIPTION

The narratives included in this chapter, written by experienced authors, will not show you the many things that can go wrong in this kind of writing. Descriptions and narratives are among the easiest kinds of writing to do, but are probably the most difficult to do well. You need to find someone who will read your draft, not just for enjoyment, but with the promise of helping you improve it. It's always hard to see the flaws in our own writing. It's especially hard with narratives and descriptions. But you can do a good job if you are willing to work at it and can find a reliable person to help you.

As you revise, ask yourself—and ask your helper to answer—the following questions:

1. Is the point of my narrative clear? It may not be stated directly, but readers should be able to tell *why* I'm telling this story.
2. Are the events in order? Are there any gaps? Any backtracking?
3. Are there enough details to be clear and interesting?
4. Are there any details that I should take out?
5. Do the descriptions provide an image (a picture, a sound, a smell, a taste, an atmosphere, an action)?

Respond to the questions as honestly as you can—and have your reader do the same. Then keep revising until you are both happy with the results.

WHAT TO LOOK FOR IN NARRATION AND DESCRIPTION

As you read the essays in this chapter, pay attention to these characteristics:

1. *Look at the way the essay is put together.* Probably the events are told chronologically, as they happened, but if not, try to figure out why the writer departed from the usual method of organization.
2. *Decide what point the narrative makes.* Its purpose may be simply to entertain the readers, but more often it will illustrate or make a point. Look for an underlying meaning that you discover as you think about the story and the author's reasons for telling it.
3. *Consider the elements of the narrative.* Think about why these particular events, people, and descriptions are included. If they are not crucial, try to decide what they add to the story and what would be lost if they were left out.
4. *Notice the descriptive details.* Underline any sentences or phrases that appeal to your senses or put a picture in your mind.
5. *Pick out good descriptive words.* Most of these you will already have underlined. Add them to your vocabulary list.

The Arnolds feign death until the Wagners, sensing the sudden awkwardness, are compelled to leave.

Why do the Arnolds pretend to be dead? What happened during the visit?

What advice would you give the Wagners to help them avoid repeating this situation?

PREPARING TO READ

Have you ever been through a tornado, a hurricane, or a severe thunderstorm? Describe how you felt at the time. Were you frightened, excited—or did everything happen too fast? Record the thoughts and feelings you had once the incident was over.

Wind!

WILLIAM LEAST HEAT-MOON

William Least Heat-Moon began his career as a professor of English at the University of Missouri but decided to quit teaching and become a writer instead. This brief selection, taken from a much longer essay in the September 1991 *Atlantic Monthly,* uses vivid description to make the narrative come to life. The author records a story told to him by a couple who were actually carried aloft by a rip-roarin' Kansas tornado.

TERMS TO RECOGNIZE

animated *(para. 1)*	lively
tinder *(para. 1)*	material that burns easily
seersucker *(para. 3)*	a light, thin fabric with a crinkled surface
ballast *(para. 4)*	weight carried to steady a balloon
veered *(para. 7)*	shifted and went in another direction
aloft *(para. 10)*	off the ground, into a high place

Paul and Leola Evans are in their early seventies but appear a decade younger, their faces shaped by the prairie wind into strong and pleasing lines. They have no children. Paul speaks softly and to the point, and Leola is animated, the kind of woman who can take a small smoldering story and breathe it into bright flame. Paul listens to her in barely noticeable amusement and from time to time tosses tinder to her.   1

Leola says: "It was 1949, May. Paul was home from the Pacific. We'd made it through the war, then this. We were living just across the county line, near Americus, on a little farm by the Neosho River. One Friday night I came upstairs to bed, and Paul gawked at me. He said, '*What* are you doing?' I was wearing my good rabbit-fur coat and wedding rings, and I had a handful of wooden matches. It wasn't cold at all. I said I didn't know   2 but that something wasn't right, and he said, 'What's not right?' and I didn't know.

"We went to bed and just after dark it began to rain, and then the wind 3 came on and blew harder, and we went downstairs and tried to open the door, but the air pressure was so strong Paul couldn't even turn the knob. The wind had us locked in. We hunkered in the corner of the living room in just our pajamas—mine were new seersucker—and me in my fur coat. The wind got louder, then the windows blew out, and we realized we were in trouble when the heat stove went around the corner and out a wall that had just come down.

"We clamped on to each other like ticks, and then we were six feet in 4 the air, and Paul was hanging on to my fur coat—for ballast, he says now— and we went up and out where the wall had been, and then we came down, and then we went up again, longer this time, and then came down in a heap of animals: a cow and one of our dogs with a two-by-four through it. The cow lived, but we lost the dog.

"We were out in the wheat field, sixty yards from the house, and Paul 5 had a knot above his eye that made him look like the Two-Headed Wonder Boy. Splintered wood and glass and metal all over, and the electric lines down and sparking, and here we were barefoot. Paul said to walk only when the lightning flashed to see what we were stepping on. We were more afraid of getting electrocuted than cut. We could see in the flashes that the second story was gone except for one room, and we saw the car was an accordion, and our big truck was upside down.

"The old hog was so terrified she got between us and wouldn't leave 6 all the way up to the neighbors'. Their place wasn't touched. They came to the door and saw a scared hog and two things in rags covered with black mud sucked up out of the river and coated with plaster dust and blood, and one of them was growing a second head. The neighbors didn't know who we were until they heard our voices."

Paul says, "That tornado was on a path to miss our house until it hit the 7 Cottonwood and veered back on us. The Indians believe a twister will change course when it crosses a river."

Leola: "The next morning we walked back home—the electric clock 8 was stopped at nine-forty, and I went upstairs to the room that was left, and there on the chest my glasses were just like I left them, but our bedroom was gone, and our mattress, all torn up, was in a tree where we'd have been."

Paul: "We spit plaster for weeks. It was just plain imbedded in us." 9

I'm thinking, What truer children of Kansas than those taken aloft by 10 the South Wind?

RESPONDING TO READING

Did you notice that Leola and Paul never mentioned their feelings in describing their adventure? What feelings do you think they had? How would you have felt? Would their account have been more interesting if they had included their feelings? Why or why not?

GAINING WORD POWER

Leola and Paul use some lively, descriptive verbs in telling their story:

. . . Paul *gawked* at me. (para. 2)

We *hunkered* in the corner . . . (para. 3)

We *clamped* on to each other . . . (para. 4)

It was just plain *imbedded* in us. (para. 9)

We repeat the sentences below, minus the verbs. Fill in each blank with your definition of the missing word.

Paul _____ at me.

We _____ in the corner.

We _____ on to each other.

It was just plain _____ in us.

What specific meanings are lost or changed in the second set of sentences? Which sentences do you prefer?

CONSIDERING CONTENT

1. What was unusual about Leola's appearance when she came upstairs to bed on the night of the tornado?
2. After they went downstairs, why was Paul unable to open the door?
3. Where, exactly, did the tornado set the couple down?
4. What two hazards made walking to the neighbors' house in the dark dangerous?
5. Why did the neighbors not recognize Paul and Leola?
6. Paul says the tornado was "on a path to miss our house," but "it veered back on us." What does he think might have caused the twister to change course?
7. What happened to Leola's glasses?

CONSIDERING METHOD

1. Why do you think William Least Heat-Moon chose to let Leola and Paul tell the story in their own voices?

2. Leola begins her tale by saying, "We'd made it through the war, then this." Does that strike you as a good way to introduce the episode— or do you think she should have left out that detail? Explain your response.

3. Leola's description is fascinating largely because she uses details that bring a picture to your mind. For instance, she says that she and Paul "came down in a heap of animals" (paragraph 4). Find three more "pictures" that you can see in your mind's eye.

4. This selection also contains a few **metaphors**—imaginative comparisons that put pictures in the readers' minds. Here, for example, is a metaphor:

   The tornado was a twisted black ribbon in the sky.

   And here is a **simile** (a metaphor introduced by *like* or *as*):

   The tornado looked like a twisted black ribbon in the sky.

   Now, find a simile in paragraph 4 and a metaphor in paragraph 5.

5. Does this selection have a thesis sentence? If not, why not?

WRITING STEP BY STEP

Think about a catastrophe—a flood, a fire, an auto wreck, a boating accident, a plane crash, an earthquake, a tornado or hurricane—that you witnessed or were involved in. Jot down as many specific details as you can remember. Then write a short narrative describing the experience.

A. Begin by describing the people who were involved.

B. Give a brief statement of the background information: where and when did this story take place?

C. Then recount the story as it happened, from beginning to end. Describe the events as specifically as you can, but do not include a thesis sentence. If your narrative has a point, let your readers guess what it is from what you imply.

D. Use "I" in referring to yourself and "we" if others join you in the action. If you speak directly to the readers, address them as "you."

E. Use direct quotations to report interesting remarks that people made.

F. Keep your feelings out of your account. Instead, let the readers experience your emotions through your forceful description.

G. Use plenty of specific details, and make them as descriptive as possible. Put pictures in your readers' minds. Lively verbs can create striking images—words like *tosses, gawked, hunkered,* and *clamped.*

H. Experiment with a couple of metaphors (or similes).

I. Write a final sentence that brings the story to a definite close. Don't let your narrative just trail off at the end.

OTHER WRITING IDEAS

1. Write an essay describing a solitary experience you once had—going to the movies alone for the first time; taking a relaxing, long, soaking bath; hiking alone on your favorite trail. Include your feelings; in fact, try to recapture your sensuous responses and convey whether the occasion was positive or negative.

2. Tell the story of the first time you were punished, either at school or at home. Explain briefly what you were being punished for, but focus on specific details about how the person doing the punishing looked to you and how you reacted. Try to remember what words were spoken—or else invent them. Conclude by telling how you felt about the punishment at the time and how you feel about it looking back on it today.

3. Write a narrative to support or disprove some familiar proverb or saying, like "A winner never quits," "Home is where the heart is," "Crime doesn't pay," or "Virtue is its own reward." Get together with several classmates before you begin writing to help one another decide what saying would make a good choice and what story might provide a convincing illustration.

EDITING SKILLS: ELIMINATING EXCESSIVE *ANDS*

Because William Least Heat-Moon is reproducing Leola and Paul's speech throughout most of the reading selection, he uses far more *and*s than would usually appear in an edited essay—thirty-seven, to be exact, in just ten paragraphs. Since people do, indeed, talk that way, the *and*s are effective in making the narrative sound authentic.

Most of the time you would not want to use that many *and*s in writing. So, for practice, try editing a few of them out:

- First, underline all the *and*s in paragraphs 2, 3, and 4 of "Wind!"
- Then, rewrite the sentences to eliminate all the *and*s that have commas in front of them.
- Try to give the sentences more variety as you decide how to change them. In other words, make them sound like written text, rather than spoken.

As an example, here are several ways to go about eliminating the second *and* from the following sentence:

Paul speaks softly and to the point, and Leola is animated.

1. Replace the *and* with a period:

   Paul speaks softly and to the point. Leola is animated.

2. Replace the *and* with a semicolon:

   Paul speaks softly and to the point; Leola is animated.

3. Replace the *and* with another connecting word:

   Paul speaks softly and to the point, while Leola is animated.

4. Begin the sentence a different way:

   Although Paul speaks softly, Leola is animated.

Write several versions of each sentence in paragraphs 2, 3, and 4.

Now examine the essay you just wrote to see how many *and*s you used. Rewrite any sentences that can be improved by eliminating unnecessary *and*s.

PREPARING TO READ

Did you ever have an experience that changed the way you look at the world—perhaps while traveling, or getting to know a stranger, or having a serious illness, or being inspired by a teacher?

Jackie's Debut: A Unique Day

MIKE ROYKO

When Chicago native Mike Royko, a lifelong newspaper journalist, died in 1997, he was a columnist for the *Chicago Tribune*. Throughout his career, his sharp-tongued observations about everyday urban life brought him national recognition, including a Pulitzer Prize. His columns often ridiculed human greed, vanity, and stupidity. The piece reprinted here is perhaps not typical, as it focuses on an uplifting event—a step toward reversing the usual pattern of ignorant prejudice. This column appeared in the *Chicago Daily News* on Wednesday, October 15, 1972, the day after Jackie Robinson died.

Royko's paragraphing may strike you as short and choppy, but newspaper articles typically are printed with lots of paragraph breaks to make the narrow columns of type easier to read. If you enjoy this article about Jackie Robinson, you might want to read Robinson's autobiography, *I Never Had It Made*.

TERMS TO RECOGNIZE

scalpers *(para. 8)* people selling tickets at higher than regular prices
Ls *(para. 10)* elevated trains
caromed *(para. 25)* hit and bounced
chortling *(para. 26)* chuckling and snorting with laughter

all that Saturday, the wise men of the neighborhood, who sat in chairs 1
on the sidewalk outside the tavern, had talked about what it would do to baseball.

I hung around and listened because baseball was about the most impor- 2
tant thing in the world, and if anything was going to ruin it, I was worried.

Most of the things they said, I didn't understand, although it sounded 3
terrible. But could one man bring such ruin?

They said he could and would. And the next day he was going to be in 4
Wrigley Field for the first time, on the same diamond as Hack, Nicholson,
Cavarretta, Schmidt, Pafko, and all my other idols.

I had to see Jackie Robinson, the man who was going to somehow 5
wreck everything. So the next day, another kid and I started walking to the
ball park early.

We always walked to save the streetcar fare. It was five or six miles, but 6
I felt about baseball the way Abe Lincoln felt about education.

Usually, we could get there just at noon, find a seat in the grandstands 7
and watch some batting practice. But not that Sunday, May 18, 1947.

By noon, Wrigley Field was almost filled. The crowd outside spilled off 8
the sidewalk and into the streets. Scalpers were asking top dollar for box
seats and getting it.

I had never seen anything like it. Not just the size, although it was a new 9
record, more than 47,000. But this was 25 years ago, and in 1947 few blacks
were seen in the Loop, much less up on the white North Side at a Cub
game.

That day, they came by the thousands, pouring off the northbound Ls 10
and out of their cars.

They didn't wear baseball-game clothes. They had on church clothes 11
and funeral clothes—suits, white shirts, ties, gleaming shoes, and straw hats.
I've never seen so many straw hats.

Big as it was, the crowd was orderly. Almost unnaturally so. People didn't 12
jostle each other.

The whites tried to look as if nothing unusual was happening, while the 13
blacks tried to look casual and dignified. So everybody looked slightly ill
at ease.

For most, it was probably the first time they had been that close to each 14
other in such great numbers.

We managed to get in, scramble up a ramp and find a place to stand 15
behind the last row of grandstand seats. Then they shut the gates. No place
remained to stand.

Robinson came up in the first inning. I remember the sound. It wasn't 16
the shrill, teen-age cry you now hear, or an excited gut roar. They applauded,
long, rolling applause. A tall middle-aged black man stood next to me, a
smile of almost painful joy on his face, beating his palms together so hard
they must have hurt.

When Robinson stepped into the batter's box, it was as if someone had 17
flicked a switch. The place went silent.

He swung at the first pitch and they erupted as if he had knocked it over 18
the wall. But it was only a high foul that dropped into the box seats. I

remember thinking it was strange that a foul could make that many people happy. When he struck out, the low moan was genuine.

I've forgotten most of the details of the game, other than that the Dodgers won and Robinson didn't get a hit or do anything special, although he was cheered on every swing and every routine play. 19

But two things happened I'll never forget. Robinson played first, and early in the game a Cub star hit a grounder and it was a close play. 20

Just before the Cub reached first, he swerved to his left. And as he got to the bag, he seemed to slam his foot down hard at Robinson's foot. 21

It was obvious to everyone that he was trying to run into him or spike him. Robinson took the throw and got clear at the last instant. 22

I was shocked. That Cub, a home-town boy, was my biggest hero. It was not only an unheroic stunt, but it seemed a rude thing to do in front of people who would cheer for a foul ball. I didn't understand why he had done it. It wasn't at all big league. 23

I didn't know that while the white fans were relatively polite, the Cubs and most other teams kept up a steady stream of racial abuse from the dugout. I thought all they did down there was talk about how good Wheaties are. 24

Later in the game, Robinson was up again and he hit another foul ball. This time it came into the stands low and fast, in our direction. Somebody in the seats grabbed for it, but it caromed off his hand and kept coming. There was a flurry of arms as the ball kept bouncing, and suddenly it was between me and my pal. We both grabbed. I had a baseball. 25

The two of us stood there examining it and chortling. A genuine, major-league baseball that had actually been gripped and thrown by a Cub pitcher, hit by a Dodger batter. What a possession. 26

Then I heard a voice say: "Would you consider selling that?" 27

It was the black man who had applauded so fiercely. 28

I mumbled something. I didn't want to sell it. 29

"I'll give you $10 for it," he said. 30

Ten dollars. I couldn't believe it. I didn't know what $10 could buy because I'd never had that much money. But I knew that a lot of men in the neighborhood considered $60 a week to be good pay. 31

I handed it to him, and he paid me with ten $1 bills. 32

When I left the ball park, with that much money in my pocket, I was sure that Jackie Robinson wasn't bad for the game. 33

Since then, I've regretted a few times that I didn't keep the ball. Or that I hadn't given it to him free. I didn't know, then, how hard he probably had to work for that $10. 34

But Tuesday I was glad I had sold it to him. And if that man is still around, and has that baseball, I'm sure he thinks it was worth every cent. 35

RESPONDING TO READING

Reread Royko's next-to-the-last paragraph. Explain in your journal why he wishes, as an adult, that he had given the baseball to the man who bought it from him. Do you think you would feel the same way?

GAINING WORD POWER

Following is the vocabulary entry for the word *unique,* which appears in Mike Royko's title. It comes from the *Webster's New World Dictionary,* third college edition, published by Simon & Schuster. Can you make sense of it?

u | nique (yo͞o nēk′) *adj.* [[Fr < L *unicus,* single < *unus,* ONE]] 1 one and only; sole *[a unique* specimen*]* 2 having no like or equal; unparalleled *[a unique* achievement*]* 3 highly unusual, extraordinary, rare, etc.: a common usage still objected to by some—**u | nique′ly** *adv.*—**u | nique′ness** *n.*

All dictionaries are unique, but here's how to read this entry from the *New World:*

1. The boldfaced word itself tells you how to spell it, and the thin line (between the *u* and the *n*) shows where it divides into syllables. Some dictionaries use centered dots instead.
2. The symbols inside the parentheses (some dictionaries use slash marks) let you know how to pronounce the word. If you don't understand the symbols, check inside the front or back cover or at the bottom of the page.
3. The boldfaced abbreviation tells you the part of speech. Notice that further down in the entry you'll see other forms of the same word that are different parts of speech (*uniquely* adv. and *uniqueness* n.). Sometimes those other parts of speech have different meanings listed.
4. Those weird notations inside the double brackets give the **etymology** of the word—that is, they tell us how it came into our language. The entry reads this way: "The word *unique* comes to us from the French, derived from the Latin *unicus,* meaning *single,* derived from *unus,* meaning *one.*" Check the explanatory notes in your dictionary to learn how to figure out the etymologies.
5. Various meanings are numbered. Some dictionaries list the most common meaning first; others begin with the oldest meaning, which would often be the least common. So, again, check your dictionary's explanatory notes. The *New World* lists meanings from oldest to newest.

6. All dictionaries give warnings about usage. If you look up the word *ain't*, you will find it labeled *slang* or *nonstandard*, perhaps even with a warning that some people have strong objections to it. In the entry for *unique*, the third meaning of "highly unusual, extraordinary, rare, etc." is followed by a caution that this is "a common usage still objected to by some." Those *some* often include English teachers, so avoid writing *most unique* or *quite unique* or *very unique*. Remember the etymology.

Now, to practice what you just learned, look up the word *debut* in Royko's title, and answer the following questions:

1. How many syllables does it have?
2. What different ways can it be correctly pronounced?
3. What parts of speech can it be?
4. What language did it come from?
5. What are two meanings of the word?
6. Are there any usage labels or warnings?

CONSIDERING CONTENT

1. What made the old men of the neighborhood say that Jackie Robinson would ruin the game of baseball?
2. How did young Royko and his friend get to Wrigley Field, and why did he choose that way to get there?
3. What does he mean when he says, "I felt about baseball the way Abe Lincoln felt about education" (para. 6)?
4. Why was he surprised to see so many black people at the game?
5. Why were the black people wearing their good clothes?
6. When the young narrator says, "It wasn't at all big league" (para. 23), what does he mean?

CONSIDERING METHOD

1. How does Royko get the readers' attention in the opening paragraph?
2. How does he let us know that the "wise men of the neighborhood" are not truly wise—that he is being sarcastic? What small detail in the sentence gives us the clue?
3. Why does Royko tell most of the narrative through the thoughts of himself as a young boy?
4. In paragraph 7, why does he give the exact date—Sunday, May 18, 1947?
5. When you think about all the details he could have included in describing the crowd at the baseball game, why do you think he chose to relate how the black people were dressed?

6. The point of view shifts briefly in paragraph 24, as Royko tells us something he learned later. How does he handle this shift so that we scarcely notice it?

7. In paragraphs 27 and 30, why does he give us the exact words of the man who wants to buy the baseball?

8. Explain why the final paragraph makes a good conclusion.

WRITING STEP BY STEP

Using Mike Royko's column as an example, write a narrative essay about a childhood experience that suddenly let you see some less than admirable aspect of the adult world. Royko, after making it clear that he grew up in a white section of the city, lets us see how the vicious action of his former hero on the Cub team opened his eyes to racial prejudice.

Think of a similar experience in your own past that will allow you to show the unfairness of some human behavior or the pain caused by some human weakness. Perhaps you could tell about your accidental discovery of disloyalty or cheating by someone you admired and trusted. Or you could tell the story of the first time you observed adult violence or adult cruelty.

A. Think about the story and the insight you gained from it. Write out the meaning of the incident as a thesis statement, but do not include it in the essay. Just keep it in mind as a guide in selecting details.

B. Jot down the events you want to cover, leaving lots of space between them. Next, go over the events, and fill in the spaces with all the details you can think of about each event. Then, go through the whole sheet again, and carefully decide just which events and which details you want to use in your narrative. Select only the most descriptive details that will allow your readers to experience the event as you did.

C. Use *I* in telling your story. Consider narrating it from the point of view of yourself as a child, as Royko does. Try to remember how you actually saw things when you were young and innocent, and tell the story that way. See Royko's paragraphs 2, 23, and 31 for good examples.

D. Begin, as Royko does, by briefly setting the scene. Be sure to work in the time, either here or later (as Royko does in paragraph 7).

E. Don't give away the point of your story, but try to work in a teaser (or a *delay*), as he does in his opening. The men are talking about what "it" would do to baseball, while we readers have no clue what "it" means and read on to find out.

F. In your conclusion, try to let your readers understand what you learned from the incident, but don't tell them straight out. See Royko's last three paragraphs, in which he tells us how he felt as a child and how he feels now as a man—and both are positive feelings. He lets us see how wrong racial prejudice is and at the same time reminds us of how proud blacks could feel about Jackie Robinson's success.

G. If exactly what people say is important to the story, put the speech in direct quotations, as Royko does in paragraphs 27 and 30.

OTHER WRITING IDEAS

1. Did you ever do something quite wrong in response to peer pressure? Tell the story of how this happened and how you felt about it at the time—and how you feel about it now.

2. Write a narrative to illustrate one of the following:

   Mother was right.

   Winning is not all.

   Nice guys finish last.

   I learned _____ the hard way.

3. With a group of classmates, discuss difficult ethical and moral decisions you have faced and how you responded. For many, deciding whether to cheat, steal, or tattle creates their first moral crisis. Then, tell the story of a tough decision you had to make and what happened as a result.

EDITING SKILLS: PUNCTUATING CONVERSATION

When adding conversation to your narrative, you know, of course, to use quotation marks around other people's words. But you also need to notice how other marks are used with those quotation marks. Look at the punctuation in these sentences from Royko's essay:

Then I heard a voice say: "Would you consider selling that?"
"I'll give you $10 for it," he said.

The words telling who is talking—called a **tag**—need to be separated from the quotation. When the tag comes *before* the quotation, you can use either a comma or a colon to separate. When the tag comes *after* the quoted words, use a comma.

Sometimes you may want to put the tag in the middle:

"I don't want to sell it," I mumbled; "it's mine!"
"Go away!" I yelled, "or I'll call a cop."
"I'm going home," I told Joe, "before I lose this ball."

If you start a new sentence after the tag, you need a semicolon or a period, just as you would in any other writing.

And don't stack up punctuation. If you use an exclamation mark or a question mark, omit the comma or period.

Notice that periods and commas go before the ending quotation marks. But with question marks (and exclamation marks), you have to decide whether the tag is a question (or an exclamation) or whether the quoted words are.

"Oh, well," Jamal said, "it takes all kinds!"
Can you believe Jamal said, "It takes all kinds"?

Finally, whenever you change speakers, begin a new paragraph.

As you read your way through the selections in this text, pay attention to the way quoted material is punctuated.

EXERCISE

Now, for practice, put the necessary punctuation in the following sentences.

Oh, heaven help us Marvin exclaimed I forgot to do our income taxes
We'd better get started on them fast then responded Rosa
Marvin groaned You get the receipts together while I try to find the calculator
How am I supposed to know where to find the receipts asked Rosa
Surely roared Marvin you've been keeping them all together some place
Rosa was silent during a long pause, then asked Was I supposed to
Marvin slapped his palm against his forehead and yelled We're doomed
Don't worry, honey soothed Rosa they never send you to Leavenworth on a first offense
Oh, you think not countered Marvin What about Leona Helmsley
They just wanted to make an example of her explained Rosa
Yeah growled Marvin an example for people like you and me
Let's get busy and write a letter to the IRS begging for mercy

Go back and look at the essay you just wrote. Did you punctuate the conversations accurately? Check all your quotations carefully, and make any necessary corrections.

PREPARING TO READ

How do you picture a typical prison guard? Have your ideas been shaped by movies and television? In your journal, write a brief description of how you think a prison guard would look, talk, and act.

A Guard's First Night on the Job

WILLIAM RECKTENWALD

William Recktenwald is a journalist who once served as a guard in a maximum security prison in Pontiac, Illinois. The following firsthand account first appeared in the *St. Louis Globe Democrat* in 1978. Because this article was published in narrow columns in a newspaper, the paragraphs are unusually short.

TERMS TO RECOGNIZE

orientation *(para. 1)*	an introduction to and explanation of an activity or a job
contraband *(para. 4)*	smuggled goods
cursory *(para. 4)*	hasty, not complete or thorough
apprehensive *(para. 16)*	worried, anxious, uneasy
virtually *(para. 16)*	for all practical purposes
ruckus *(para. 17)*	noisy disturbance
din *(para. 18)*	loud, continuous noise
equivalent *(para. 25)*	the equal of, the same as

When I arrived for my first shift, 3 to 11 P.M., I had not had a minute of training except for a one-hour orientation lecture the previous day. I was a "fish," a rookie guard, and very much out of my depth. 1

A veteran officer welcomed the "fish" and told us: "Remember, these guys don't have anything to do all day, 24 hours a day, but think of ways to make you mad. No matter what happens, don't lose your cool. Don't lose your cool!" 2

I had been assigned to the segregation unit, containing 215 inmates who are the most trouble. It was an assignment nobody wanted. 3

To get there, I passed through seven sets of bars. My uniform was my only ticket through each of them. Even on my first day, I was not asked for any identification, searched, or sent through a metal detector. I could 4 have been carrying weapons, drugs, or any other contraband. I couldn't believe this was what's meant by a maximum-security institution. In the week I worked at Pontiac, I was subjected to only one check, and that one was cursory.

The segregation unit consists of five tiers, or galleries. Each is about 300 [5] feet long and has 44 cells. The walkways are about 3 1/2 feet wide, with the cells on one side and a rail and cyclone fencing on the other. As I walked along one gallery, I noticed that my elbows could touch cell bars and fencing at the same time. That made me easy pickings for anybody reaching out of a cell.

The first thing they told me was that a guard must never go out on a [6] gallery by himself. You've got no weapons with which to defend yourself, not even a radio to summon help. All you've got is the man with whom you're working.

My partner that first night was Bill Hill, a soft-spoken six-year veteran [7] who immediately told me to take the cigarettes out of my shirt pocket because the inmates would steal them. Same for my pen, he said—or "They'll grab it and stab you."

We were told to serve dinner on the third tier, and Hill quickly tried to [8] fill me in on the facts of prison life. That's when I learned about cookies and the importance they have to the inmates.

"They're going to try and grab them, they're going to try and steal them [9] any way they can," he said. "Remember, you only have enough cookies for the gallery, and if you let them get away, you'll have to explain to the guys at the end why there weren't any for them."

Hill then checked out the meal, groaning when he saw the drippy ravi- [10] oli and stewed tomatoes. "We're going to be wearing this," he remarked, before deciding to simply discard the tomatoes. We served nothing to drink. In my first six days at Pontiac, I never saw an inmate served a beverage.

Hill instructed me to put on plastic gloves before we served the meal. [11] In view of the trash and waste through which we'd be wheeling the food cart, I thought he was joking. He wasn't.

"Some inmates don't like white hands touching their food," he [12] explained.

Everything went routinely as we served the first 20 cells, and I wasn't [13] surprised when every inmate asked for extra cookies.

Suddenly, a huge arm shot through the bars of one cell and began swing- [14] ing a metal rod at Hill. As he ducked away, the inmate snared the cookie box.

From the other side of the cart, I lunged to grab the cookies—and was [15] grabbed in turn. A powerful hand from the cell behind me was pulling my arm. As I jerked away, objects began crashing about, and a metal can struck me in the back.

Until that moment I had been apprehensive. Now I was scared. The   16
food cart virtually trapped me, blocking my retreat.

Whirling around, I noticed that mirrors were being held out of every   17
cell so the inmates could watch the ruckus. I didn't realize the mirrors
were plastic and became terrified that the inmates would start smashing
them to cut me up.

The ordinary din of the cell house had turned into a deafening roar. For   18
the length of the tier, arms stretched into the walkway, making grabbing
motions. Some of the inmates swung brooms about.

"Let's get out of here—now!" Hill barked. Wheeling the food cart   19
between us, we made a hasty retreat.

Downstairs, we reported what had happened. My heart was thumping,   20
my legs felt weak. Inside the plastic gloves, my hands were soaked with
sweat. Yet the attack on us wasn't considered unusual by the other guards,
especially in segregation. That was strictly routine, and we didn't even file
a report.

What was more shocking was to be sent immediately back to the same   21
tier to pass out medication. But as I passed the cells from which we'd been
attacked, the men in them simply requested their medicine. It was as if what
had happened minutes before was already ancient history. From another
cell, however, an inmate began raging at us. "Get my medication," he said.
"Get it now, or I'm going to kill you." I was learning that whatever you're
handing out, everybody wants it, and those who don't get it frequently
respond by threatening to kill or maim you. Another fact of prison life.

Passing cell no. 632, I saw that a prisoner I had helped take to the hospi-   22
tal before dinner was back in his cell. When we took him out, he had been
disabled by mace and was very wobbly. Hill and I had been extremely
gentle, handcuffing him carefully, then practically carrying him down the
stairs. As we went by his cell this time, he tossed a cup of liquid on us.

Back downstairs, I learned I would be going back to that tier for a third   23
time, to finish serving dinner. This time, we planned to slip in the other
side of the tier so we wouldn't have to pass the trouble cells. The plates were
already prepared.

"Just get in there and give them their food and get out," Hill said. I   24
could see he was nervous, which made me even more so. "Don't stop for
anything. If you get hit, just back off, 'cause if they snare you or hook you
some way and get you against the bars, they'll hurt you real bad."

Everything went smoothly. Inmates in the three most troublesome cells   25
were not getting dinner, so they hurled some garbage at us. But that's something else I had learned; getting no worse than garbage thrown at you is
the prison equivalent of everything going smoothly.

RESPONDING TO READING

After reading the essay, write a paragraph in your journal describing what kind of person you think William Recktenwald is and how he responds to his new job. In another paragraph, note any ways in which he is different from your expectations of a typical prison guard.

GAINING WORD POWER

Since our brief definitions are sometimes cursory, look up in a college-size dictionary the following words from the "Terms to Recognize" list. Then write a sentence using each word.

orientation   apprehensive
contraband   equivalent
cursory

CONSIDERING CONTENT

1. What was the only piece of advice the author got during his orientation as a rookie guard?
2. What can you tell about race relations in Pontiac prison? Are the guards white and the prisoners black?
3. What qualities would a prison guard need in order to work in the segregation unit?
4. Why is the width of the galleries an important detail?
5. What kind of weapons does a guard carry?
6. At the end of the essay, why are the guards not much bothered by having garbage thrown at them?

CONSIDERING METHOD

1. Why does the writer quote directly the "welcoming" advice given by the veteran police officer?
2. The descriptive details in paragraph 4 have no vivid appeal to the senses. Why, then, are they included?
3. Look at the action verbs in paragraph 14: *shot, ducked,* and *snared.* Why are they more effective than *came, moved,* and *took*? What extra feelings do Recktenwald's verbs add? Find five more examples of verbs that you think add color and feeling.
4. In paragraphs 11 and 16, the writer uses short-short sentences: "He wasn't" and "Now I was scared." Why do you think he uses such short statements?
5. How is the essay organized?
6. What sentence serves as a thesis statement to tell readers what the essay is about?

7. What is the author's purpose?
8. Do you think the conclusion is effective? Can you explain why?

WRITING STEP BY STEP

Did you ever hold a difficult job? If so, write an essay describing a bad day. Use specific details that will let your readers share your experience. Follow the form of "A Guard's First Night on the Job." If you don't have a job to write about, describe a bad day at home or at school.

A. Begin by giving your readers a brief orientation—that is, explaining where you work, what you do, maybe what time you begin, if you have a shift job.
B. At the end of your introduction, let your readers know that the essay will be about a bad day on the job. Your purpose may be to entertain, if you have some humorous incidents to relate; or you may write simply to inform your readers about how trying your job is, as William Recktenwald does; or maybe you want to make the point that your line of work is pitifully underpaid for the stress it causes you.
C. Use the informal "you" to speak directly to your readers.
D. Think of one particularly troublesome detail of your job that bothers you repeatedly (like Recktenwald's problems with the cookies) and focus on that. Or jot down a number of incidents that drive you crazy and relate those in the order in which they typically occur.
E. Include specific details (like the cigarettes, pen, plastic gloves, plastic mirrors) as you describe incidents.
F. Use action verbs whenever possible (like Recktenwald's *shot, snared, lunged, grabbed, jerked, barked, hooked,* and *hurled*) to give your readers a picture of what happened.
G. If you include people, briefly identify them ("Bill Hill, a soft-spoken, six-year veteran").
H. Write a closing that reinforces how bad your day can be without actually saying so, as Recktenwald does when he concludes that merely having garbage thrown at him means his shift is "going smoothly."

OTHER WRITING IDEAS

1. Write an essay explaining how you think prisons should be run. Try to offer concrete ideas for improving them.
2. Describe the most stressful vacation you ever took (or the most stressful picnic or wedding or trip to the zoo or any activity that you would expect to be pleasurable).
3. Get together with classmates or friends and talk about memorable "firsts," like your first day of school, your first date, your first rock

concert, or your first family reunion. See how many "firsts" the group can come up with. Then choose the experience from your own life that will make the most interesting story and write about it.

EDITING SKILLS: COMMAS AFTER DEPENDENT ELEMENTS

Copy these sentences from the reading exactly. As you write, look for a pattern they all follow.

As he ducked away, the inmate snared the cookie box.

When we took him out, he had been disabled by mace and was very wobbly.

As we went by his cell this time, he tossed a cup of liquid on us.

Each of these sentences has two parts. Notice that the second part, after the comma, can stand alone as a sentence; it's called **independent.** If you read the first part alone, it does not sound complete. The first part is called **dependent** for this reason. When you write a sentence in which the *independent* part comes after a *dependent* part, you need to insert a comma to separate the two.

EXERCISE

Put commas in the following sentences:

While planning is important do not overschedule your time.

Since the best courses fill up early plan at least a term or two in advance.

If you cannot write well you will be at a disadvantage.

Now fill in the blanks to make the following sentences complete:

While studying is the major task of college life, _____ _____.

Since grades are important to some employers, _____ _____.

_____, Henry went to the basketball game.

Next, write three sentences in this dependent-comma-independent pattern.

Finally, check your essay to be sure that you have included the commas in sentences like these.

PREPARING TO READ

Did you ever think of houses as having tales to tell about the lives of the people who live in them? In your journal, write the story that a house you are familiar with might tell—if it could.

More Room

JUDITH ORTIZ COFER

Born in Puerto Rico, Judith Ortiz Cofer moved with her family to the United States in 1955 and settled in Paterson, New Jersey. Besides essays, she writes poetry and fiction. The following piece appeared in *Silent Dancing: A Partial Remembrance of a Puerto Rican Childhood,* published in 1990.

TERMS TO RECOGNIZE

geneology *(para. 2)*	family history
acrid *(para. 4)*	harsh, bitter
malingering *(para. 4)*	pretending to be ill
inviolate *(para. 5)*	pure, virginal (never entered)
obligatory *(para. 6)*	required
purgatives *(para. 6)*	medicines to cleanse the body
animosity *(para. 9)*	hostility, resentment
coup *(para. 9)*	brilliant, surprising tactic that overcomes an opponent
vortex *(para. 9)*	whirlpool
fecund *(para. 9)*	fruitful in offspring
acceded *(para. 10)*	gave in to, went along with
emanate *(para. 12)*	to emit, to give off

m y grandmother's house is like a chambered nautilus; it has many rooms, yet it is not a mansion. Its proportions are small and its design simple. It is a house that has grown organically, according to the needs of its inhabitants. To all of us in the family it is known as *la casa de Mamá.* It is the place of our origin; the stage for our memories and dreams of Island life.

I remember how in my childhood it sat on stilts; this was before it had a downstairs—it rested on its perch like a great blue bird—not a flying sort of bird, more like a nesting hen, but with spread wings. Grandfather had built it soon after their marriage. He was a painter and housebuilder by trade—a poet and meditative man by nature. As each of their eight children were born, new rooms were added. After a few years, the paint didn't exactly match, nor the materials, so that there was a chronology to it, like the rings of a tree, and Mamá could tell you the history of each room in her *casa,* and thus the geneology of the family along with it.

Her own room is the heart of the house. Though I have seen it recently—and both woman and room have diminished in size, changed by the new perspective of my eyes, now capable of looking over countertops and tall beds—it is not this picture I carry in my memory of Mamá's *casa.* Instead, I see her room as a queen's chamber where a small woman loomed large, a throne room with a massive four-poster bed in its center, which stood taller than a child's head. It was on this bed, where her own children had been born, that the smallest grandchildren were allowed to take naps in the afternoons; here too was where Mamá secluded herself to dispense private advice to her daughters, sitting on the edge of the bed, looking down at whoever sat on the rocker where generations of babies had been sung to sleep. To me she looked like a wise empress right out of the fairy tales I was addicted to reading.

Though the room was dominated by the mahogany four-poster, it also contained all of Mamá's symbols of power. On her dresser there were not cosmetics but jars filled with herbs: *yerba* we were all subjected to during childhood crises. She had a steaming cup for anyone who could not, or would not, get up to face life on any given day. If the acrid aftertaste of her cures for malingering did not get you out of bed, then it was time to call *el doctor.*

And there was the monstrous chifforobe she kept locked with a little golden key she did not hide. This was a test of her dominion over us; though my cousins and I wanted a look inside that massive wardrobe more than anything, we never reached for that little key lying on top of her Bible on the dresser. This was also where she placed her earrings and rosary when she took them off at night. God's word was her security system. This chifforobe was the place where I imagined she kept jewels, satin slippers, and elegant silk, sequined gowns of heartbreaking fineness. I lusted after those imaginary costumes. I had heard that Mamá had been a great beauty in her youth, and the belle of many balls. My cousins had ideas as to what she kept in that wooden vault: its secret could be money (Mamá did not hand cash to strangers, banks were out of the question, so there were stories that her mattress was stuffed with dollar bills, and that she buried coins in jars in her garden under rose-bushes, or kept them in her inviolate chifforobe); there might be that legendary gun salvaged from the Spanish-American conflict over the Island. We went wild over suspected treasures that we made up simply because children have to fill locked trunks with something wonderful.

On the wall above the bed hung a heavy silver crucifix. Christ's agonized head hung directly over Mamá's pillow. I avoided looking at this weapon suspended over where her head would have lain; and on the rare occasions

3

4

5

6

when I was allowed to sleep on that bed, I scooted down to the safe middle of the mattress, where her body's impression took me in like mother's lap. Having taken care of the obligatory religious decoration with the crucifix, Mamá covered the other walls with objects sent to her over the years by her children in the States. *Los Nueva Yores* was represented by, among other things, a postcard of Niagara Falls from her son Heman, postmarked Buffalo, N.Y. In a conspicuous gold frame hung a large color photograph of her daughter Nena, her husband and their five children at the entrance to Disneyland in California. From us she had gotten a black lace fan. Father had brought it to her from a tour of duty with the Navy in Europe. (On Sundays she would remove it from its hook on the wall to fan herself at Sunday mass.) Each year more items were added as the family grew and dispersed, and every object in the room had a story attached to it, a *cuento,* which Mamá would bestow on anyone who received the privilege of a day alone with her. It was almost worth pretending to be sick, though the bitter herb purgatives of the body were a big price to pay for the spirit revivals of her storytelling.

Except for the times when a sick grandchild warranted the privilege, or when a heartbroken daughter came home in need of more than herbal teas, Mamá slept alone on her large bed.   7

In the family there is a story about how this came to be.   8

When one of the daughters, my mother or one of her sisters, tells the   9 *cuento* of how Mamá came to own her nights, it is usually preceded by the qualification that Papá's exile from his wife's room was not a result of animosity between the couple. But the act had been Mamá's famous bloodless coup for her personal freedom. Papá was the benevolent dictator of her body and her life who had had to be banished from her bed so that Mamá could better serve her family. Before the telling, we had to agree that the old man—whom we all recognize in the family as an *alma de Dios,* a saintly, soft-spoken presence whose main pleasures in life, such as writing poetry and reading the Spanish large-type editions of *Reader's Digest,* always took place outside the vortex of Mamá's crowded realm, was not to blame. It was not his fault, after all, that every year or so he planted a baby-seed in Mamá's fertile body, keeping her from leading the active life she needed and desired. He loved her and the babies. He would compose odes and lyrics to celebrate births and anniversaries, and hired musicians to accompany him in singing them to his family and friends at extravagant pig-roasts he threw yearly. Mamá and the oldest girls worked for days preparing the food. Papá sat for hours in his painter's shed, also his study and library, composing the songs. At these celebrations he was also known to give long speeches in praise of God, his fecund wife, and his beloved Island. As a middle child, my mother remembers these occasions as a time when the women sat in the kitchen and lamented their burdens while the men feasted out in the patio, their rum-thickened voices rising in song and praise of each other, *companeros* all.

It was after the birth of her eighth child, after she had lost three at birth   10
or infancy, that Mamá made her decision. They say that Mamá had had a special way of letting her husband know that they were expecting, one that had begun when, at the beginning of their marriage, he had built her a house too confining for her taste. So, when she discovered her first pregnancy, she supposedly drew plans for another room, which he dutifully executed. Every time a child was due, she would demand, *More space, more space.* Papá acceded to her wishes, child after child, since he had learned early that Mamá's renowned temper was a thing that grew like a monster along with a new belly. In this way Mamá got the house that she wanted, but with each child she lost in health and energy. She had knowledge of her body and perceived that if she had any more children, her dreams and her plans would have to be permanently forgotten, because she would be a chronically ill woman, like Flora with her twelve children, asthma, no teeth; in bed more than on her feet.

And so after my youngest uncle was born, she asked Papá to build a large   11
room at the back of the house. He did so in joyful anticipation. Mamá had asked him for special things this time: shelves on the walls, a private entrance. He thought that she meant this room to be a nursery where several children could sleep. He thought it was a wonderful idea. He painted it his favorite color—sky blue—and made large windows looking out over a green hill and the church spires beyond. But nothing happened. Mamá's belly did not grow, yet she seemed in a frenzy of activity over the house. Finally, an anxious Papá approached his wife to tell her that the new room was finished and ready to be occupied. And Mamá, they say, replied: "Good, it's for you."

And so it was that Mamá discovered the only means of birth control   12
available to a Catholic woman of her time: sacrifice. She gave up the comfort of Papá's sexual love for something she deemed greater: the right to own and control her body, so that she might live to meet her grandchildren, me among them, so that she could give more of herself to the ones already there, so that she could be more than a channel for other lives, so that even now that time has robbed her of the elasticity of her body and of her amazing reservoir of energy, she can still emanate the calm joy that can only be achieved by living according to the dictates of one's own heart.

RESPONDING TO READING

What do you think of Mamá's chosen method of birth control? Why do you think Papá agreed to it without resentment?

GAINING WORD POWER

Cofer uses lots of unusual descriptive terms. Here is a list of nine of them.

massive (para. 3)	agonized (para. 6)
steaming (para. 4)	conspicuous (para. 6)
monstrous (para. 5)	benevolent (para. 9)
elegant (para. 5)	frenzy (para. 11)
heartbreaking (para. 5)	

Use each of these words in a sentence of your own. If the term is new to you, look it up in your dictionary before writing the sentence, and add it to your vocabulary list after you finish.

CONSIDERING CONTENT

1. What is a chambered nautilus, and how is one formed? What is a chifforobe (para. 5)? Why are the children fascinated by Mamá's? Why is it kept locked, even though the key is in plain sight?

2. How are Mamá's bedroom walls decorated (para. 6)? What do these decorations tell you about her character? Why is the detail about the crucifix especially significant?

3. What is a "benevolent dictator" (para. 9)? What sort of man is Papá? What details let you know what he is like?

4. What is a "bloodless coup" (para. 9)? Explain how Mamá pulls hers off. Why is the nature of Papá's character important in understanding her success?

5. What meaning did you derive from Cofer's narrative?

CONSIDERING METHOD

1. Besides being an *analogy* (see Glossary), the description in the opening sentence of Mamá's house as "like a chambered nautilus" is also a *simile* (see Glossary). Can you find other similes in paragraphs 2 and 3? Explain why they are effective.

2. What do you call the figure of speech in the first sentence of paragraph 3: "Her room is the heart of the house"? What does that description tell you, in a word, about Mamá?

3. Papá is referred to as a "benevolent dictator," but Cofer lets us know that Mamá also wields power in the family. What details convey this information?

4. What is the function of the single short sentence punctuated as a paragraph (para. 8)? Why does Cofer divide the essay with a space break following that sentence?

5. How does the concluding paragraph clarify the meaning of the whole piece?

WRITING STEP BY STEP

Write an essay in which you explain how you brought off some "blood-less coup" of your very own. In other words, tell how you managed to get your way in some matter (large or small) by outmaneuvering a person who had authority over you—a parent, teacher, older sibling, boss, coach, or law enforcement officer. Or maybe in an equal relationship with your spouse or roommate, you managed to slither out of some obligation that you felt justified in dodging, as Mamá does in Cofer's essay.

A. Tell your story, as Cofer does, in the first person, using *I* and *me, we, us,* and *our.*

B. Begin by setting the scene—the when and where. If your story happened in the past, let your readers know in a phrase how long ago, like Cofer's "I remember how in my childhood . . ." (para. 2). Describe, with plenty of visual details (the way Cofer presents Mamá's room), where you were—at home, in a car, in a classroom, in an office, on a football field—when you encountered the problem, disagreement, or conflict that you eventually resolved to your satisfaction.

C. Then, briefly explain the situation that gave rise to the problem, including only enough background details to let your readers understand how the difficulty arose.

D. Next, describe the personality of the other person involved. Use concrete details, as Cofer does in telling us the sort of man her grandfather was: "a saintly, soft-spoken presence," who enjoyed "the Spanish large-type editions of *Reader's Digest*," who loved his wife and children, who wrote poetry and sang songs, who threw "extravagant pig-roasts" with hired musicians, and who "gave long speeches in praise of God, his fecund wife, and his beloved Island" (para. 9).

E. Compose a short transitional sentence (like Cofer's single sentence in para. 8) saying that you are now going to let your readers know the way you resolved your difficulty. Make the sentence a complete paragraph.

F. Finally, present the clever strategy you used in pulling off your "blood-less coup." If you achieved some resulting benefit (as Mamá does in Cofer's final paragraph), you could mention that in your conclusion.

OTHER WRITING IDEAS

1. Tell the story of an episode that allowed you to see another side of a person you thought you knew quite well. Begin by describing the

person's character as you first observed it. Then narrate the incident that changed your perception. Conclude by describing briefly how you saw the person's character afterward.

2. Discuss with a group of friends or classmates whether the familiar saying "Sports build character" is true or not. After you decide how you feel about the matter, think of an incident that illustrates your belief, and use the story to make your point in a narrative essay.

3. In Cofer's essay, Mamá regains "the right to own and control her body" (para. 12). Write a narrative telling how you discovered the need to gain control of something in your life—your living expenses; your calorie intake; your large, unruly Dalmatian; your wedding plans; your TV watching. Conclude by letting your readers know whether or not you were successful.

EDITING SKILLS: USING COORDINATION

Experienced writers vary their sentence types and lengths to make their writing more interesting. Even Ernest Hemingway, who was noted for his lean, simple sentences, often put two or more together to make longer ones, as Cofer does in the following example:

> In this way Mamá got the house that she wanted, but with each child she lost in health and energy.

These are the sentences that are put together:

> In this way Mamá got the house that she wanted.
> With each child she lost in health and energy.

To make short sentences into one longer sentence, you splice them together with coordinating conjunctions. There are only seven of them: *and, but, for, or, nor, yet,* and *so.* Put a comma after each short sentence you are combining, but put a period at the very end, as in these examples:

> Mamá's belly did not grow, yet she seemed in a frenzy of activity over the house.
> [The house] has many rooms, yet it is not a mansion.

If you are dissatisfied with your writing because it sounds choppy, this method will help you achieve longer sentences.

Go back to your essay and combine two sentences into one long one, using a coordinating conjunction. Read the new sentence out loud. If you like the effect, leave it in your essay.

Student Essay Using Description and Narration

Domestic Abuse

Kelly Berlin

It was the summer of my freshman year, and I had   1
been baby-sitting my two-year-old niece, Briana, at my
sister's house every weekday for the past couple
months. It was late in the afternoon on a Friday, so
I couldn't wait for my sister Kim to come home from
work. Since she was already a half an hour late, I
decided to take a shower so I wouldn't be late for my
date later that evening. I was in the bathroom blow-
drying my hair when my sister and her boyfriend Scott
came home.

My sister and Scott had been dating a couple of   2
years, despite the disapproval from my family. Scott,
even though he had a child, was not a good "father
figure" for my niece. Scott was a regular drinker and
smoker, and his appearance did nothing for him. He
was over six feet tall with big, bulging muscles; he
wore tight clothes; and he had long, shaggy hair. My
sister, on the other hand, standing only five feet
five inches tall, was slender with long, curly brown
hair and a beautiful white smile.

I finished blow-drying my hair and was going to   3
ask my sister to take me home, but I heard her and
Scott fighting in the bedroom. I went into the living
room to watch television with my niece and to keep
her mind off the shouting. I started to become
worried because the yelling became more intense. All
of a sudden, I heard a loud noise--not a boom, but
more like a crack, a board breaking. The shouting
stopped.

"Briana, stay here!" I left my niece in the   4
living room and ran into the bedroom. "Scott, what in
the hell did you do to her? Get away from her!" My
sister was lying limp on her bed with her face down.

"It's none of your business. Get out of here," he   5
yelled at me with a fierce look in his eyes.

I was shaking but yelled back at him with just as   6
much determination and strength. "Bullshit, if it's

not my business. She's my sister. Don't think I'm just going to sit here while you push her around!" I turned, looked at my sister, and asked gently, "Kim, are you all right?"

"Yeah," Kim told me in a shaky voice. "I'll be all right. But my legs hurt because I hit the foot board when he pushed me down." 7

"Scott, leave NOW!" I said with all the authority I could manage. 8

"Shut up, Kelly. This isn't your house, and I'll leave whenever I please." 9

My sister pleaded with him. "Scott, please leave me alone. Just leave me alone." 10

He stormed out of the bedroom and out of the house like a raging bull. I helped my sister sit up and looked at her legs. She had two long, wide bruises forming across her upper thighs from where they hit the foot board. I told her to stay on her bed while I checked on Briana and called my mom for help. 11

My mom arrived about ten minutes later, and I told her what had happened. She was furious and was determined to do something about it. We called the police to report the incident and file charges. When the police arrived at the house, I described the scene and signed my name to the papers to file charges. Then, they took photographs of my sister's bruises and recorded her statement. But she wouldn't sign the papers. She had decided not to press charges. Well, I was confused, but I thought I could still press charges against him. I was wrong. I hadn't actually seen Scott push my sister. I had only heard them fighting and had found her lying on the bed. We tried to convince my sister to press charges against Scott, but she refused. She believed that he'd just gotten carried away, that he wouldn't do it again. We tried to make her realize that he could very well do it again, but she wouldn't believe us. 12

As it turned out, my sister was mistaken. Scott continued to beat her and control her life, and she continued to refuse to press charges. Finally, she 13

realized he was not going to stop, so she left Scott.
At one time, she put a restraining order on him,
which kept him away temporarily. And fortunately, he
lost his license due to DUIs, so he had no legal
transportation to get to her house. Now, the only
time he harasses her is when he's high on drugs. But
as time and experience have taught my sister, she now
calls the police herself.

C h a p t e r

STRATEGIES FOR MAKING A POINT

Example and Illustration

There's an old saying that a picture is worth a thousand words. It may be true. But we can't always communicate with pictures. Most of the time we have to convey our ideas with words—often with written words. You will find that your skills in describing and narrating can be put to good use in providing examples and illustrations to make a point.

Did you ever read a passage that seemed hard to get the meaning of— that remained fuzzy in your mind no matter how many times you plowed through it? Here's an example of the kind of writing we mean:

> A democratic plan of education includes more than the mere transmission of the social heritage and an attempt to reproduce existing institutions in a static form. The democratic school is also required to indoctrinate individuals with the democratic tradition which, in turn, is based on the agitative liberties of the individual and the needs of society.

If a person spoke those words to you, you could say, "What was that again?" or "Could you give me an example, please?" or "What do you mean by *agitative liberties?*" But you can't question the written page, so the meaning of whatever that writer had in mind is lost.

The difference between an **illustration** and an **example** is not clear cut. Some people use the terms to mean the same thing; some people use *illustration* to mean several short examples or a fairly long example, like a brief narrative used within an essay. We don't think it makes a whole lot of difference what you call them—just be sure to use them.

THE POINT OF EXAMPLE AND ILLUSTRATION

Good writers use examples or illustrations to make their writing clear and convincing. As a bonus, concrete examples make writing interesting.

Using Examples to Explain and Clarify

The paragraph about democratic education shows that writing that uses only general statements is vague and unclear. Here's another illustration to show how examples help in explaining ideas. We have deliberately taken the examples out of the following paragraph. See how much you can get out of it:

> You should define what you mean when any abstract, ambiguous, or controversial terms figure importantly in your writing. Serious miscommunications can occur when audience and writer do not share the same idea about what a word or phrase means, either *connotatively* or *denotatively.*

That's not very clear, is it? But now read it with the examples that were included in the original:

> You should define what you mean when any abstract, ambiguous, or controversial terms figure importantly in your writing. Serious miscommunications can occur when audience and writer do not share the same idea about what a word or phrase means, either *connotatively* (by its associations) or *denotatively* (by its direct meaning). Consider, for instance, the connotations of these words: *daddy, father, old man.* All denote *male parent,* but their understood meanings are quite different. Also, the phrase *good writing* seems clear, doesn't it? Yet three English teachers can argue endlessly about what constitutes good writing if teacher A thinks that good writing is honest, direct, and completely clear; if teacher B thinks that good writing is serious, formal, and absolutely correct; and if teacher C thinks that good writing is flashy, spirited, and highly entertaining.

A couple of the examples in that paragraph are definitions; the others explain the need for definitions. All of the examples add clarity and meaning to the passage.

Using Examples and Illustrations to Convince

Consider this letter to the editor, published a few years ago in an urban newspaper:

> Liquor is something we can get along without to a very good advantage. The problem of jazz music is a very grave one in this city, also, as it produces an attitude of irresponsibility in the listener.
>
> Let's keep Kansas attractive to God-fearing people. This is the type industry is interested in hiring and this is the type needed in government and the armed forces.

Are you persuaded? Not likely, unless you agreed with the opinions before reading the letter. The writer offers nothing but unsupported personal opinions.

Examples and illustrations are essential in making a point—that is, as evidence to convince your readers that what you say is right. If you want to convince readers that they should run out and rent *Batman Forever,* you have to provide examples to explain why. You will need to discuss the thrill-packed plot, the wonderful gizmos and toys (including a Batmobile that climbs walls), the deadpan jokes, the uproarious physical humor of Jim Carrey, and Chris O'Donnell's spirited performance as Robin. The more illustrations of this sort you can provide, the more persuasive your essay will be.

THE PRINCIPLES OF EXAMPLE AND ILLUSTRATION

The success of a piece of writing often depends on how well you choose your supporting evidence.

Select Appropriate Examples

You must be sure, first of all, that the examples actually do illustrate the point you want to make. If, for instance, you are explaining how you feel about people who borrow a book and then write their own comments in the margins, be sure to focus on your feelings—of interest, of outrage, of violation, of loss, or whatever you felt. Do not slide off the subject to discuss the interesting philosophy course you bought the book for and the time you accidentally left the book on a lunchroom counter and were quite sure you had lost it forever only to have the guy who sat behind you in class return it, saying he found it when he happened to stop in for a late lunch in the same greasy spoon that afternoon. When people do that sort of free associating in conversation, we tend to suffer through it, even as our eyes glaze over. But it will not do in writing.

Give Plenty of Examples

Keep in mind, though, that you need to supply enough examples to make your ideas clear and convincing. Say that you want to persuade your readers that becoming a vegetarian is the key to a long life in a healthy body. If you offer only the single illustration of your uncle Seymour who never ate meat, never had a cold, always felt frisky, and ran in the Boston Marathon to celebrate his seventy-ninth birthday, you are not likely to sway many readers. They'll just think, "Well, wasn't he lucky?" You need either to dig up more examples—perhaps even some statistics about low-fat diets and heart disease—or else change your thesis to focus on Uncle Seymour's personal recipe for keeping fit. There's nothing wrong with using one long illustration, if that single illustration really does prove your point.

Include Specific Information

Finally, you need to develop your examples and illustrations with plenty of specific, graphic details. If you say that riding motorcycles is dangerous, you need to follow up with examples more specific than "Every year many people are injured in motorcycle accidents" and "The person on the motor-cycle can't always tell what motorists are going to do." Instead, describe what happens when an automobile unexpectedly turns left in front of a motorcyclist traveling forty miles an hour. Mention the crushed noses, the dislocated limbs, the fractured femurs, the broken teeth, and the shattered skulls that such accidents cause. As a general rule, if you use an abstract word, like *dangerous,* follow it soon with a specific example, like "His splin-tered kneecap never did heal properly."

THE PITFALLS OF EXAMPLE AND ILLUSTRATION

If you are writing an essay developed almost entirely through the use of examples, you need to make sure those examples are connected smoothly when you furnish several in a row. Notice how the italicized transitions introduce the examples in this paragraph defining a psycho-logical term:

> People who use reaction formation avoid facing an unpleasant truth by acting exactly opposite from the way they truly feel. *For example,* you may have known somebody who acts like the life of the party, always laughing and making jokes, but who you suspect is trying to fool

everybody—including herself—into missing the fact that she is sad and lonely. *Another example* of reaction formation involves the person who goes overboard to be open-minded, insisting, "I'm not prejudiced! Why some of my best friends are _____!"

—Ronald Adler and Neil Towne, "Defense Mechanisms"

Here are some other transitional expressions that you may find useful:

such as	that is	in the following way
namely	in this case	as an illustration
for instance	in addition	at the same time

It's quite possible to use too many transitions. Ask the friend or classmate who helps you edit your first draft to let you know if you've put in more than you need.

As you prepare to revise your essay, ask yourself (and your editorial helper) the following questions:

1. Does each of my examples really illustrate the point I'm trying to make?
2. Have I included enough examples to be convincing?
3. If I'm using a single illustration in some paragraphs, is that convincing?
4. Do any of my illustrations begin to prove the point and then stray from it?
5. Are any of my examples too short or my illustrations too long?
6. Have I used enough specific details?

WHAT TO LOOK FOR IN EXAMPLE AND ILLUSTRATION

As you study the essays in this chapter, focus on the way examples and illustrations are used.

1. In the paragraphs that have a **topic sentence** (the sentence that tells what the paragraph is about), look at the examples or illustrations and decide how convincing they are—that is, how well they explain, support, or enlarge on that idea.
2. Look for concrete, specific, sometimes visual details in the examples and illustrations themselves. Ask yourself what would be lost if these were omitted.
3. Underline the transitional terms used to introduce the examples and illustrations, and keep a list of them in your journal.

This cartoon uses three general examples of "Real-Life Toy Instructions": flying toys, models, and board games.

Can you think of other kinds of toys that would fit this cartoon?

Can you think of specific examples for each of the general categories? (The drawings around the boxed-in instructions will give you some ideas.)

Can you think of an experience you had that would illustrate the point of this cartoon?

When you snatch a tissue, grab a paper towel, toss out a diaper, or pitch a paper napkin, do you ever give a thought to the tree that had to die for that convenience?

Down with Forests

CHARLES KURALT

For more than forty years, Charles Kuralt was one of America's most respected broadcasters. He charmed millions with his *On the Road* TV programs presenting human interest stories found while traveling in a lumbering recreational vehicle to remote corners of America. The piece reprinted here is the text from one of his *Dateline America* series that appeared on the CBS evening news.

TERMS TO RECOGNIZE

habitat *(para. 3)*   the place or region where a plant, animal, or person lives

colleagues *(para. 4)*   people working in the same profession

b altimore, Maryland. I was waiting for breakfast in a coffee shop the 1
other morning and reading the paper. The paper had sixty-six pages.
The waitress brought a paper place mat and a paper napkin and took my order, and I paged through the paper.

I put the paper napkin in my lap, spread the paper out on the paper place 2
mat, and read on: "The House Agriculture Committee," it said, "is looking over legislation that would once again open national forests to the clear-cutting of trees by private companies under government permits."

The waitress brought the coffee. I opened a paper sugar envelope and 3
tore open a little paper cup of cream and went on reading the paper: "The Senate voted without dissent yesterday to allow clear-cutting," the paper said. "Critics have said clear-cutting in the national forests can lead to erosion and destruction of wildlife habitats. Forest Service and industry spokesmen said a flat ban on clear-cutting would bring paralysis to the lumber industry." And to the paper industry, I thought. Clear-cutting is one way to get a lot of paper, and we sure seem to need a lot of paper.

The waitress brought the toast. I looked for the butter. It came on a little   4
paper tray with a covering of paper. I opened a paper package of marmalade
and read on, "Senator Jennings Randolph, Democrat of West Virginia,
urged his colleagues to take a more restrictive view and permit clear-cutting
only under specific guidelines for certain types of forest. But neither he nor
anyone else voted against the bill, which was sent to the House on a 90 to
0 vote."

The eggs came, with little paper packages of salt and pepper. I finished   5
breakfast, put the paper under my arm, and left the table with its used and
useless paper napkin, paper place mat, paper salt and pepper packages, paper
butter and marmalade wrappings, paper sugar envelope, and paper cream
holder, and I walked out into the morning wondering how our national
forests can ever survive our breakfasts.

RESPONDING TO READING

What do you, your family, or friends do (if anything) to preserve our
natural environment? Is organized recycling done in your community? If
so, is it voluntary or required?

GAINING WORD POWER

Sometimes little words can mean a lot. What, for instance, does the word
flat mean in the following sentence?

> Forest Service and industry spokesmen said a *flat* ban on clear-cutting
> would bring paralysis to the lumber industry.

Get together with several of your classmates and see how many other
meanings of the word the group can come up with. Then look it up in a
dictionary. Did you think of most of them?

Now think about the word *set*. See how many sentences the group can
write using *set* with a different meaning in each one. Do at least five. Then
check the dictionary to see how many there are. Surprising, isn't it, how
much meaning can be packed into such a simple little word?

CONSIDERING CONTENT

1. How many times does the word *paper* appear in this brief piece?
2. Make a list of paper products that might have been used if the
   writer had been eating a fast-food lunch instead of breakfast.
3. Do you think the critics of clear-cutting who are quoted by Kuralt
   in paragraph 3 are right about what happens as a result of that kind
   of logging?

4. Why do you think the senators voted so overwhelmingly to allow clear-cutting again in our national forests?
5. How would you have voted? How do you think Kuralt would have voted?
6. What is the point of the essay? How do you know? Can you find a thesis statement?

CONSIDERING METHOD

1. How does the writer get our interest in the opening paragraph?
2. Besides the timber industry and the paper industry, who else shares responsibility for the destruction of forests? Point out specific sentences that let you know this.
3. The examples Kuralt selected to describe his breakfast are carefully chosen to illustrate what point?
4. Why do you think he decided not to tell us the name of the cafe, what it looked like, whether the service was fast or slow, or any of the dozens of other details he could have included?
5. In virtually every paragraph, he begins with details about his breakfast and then shifts to examples quoted from the morning paper. Would the piece have been as effective if he had reversed the order—quoted first and then supplied examples about his breakfast?
6. What makes the conclusion effective?

WRITING STEP BY STEP

Perhaps you noticed that Kuralt's essay is a short, simple narrative—the story of someone's breakfast one morning. Not exactly an exciting, action-packed adventure, is it? So what makes the piece effective? Probably its success lies in the skillful way Kuralt arranges the examples to prove his point, without ever having to tell us directly what the point is.

Write a brief essay, or perhaps just one well-developed paragraph, using Kuralt's technique.

A. Think of something you do often that has become a nuisance (like prying open safety seals on food) or that serves as a convenience (like tossing out disposable food containers).
B. Then think of a little story that will allow you to use five or six examples to illustrate either the nuisance (of having to peel off all those pesky pieces of plastic in the middle of getting lunch) or the convenience (of just throwing all the mess out when cleaning up after a party).

C. Make a list of examples to use. Trade lists with a classmate and help each other add to the lists.

D. Begin your piece, as Kuralt does, by establishing the setting ("I was trying to fix lunch in a hurry before my one o'clock appointment when I reached for the mustard" or "I was still half asleep when I faced up to clearing out the remains of the party").

E. Present your examples as concretely as possible ("Circling the top of the mustard container was a tight band of clear plastic, impossible to break with mere fingers," or "Into the trash went the revolting remains of the onion dip in its plastic container").

F. Close by making some observation about your story to make a point about the nuisance ("I think it's grossly unfair that we all have to struggle to open even a jar of mayonnaise just because years ago some crazy person poisoned the Tylenol") or the convenience ("Cleaning up was a breeze, but what's going to happen when all the landfills are full of plastic pop bottles and sour cream cartons?").

OTHER WRITING IDEAS

1. Would you be willing to give up using some paper products in order to slow the destruction of our forests? If so, write an essay telling which ones you could do without and what you would use instead, guessing how much time and effort the change would cost you, then figuring how much money you could save in a year. Conclude by urging your readers to do the same.

2. Discuss the problem of excessive packaging of products in our society, offering specific examples and posing possible solutions, if you have any.

3. Write an essay explaining a good, easy method of recycling some product, like paper, aluminum cans, plastic bottles, or glass containers.

EDITING SKILLS: USING COMMAS IN SERIES

Notice where the commas are placed in the following examples containing items in series. (The strings of **ellipsis** dots tell you that we have left some words out—that is, we quote only part of Kuralt's sentence.)

I put the paper napkin in my lap, spread the paper out on the paper place mat, and read on. . . .

I finished breakfast, put the paper under my arm, and left the table with its used and useless paper napkin, paper place mat, paper salt and pepper packages, paper butter and marmalade wrappings, paper sugar envelope, and paper cream holder. . . .

The commas are necessary to let you know when one item ends and another begins. Try making sense of those words without the commas to see what a hopeless task reading would be without commas:

> . . . the table with its used and useless paper napkin paper place mat paper salt and pepper packages paper butter and marmalade wrappings paper sugar envelope and paper cream holder. . . .

Notice that in all of the series we just quoted, Kuralt places a comma before the *and* attaching the last item but not before the *and* in *paper salt and pepper packages* or *paper butter and marmalade wrappings.* The comma used before the *and* connecting the last item in a series is optional these days. But we recommend using it to avoid confusing items like *salt and pepper* with the final item in the list.

Now check your essay to be sure that any items in series are properly punctuated.

PREPARING TO READ

Do you feel safe when you go out alone at night? Are there certain sections of town that you would refuse to enter alone after dark? Does the fear, or lack of fear, in any way relate to your gender, your age, or the color of your skin?

'Just Walk on By': A Black Man Ponders His Power to Alter Public Space

BRENT STAPLES

Born in 1951 in Chester, Pennsylvania, Brent Staples is a journalist who also holds a Ph.D. in psychology from the University of Chicago. He is presently an editor at the *New York Times*. The selection reprinted here was first published in *Ms.* magazine in September 1986. An excerpt, entitled "Black Men and Public Space," appeared in the December 1986 issue of *Harper's*.

TERMS TO RECOGNIZE

uninflammatory *(para. 1)*	not likely to cause violence or excitement
unwieldy *(para. 2)*	hard to manage or to deal with
indistinguishable *(para. 2)*	not clearly different from
elicit *(para. 3)*	draw forth
warrenlike *(para. 5)*	narrow and crowded like a hutch where rabbits are kept
bandolier *(para. 5)*	a belt holding bullets, draped across the chest
lethality *(para. 6)*	being lethal or deadly
bravado *(para. 6)*	pretended courage or false confidence
ad hoc *(para. 7)*	for this case only
labyrinthine *(para. 7)*	like the winding, confusing passages in a maze
berth *(para. 9)*	enough space at sea to avoid hitting another ship or the shore
skittish *(para. 9)*	jumpy, easily frightened
constitutionals *(para. 10)*	walks to improve one's health

m y first victim was a woman—white, well dressed, probably in her 1
early 20s. I came upon her late one evening on a deserted street in
Hyde Park, a relatively affluent neighborhood in an otherwise mean,
impoverished section of Chicago. As I swung onto the avenue behind her,
there seemed to be a discreet, uninflammatory distance between us. Not
so. She cast back a worried glance. To her, the youngish black man—a
broad six feet two inches with a beard and billowing hair, both hands
shoved into the pockets of a bulky military jacket—seemed menacingly
close. She picked up her pace and was soon running in earnest. Within
seconds she disappeared into a cross street.

That was more than a decade ago. I was 22 years old, a graduate student 2
newly arrived at the University of Chicago. It was in the echo of that terrified woman's footfalls that I first began to know the unwieldy inheritance
I'd come into—the ability to alter public space in ugly ways. It was clear
that she thought of herself as the quarry of a mugger, a rapist, or worse.
Suffering a bout of insomnia, however, I was stalking sleep, not defenseless
wayfarers. As a softy who is scarcely able to take a knife to a raw chicken—
let alone hold one to a person's throat—I was surprised, embarrassed, and
dismayed all at once. Her flight made me feel like an accomplice in tyranny.
It also made it clear that I was indistinguishable from the muggers who
occasionally seeped into the area from the surrounding ghetto. I soon gath-
ered that being perceived as dangerous is a hazard in itself: Where fear and
weapons meet—as they often do in urban America—there is always the
possibility of death.

In that first year, my first away from my hometown, I was to become 3
thoroughly familiar with the language of fear. At dark, shadowy intersections,
I could cross in front of a car stopped at a traffic light and elicit the *thunk,*
thunk, thunk, thunk of the driver—black, white, male, female—hammering
down the door locks. On less traveled streets after dark, I grew accustomed
to but never comfortable with people crossing to the other side of the street
rather than pass me. Then there were the standard unpleasantries with police-
men, doormen, bouncers, cabdrivers, and others whose business it is to
screen out troublesome individuals *before* there is any nastiness.

I moved to New York nearly two years ago and I have remained an avid 4
night walker. In central Manhattan, the near-constant crowd covers the tense
one-on-one street encounters. Elsewhere, things can get very taut indeed.

After dark, on the warrenlike streets of Brooklyn where I live, I often 5
see women who fear the worst from me. They seem to have set their faces
on neutral, and with their purse straps strung across their chests bandolier-
style, they forge ahead as though bracing themselves against being tackled.
I understand, of course, that the danger they perceive is not a hallucina-
tion. Women are particularly vulnerable to street violence, and young black

males are drastically overrepresented among the perpetrators of that violence. Yet these truths are no solace against the alienation that comes of being ever the suspect, an entity with whom pedestrians avoid making eye contact.

It is not altogether clear to me how I reached the ripe old age of 22 without being conscious of the lethality nighttime pedestrians attributed to me. Perhaps it was because in Chester, Pa., the small, angry industrial town where I came of age in the 1960s, I was scarcely noticeable against a backdrop of gang warfare, street knifings, and murders. I grew up one of the good boys, had perhaps a half-dozen fistfights. In retrospect, my shyness of combat has clear sources. As a boy, I saw countless tough guys locked away; I have since buried several, too. They were babies, really—a teen-age cousin, a brother of 22, a childhood friend in his mid-20s—all gone down in episodes of bravado played out in the streets. I chose, perhaps unconsciously, to remain a shadow—timid, but a survivor.

The fearsomeness mistakenly attributed to me in public places often has a perilous flavor. The most frightening of these confusions occurred in the late 1970s and early 1980s, when I worked as a journalist in Chicago. One day, rushing into the office of a magazine I was writing for with a deadline story in hand, I was mistaken for a burglar. The office manager called security and, with the speed of an ad hoc posse, pursued me through the labyrinthine halls, nearly to my editor's door. I had no way of proving who I was. I could only move briskly toward the company of someone who knew me.

Relatively speaking, however, I never fared as badly as another black male journalist. He went to nearby Waukegan, Ill., a couple of summers ago to work on a story about a murderer who was born there. Mistaking the reporter for the killer, police officers hauled him from his car at gunpoint and but for his press credentials would probably have tried to book him. Such episodes are not uncommon. Black men trade tales like this all the time.

Over the years, I learned to smother the rage I felt at so often being mistaken for a criminal. Not to do so would surely have led to madness. I now take precautions to make myself less threatening. I move about with care, particularly late in the evening. I give a wide berth to nervous people on subway platforms during the wee hours. If I happen to be entering a building behind some people who appear skittish, I may walk by, letting them clear the lobby before I return, so as not to seem to be following them. I have been calm and extremely congenial on those rare occasions when I've been pulled over by the police.

And on late-evening constitutionals I employ what has proved to be an excellent tension-reducing measure: I whistle melodies from Beethoven and Vivaldi and the more popular classical composers. Even steely New Yorkers hunching toward nighttime destinations seem to relax, and occasionally they even join in the tune. Virtually everybody seems to sense that a mugger wouldn't be warbling bright, sunny selections from Vivaldi's "Four Seasons." It is my equivalent of the cowbell that hikers wear when they are in bear country.

RESPONDING TO READING

Why don't we expect muggers to be whistling melodies from Beethoven and Vivaldi? In your journal, write a brief explanation of the possible reasons.

GAINING WORD POWER

The following words appear in the reading but are not included in the "Terms to Recognize." Look up each one in your dictionary and use it in a sentence of your own.

1. affluent (para. 1)
2. menacingly (para. 1)
3. dismayed (para. 2)
4. taut (para. 4)
5. vulnerable (para. 5)
6. solace (para. 5)
7. entity (para. 5)
8. attributed (para. 7)
9. precautions (para. 9)
10. congenial (para. 9)

CONSIDERING CONTENT

1. How does the author describe his physical appearance in the opening paragraph?
2. Why does the woman take him for "a mugger, a rapist, or worse"?
3. What does the writer mean when he says that "being perceived as dangerous is a hazard in itself"? What illustrations does he offer to prove his point?
4. What kind of hometown background did Brent Staples have? What kind of person did he turn out to be?
5. At the end of paragraph 6, he speaks of three young men he was close to—"all gone down in episodes of bravado played out on the streets." Although he doesn't tell us how any of them died, can you guess? Give examples of the kind of "episodes of bravado" that may have cost them their lives.
6. How did Staples learn to deal with the problem of being a large, young black man in the city?

7. Why would hikers in bear country wear cowbells? Explain how that wilderness situation is similar to Staples's urban situation.

CONSIDERING METHOD

1. Explain how the brief narrative in the opening paragraph catches our interest.
2. The thesis of this selection is implied, not directly stated. Write out in your own words a statement of the author's main point.
3. In the first paragraph, Staples uses a two-word sentence fragment, "Not so." Turn those two words into a complete sentence, and then comment on why you think he chose the fragment.
4. How does description help to make Staples's illustrations interesting and convincing in paragraphs 1 and 5?
5. Using words that sound like the noise they describe is called **onomatopoeia** (for example, the *thunk, thunk, thunk, thunk* of the car door locks in para. 3). Explain why that word choice is effective. Can you think of other examples of words that sound like what they mean?
6. This essay is developed through example and illustration, yet Staples does not tell us how the three young men died in paragraph 6. Why does he leave out these details?
7. Explain what makes the conclusion particularly satisfying.

WRITING STEP BY STEP

Stereotypes are oversimplified groupings of people by race, gender, politics, athletic ability, ethnic origin, and so on. Staples was stereotyped because he was a young black male, and as Staples says, "young black males are drastically overrepresented among the perpetrators of . . . violence." There is usually some grain of truth behind stereotypes, but, nonetheless, they tend to be negative and unfair. Women, for instance, are stereotyped as weak, passive, fickle, timid, scatterbrained, and indecisive. Men, on the other hand, are supposed to be strong-minded and assertive, but dense and unfeeling. Stereotypes are unfair because they lump lots of people into a category whether or not the characteristics fit every individual.

A. Think of a stereotype that includes you. Choose one that you think is unfair to you; your essay will explain how you are different.
B. Begin, as Staples does, with a brief narrative, a story that illustrates how you *seem* to fit the type although you actually do not.
C. In the next paragraph, define the stereotype by giving examples of several characteristics people expect you to have—or not to have.

D. Next, explain why people would tend to place you in this stereo-type. For instance, if you are a male football player, people may take you for a clumsy hulk who can barely read and write.

E. Then, explain why you don't fit the stereotype, and tell about some influence while you were growing up that helped you to avoid the typical pattern of behavior. Provide concrete examples, as Staples does in paragraph 6 when he tells about his childhood among the gangs in Chester, Pennsylvania.

F. In conclusion, explain how you felt about being stereotyped, and tell how you have learned to cope with the mistaken views of strangers—perhaps even relatives and friends—who took you for a different kind of person than you truly are.

OTHER WRITING IDEAS

1. Write the paper outlined in the previous section, but instead illus-trate how you are the perfect example of a stereotype. You may want to think of a positive stereotype—or else make your essay humorous.

2. Write an essay about frustrations at work (or in some other area of your life). What frustrations do you have? How do you deal with them? Do you think you handle them well or poorly? If poorly, what could you do to improve? Give plenty of specific examples to explain and support your general points.

3. With a small group of classmates, discuss phobias, those irrational fears that most of us have—fear of spiders, of snakes, of high places, of flying, of closed spaces. Which ones do you have? Choose your worst or your most embarrassing phobia, and tell in an essay how it limits your activities, how it makes you feel, how you think you got it, and what you do to control it.

EDITING SKILLS: COMMAS AROUND INTERRUPTERS

An **interrupter** is just what it sounds like—a word or group of words that interrupts or breaks the flow of a sentence, like the italicized words do here:

I understand, *of course,* that the danger they perceive is not a hallucina-tion.

You need a comma before and after the interrupter as a signal to your readers that the interrupter is an addition that can be removed without changing the meaning of the sentence. The first comma signals the start of the interruption; the second comma signals the end of the interruption. It would be quite misleading in that sentence, with its flow interrupted, to use only one comma. But if you move the *of course* to the beginning or to the end of the sentence so that it no longer interrupts the flow, then a single comma is fine:

> *Of course,* I understand that the danger they perceive is not a hallucination.
>
> I understand that the danger they perceive is not a hallucination, *of course.*

The principle remains the same, even when the interrupter is longer:

> One day, *rushing into the office of a magazine I was writing for with a deadline story in hand,* I was mistaken for a burglar.

Remember to put commas *around* interrupters—one before and one after.

EXERCISE

We've omitted the commas from around the interrupters in the following sentences. Figure out where they belong, and put them back in.

1. Suffering a bout of insomnia however I was stalking sleep, not defenseless wayfarers.
2. After dark on the warrenlike streets of Brooklyn where I live I often see women who fear the worst from me.
3. I chose perhaps unconsciously to remain a shadow—timid, but a survivor.
4. The office manager called security and with the speed of an ad hoc posse pursued me through the labyrinthine halls, nearly to my editor's door.
5. Relatively speaking however I never fared as badly as another black male journalist.

Now check the essay you've just written to be sure that you have punctuated interrupters correctly. Did you always remember to include the second comma?

PREPARING TO READ

Do men or women make better schoolteachers? Does gender matter? Does the age of the students make any difference?

One Man's Kids

DANIEL MEIER

Daniel Meier received a master's degree from Harvard Graduate School of Education in 1984. Since then he has taught first grade at schools in Brookline and Boston in Massachusetts. His articles about teaching and his reviews of children's books have appeared in a number of educational journals. The essay reprinted here appeared in 1987 in the "About Men" series of the *New York Times Magazine.*

TERMS TO RECOGNIZE

complying *(para. 4)*	agreeing to someone else's request or command
singular *(para. 5)*	exceptional, unusual, distinguished by superiority
consoling *(para. 6)*	offering comfort and advice
intellectual *(para. 7)*	guided chiefly by knowledge or reason rather than by emotion or experience
hilarity *(para. 7)*	spirited merriment, cheerfulness
complimentary *(para. 12)*	given free as a courtesy or a favor

1 teach first graders. I live in a world of skinned knees, double-knotted shoelaces, riddles that I've heard a dozen times, stale birthday cakes, hurt feelings, wandering stories, and one lost shoe ("and if you don't find it my mother'll kill me"). My work is dominated by 6-year-olds.

2 It's 10:45, the middle of snack, and I'm helping Emily open her milk carton. She has already tried the other end without success, and now there's so much paint and ink on the carton from her fingers that I'm not sure she should drink it at all. But I open it. Then I turn to help Scott clean up some milk he has just spilled onto Rebecca's whale crossword puzzle.

3 While I wipe my milk- and paint-covered hands, Jenny wants to know if I've seen that funny book about penguins that I read in class. As I hunt for it in a messy pile of books, Jason wants to know if there is a new seating

arrangement for lunch tables. I find the book, turn to answer Jason, then face Maya, who is fast approaching with a new knock-knock joke. After what seems like the 10th "Who's there?" I laugh and Maya is pleased.

Then Andrew wants to know how to spell "flukes" for his crossword. As I get to "u," I give a hand signal for Sarah to take away the snack. But just as Sarah is almost out the door, two children complain that "we haven't even had ours yet." I stop the snack mid-flight, complying with their request for graham crackers. I then return to Andrew, noticing that he has put "flu" for 9 Down, rather than 9 Across. It's now 10:50.

My work is not traditional male work. It's not a singular pursuit. There is not a large pile of paper to get through or one deal to transact. I don't have one area of expertise or knowledge. I don't have the singular power over language of a lawyer, the physical force of a construction worker, the command over fellow workers of a surgeon, the wheeling and dealing transactions of a businessman. My energy is not spent in pursuing, climbing, achieving, conquering, or cornering some goal or object.

My energy is spent in encouraging, supporting, consoling, and praising my children. In teaching, the inner rewards come from without. On any given day, quite apart from teaching reading and spelling, I bandage a cut, dry a tear, erase a frown, tape a torn doll, and locate a long-lost boot. The day is really won through matters of the heart. As my students groan, laugh, shudder, cry, exult, and wonder, I do too. I have to be soft around the edges.

A few years ago, when I was interviewing for an elementary-school teaching position, every principal told me with confidence that, as a male, I had an advantage over female applicants because of the lack of male teachers. But in the next breath, they asked with a hint of suspicion why I chose to work with young children. I told them that I wanted to observe and contribute to the intellectual growth of a maturing mind. What I really felt like saying, but didn't, was that I loved helping a child learn to write her name for the first time, finding someone a new friend, or sharing in the hilarity of reading about Winnie the Pooh getting so stuck in a hole that only his head and rear show.

I gave that answer to those principals, who were mostly male, because I thought they wanted a "male" response. This meant talking about intellectual matters. If I had taken a different course and talked about my interest in helping children in their emotional development, it would have been seen as closer to a "female" answer. I even altered my language, not once mentioning the word "love" to describe what I do indeed love about teaching. My answer worked; every principal nodded approvingly.

Some of the principals also asked what I saw myself doing later in my career. They wanted to know if I eventually wanted to go into educational administration. Becoming a dean of students or a principal has never been one of my goals, but they seemed to expect me, as a male, to want to climb higher on the career stepladder. So I mentioned that, at some point, I would be interested in working with teachers as a curriculum coordinator. Again, they nodded approvingly.

If those principals had been female instead of male, I wonder whether 10 their questions, and my answers, would have been different. My guess is that they would have been.

At other times, when I'm at a party or a dinner and tell someone that I 11 teach young children, I've found that men and women respond differently. Most men ask about the subjects I teach and the courses I took in my training. Then, unless they bring up an issue such as merit pay, the conversation stops. Most women, on the other hand, begin the conversation on a more immediate and personal level. They say things like "those kids must love having a male teacher" or "that age is just wonderful, you must love it." Then, more often than not, they'll talk about their own kids or ask me specific questions about what I do. We're then off and talking shop.

Possibly, men would have more to say to me, and I to them, if my job 12 had more of the trappings and benefits of more traditional male jobs. But my job has no bonuses or promotions. No complimentary box seats at the ball park. No cab fare home. No drinking buddies after work. No briefcase. No suit. (Ties get stuck in paint jars.) No power lunches. (I eat peanut butter and jelly, chips, milk, and cookies with the kids.) No taking clients out for cocktails. The only place I take my kids is to the playground.

Although I could have pursued a career in law or business, as several of 13 my friends did, I chose teaching instead. My job has benefits all its own. I'm able to bake cookies without getting them stuck together as they cool, buy cheap sewing materials, take out splinters, and search just the right trash cans for useful odds and ends. I'm sometimes called "Daddy" and even "Mommy" by my students, and if there's ever a lull in the conversation at a dinner party, I can always ask those assembled if they've heard the latest riddle about why the turkey crossed the road. (He thought he was a chicken.)

RESPONDING TO READING

What do you think about Meier's choice of career? Do you think it's reasonable and appropriate? Why or why not?

GAINING WORD POWER

In paragraph 12 Meier uses the word *complimentary*. There is a word that's pronounced the same but has a different spelling and a different meaning—*complementary*. Do you know what each word means? English has many of these sound-alike words, and it's important to know the differences among them. They won't cause you any trouble in speaking, but they will change the meaning of your writing if you choose the wrong one.

Here is a list of words from Meier's essay. Using your dictionary, find a sound-alike word for each item in the list, and write down its meaning. Then use the word you found in a sentence.

fare	right	male
new	won	course
principal	seen	whether
through	two	hole

CONSIDERING CONTENT

1. Why did Meier write this essay? What point do you think he wants to make?
2. Meier says, "my work is not traditional male work" (para. 5). What does he mean by that statement? Do you agree?
3. What is a "singular pursuit"? Why does the author use that phrase to describe "male work"?
4. Why did the principals who interviewed Meier have "a hint of suspicion" about him (para. 7)?
5. What kind of answers did Meier give in his job interviews (para. 8)? What kind of answers did he avoid? Why didn't he mention the word "love"?
6. The author says that men and women respond differently to him when he talks about his job (para. 11). What are the differences?
7. How does Meier feel about his job? Do you think he is being defensive or apologetic about it?

CONSIDERING METHOD

1. In the first paragraph, the author says, "My work is dominated by 6-year-olds." What examples does he give to explain and support this general statement?
2. Why does Meier open his essay the way he does? Why doesn't he state his thesis until paragraph 5?
3. Find the series of words that Meier uses to describe "male work" (end of para. 5) and the words he uses to describe what he does (beginning of para. 6). What is he saying about the difference between his work and "male work"?
4. What does the author mean when he says, "In teaching, the inner rewards come from without" (para. 6)? What examples does he give to make his meaning clear?

5. What is the effect of the series of phrases that begin with "No" in paragraph 12? Why are the positive comments in parentheses? Why is the last sentence in the paragraph not in parentheses?

WRITING STEP BY STEP

Think of a workplace that you know well—a place where you have a job now or had one in the past. If your primary work is being a student, then school is your workplace.

A. First identify and briefly explain your role in the workplace ("I am a cashier, salesperson, and general trouble shooter at Posh Pups, a pet grooming and pet supply store").

B. Then name three or four personal qualities that make for success in that job ("To work at Posh Pups, you need to be loyal and good at math and to like people as much as you like animals").

C. Think about the order in which you want to present these qualities. You might start with a less important quality and build up to the most important one. Or you may see that two of them are related and need to be placed in back-to-back paragraphs. Make a scratch outline to help you decide how to arrange your main points and examples.

D. For each quality you name, give at least one example of how it is important in the job. Think of a specific time when each quality was needed. Tell the story of how you or your co-workers showed the quality (or, unfortunately, showed a lack of it).

E. If an example is long and detailed, give it its own paragraph, as Meier does in paragraphs 2, 3, and 4 of his essay. If some of your examples are only a sentence or two, try to expand them with more details that will give your readers the sights, sounds, and feel of your work.

F. Close with a summarizing statement of how you feel about this job. Or offer a recommendation to anyone who might consider going into this line of work. Try to reinforce your thesis idea without just repeating it.

G. When you revise, look at the transitions between your paragraphs. Try to fill in any gaps between your main points. Also check to see that you used transitions to lead into your examples. Ask your instructor or your classmates to help you improve the flow of your ideas.

OTHER WRITING IDEAS

1. Select one of the following general statements, or compose one of your own. Make it the central idea of an essay full of examples and

illustrations. Draw examples from your reading, your conversation, your observations, and your own experience.

    a. Action heroes in the movies today are pretty much alike.

    b. Being a good parent is probably the hardest job there is.

    c. The stereotypical female (or male) is not easy to find in our society anymore.

    d. Being a teenager can be difficult (or easy or perplexing or a lot of fun).

    e. Jealousy is a destructive emotion.

2. Discuss with your classmates some superstitions that you or members of your family or community have held. Frequently, these superstitions have to do with success or bad luck in sports, performances, weather, or work. Do they have any validity? How did they develop? Write an essay of example about the role that superstition plays in your life or in the life of someone you know.

EDITING SKILLS: USING SUBORDINATION

Writers often combine two or more ideas in a sentence by using **subordination.** When one idea is subordinate to or dependent on another, it is less important. Take a look at these sentences from Meier's essay to see how the subordinate ideas are introduced by words that make them sound less important:

> *Although* I could have pursued a career in law or business, I chose teaching instead.
>
> Then, *unless* they bring up an issue such as merit pay, the conversation stops.
>
> *If* I had taken a different course and talked about my interest in helping children in their emotional development, it would have been seen as close to a "female" answer.

As you can see, each of these sentences has two parts. Notice that the second part, after the comma, can stand alone as a sentence: that part is called **independent.** If you read the first part alone, it does not sound complete. The first part is called **dependent** for this reason. The opening words—*Although, unless,* and *If*—make the first statement of each sentence dependent. These words are called *subordinating conjunctions;* they indicate that the first idea is not as important as the rest of the sentence. (You will also notice that when the dependent part comes first, a comma separates it from the independent part.)

Subordinating conjunctions are familiar words; we use them a lot. Here's a list of the most common ones: *since, because, if, even if, unless, although, even though, though, as long as, after, before, when, whenever, while, until,* and *wherever.* Skillful writers use subordination to give variety to their sentences and to keep readers' attention focused on the main ideas.

EXERCISE

Imitate the following sentences. Each one begins with a dependent statement followed by an independent one. You don't have to imitate each sentence exactly; just follow the dependent–independent pattern and use the same subordinating conjunction as the model sentence. Put in the commas, too.

> Model: If we want clean air, then we will have to drive more fuel-efficient cars.
>
> Imitation: If you like lasagna, then you should try the new Italian restaurant on Division Street.

1. While I was eating my lunch, a friend walked in.
2. Wherever I go in this city, I run into old friends.
3. Before you gather up your books, be sure your notes are complete.
4. Although Selma is a good athlete, she sometimes swears at the umpire.
5. Unless she sees the error of her ways, Selma may get tossed off the team.

Write at least one more imitation of each of the preceding sentences.

Go back to your example essay to see how many sentences like these you've written. What subordinating conjunctions did you use? Did you include the commas? Now combine some more of your sentences by using subordinating conjunctions and the dependent–independent pattern. If they sound sensible, keep them in your essay.

PREPARING TO READ

If you are male, would you be surprised to have a female open a door for you? If a woman did, would you be pleased or annoyed? If you are female, do you expect a man you are with to open doors, including car doors, for you? Would you be disappointed if he did or did not? Or would you even notice?

Civil Rites

CAROLINE MILLER

Caroline Miller wrote the following selection as an editorial for the August 1993 issue of *Lear's*, a magazine no longer published, which was aimed at intellectual women over age forty. In this piece, Miller speculates on the confusion over what constitutes good manners now that social roles have changed as a result of the women's movement.

TERMS TO RECOGNIZE

gallantry *(para. 4)*	great courtesy
ambiguous *(para. 5)*	uncertain, unclear, in doubt
elusive *(para. 5)*	not easily grasped or pinned down
chivalry *(para. 7)*	courteous protection of women
demise *(para. 9)*	death, end
improvise *(para. 10)*	to make up or do on the spur of the moment
clamoring *(para. 11)*	making a loud, continuous noise
empathy *(para. 11)*	understanding, sensitivity
acute *(para. 11)*	pointed, sharp, extreme

I was taking my kids to school not long ago when I had one of those 1 experiences particular to parents—a moment that nobody else notices, but that we replay over and over because in it we see something new about our children.

On this morning the bus was standing-room-only as we squeezed on at 2 our regular stop. Several blocks later my son, Nick, found a free seat halfway back on one side of the bus and his little sister, Elizabeth, and I took seats on the other.

I was listening to Lizzie chatter on about something when I was 3 surprised to see Nick get up. I watched as he said something quietly to an older, not quite grandmotherly woman who didn't look familiar to me. Suddenly I understood: He was offering her his seat.

A little thing, but still I was flooded with gratitude. For all the times we have talked about what to do and what not to do on the bus—say "Excuse me," cover your mouth when you cough, don't point, don't stare at people who are unusual looking—this wasn't something I had trained him to do. It was a small act of gallantry, and it was entirely his idea. 4

For all we try to show our kids and tell them how we believe people should act, how we hope *they* will act, it still comes as a shock and a pleasure—a relief, frankly—when they do something that suggests they understand. All the more so because in the world in which Nick is growing up, the rules that govern social interaction are so much more ambiguous than they were when we were his age. Kids are exposed to a free-for-all of competing signals about what's acceptable, let alone what's admirable. It's a world, after all, in which *in your face* is the style of the moment. Civility has become a more or less elusive proposition. 5

I was reminded of this incident on the train the other day, on another crowded morning, as I watched a young man in an expensive suit slip into an open seat without so much as losing his place in *The New York Times,* smoothly beating out a silver-haired gentleman and a gaggle of young women in spike heels. 6

My first thought was that his mother would be ashamed of him. And then I thought, with some amusement, that I am hopelessly behind the times. For all I know, the older man would've been insulted to be offered a seat by someone two or three decades his junior. And the women, I suppose, might consider chivalry a sexist custom. Besides, our young executive or investment banker probably had to compete with women for the job that's keeping him in Italian loafers; why would he want to offer a potential competitor a seat? 7

Of course, this sort of confusion is about much more than etiquette on public transportation. It's about what we should do for each other, and expect of each other, now that our roles are no longer closely dictated by whether we are male or female, young or old. 8

Not for a minute do I mourn the demise of the social contract that gave men most of the power and opportunity, and women most of the seats on the bus. But operating without a contract can be uncomfortable, too. It's as if nobody quite knows how to behave anymore; the lack of predictability on all fronts has left all our nerve endings exposed. And the confusion extends to everything from deciding who goes through the door first to who initiates sex. 9

Under the circumstances, civility requires a good deal more imagination than it once did, if only because it's so much harder to know what the person sitting across from you—whether stranger or spouse—expects, 10 needs, wants from you. When you don't have an official rulebook, you have to listen harder, be more sensitive, be ready to improvise.

But of course improvising is just what Americans do best. And unlike 11 the European model, our particular form of civility here in the former colonies aims to be democratic, to bridge our diverse histories with empathy and respect. At a moment when so many people are clamoring for attention, and so many others are nursing their wounds, the need for empathy and respect is rather acute.

And so, as we encourage our children to define themselves actively, to 12 express themselves with confidence, we hope they will also learn to be generous—with those they don't know, as well as with those they love. And we hope they will care enough, and be observant enough, to be able to tell when someone else needs a seat more than they do.

RESPONDING TO READING

What kinds of behavior are necessary for good manners in dealing with the opposite sex—or do you think there is no need for two different sets of polite behavior? Think of very specific examples, like holding coats, opening doors, using four-letter words, giving up seats, removing hats, and so on.

GAINING WORD POWER

Miller uses the word *civil* in her title; then in paragraphs 10 and 11, she speaks of *civility.* If the word *civil* means "polite or courteous," then the word *civility* means "politeness or courteousness." Can you tell from that change in meaning how the suffix *-ity* works? If you aren't sure, look it up in your dictionary.

First, use each of the following words in a sentence. Then, add the suffix *-ity* to each one, dropping the final *e* if the word has one. Next, look up each new word to see how the pronunciation changes. Finally, write another set of sentences in which you use each new word in a reasonable way.

1. timid
2. equal
3. productive
4. specific
5. passive
6. active
7. possible
8. diverse
9. scarce
10. inferior

CONSIDERING CONTENT

1. Explain what Miller means by the "rules that govern social interaction" (para. 5). Are these "rules" written down anywhere? How could you learn them?
2. The essay focuses on *etiquette* (para. 8). Look the word up in your dictionary, and explain what it means.

3. What synonyms (terms meaning the same thing) for *etiquette* does Miller use?
4. What has led to the present confusion about good manners?
5. What impression of the "young women in spike heels" do you get from Miller's choice of the word *gaggle* to describe them? Look up the word if you don't know what it means.
6. What quality does Miller hope will be learned by children who are growing up now?

CONSIDERING METHOD

1. How does Miller capture our interest at the beginning of her essay?
2. How do these details in paragraph 6—the expensive suit, the silver hair, and the spike heels—contribute to our understanding of the incident she describes?
3. Can you figure out why Miller delays her thesis statement until paragraph 8?
4. The final sentence echoes an element in the introduction, giving the essay a pleasing unity. What does she echo?
5. Explain the play on words in the title.

WRITING STEP BY STEP

A. Think about dating rituals. You may have put dating behind you— or perhaps you are going through it for the second or third time. Get together with a small group of classmates or friends, and brainstorm about dating etiquette—who does what, when, and for whom.
B. Talk about and take notes on all the particulars—who calls first, who drives, who picks up the check, what strings may be attached to an expensive dinner. Decide which "rules" you think are just fine and which ones should be ignored.
C. Jot down incidents from your own life and from experiences of the group that illustrate how the dating rules work.
D. Then write an essay focusing on dating rituals. Decide whether you think they are mainly useful in selecting a suitable mate—or mostly silly, outdated, and unfair.
E. Develop your essay with illustrations and examples. Select material from your brainstorming to support your viewpoint, and organize your details around one typical date or around a typical courtship.
F. Begin with an illustration, as Miller does. Depending on your view-point, choose something touching (like orchids arriving unexpectedly at your door) or something agonizing (like waiting endlessly for the phone to ring).

G. For your conclusion, find one example of some practice you think is a good idea from the other side of the issue. For instance, if you are writing in favor of current etiquette, you might want to suggest that although most of the rules are fine, the dating ritual could be improved if males didn't always have to pick up the check.

H. If you can't think of anything wrong with the current custom—or if you can't think of anything *good* about it—conclude with an echo of the incident you began with, as Miller does in her last sentence.

OTHER WRITING IDEAS

1. "Miss Manners" is the pen name of a newspaper columnist who, like Ann Landers and Dear Abby, gives advice—but Miss Manners offers advice about etiquette. Write a letter to Miss Manners, asking how to behave in a certain social situation—something like, "Is it acceptable to kiss the groom as well as the bride after a wedding?" Then pretend to be Miss Manners and write a response to the letter.

2. Using lots of examples, explain a ritual from another culture that you are familiar with.

3. Write an essay developing this thesis: "I wish my family (or mate or roommate or dog) had better manners," citing examples of behavior that annoys you.

EDITING SKILLS: SEMICOLONS BETWEEN SENTENCES

If you tend to write mainly short, simple sentences, you may need to add some variety. Here's an easy way. If you have two sentences *that are closely connected in meaning,* you can put them together—separated by a semicolon—as Miller does here:

It's as if nobody quite knows how to behave anymore; the lack of predictability on all fronts has left all our nerve endings exposed.

She could, of course, have used a comma plus a coordinating conjunction (*and, but, or, for, nor, yet,* or *so*) between the sentences:

It's as if nobody quite knows how to behave anymore, *for* the lack of predictability on all fronts has left all our nerve endings exposed.

But you don't get much variety that way, as it's a common way to join sentences.

Find another example of sentences joined with a semicolon in paragraph 7 of Miller's essay.

Now, go through the essay you just wrote to see whether you have any short, closely related sentences that come one right after the other. If so, try taking out the period, putting in a semicolon, and making the capital letter lowercase.

A word of caution: be sure to use a *semicolon* in joining sentences; a comma definitely will not do. Also, be sure that the sentences really are closely related—that is, focused on the same idea.

Student Essay Using Examples

My Key Chain

David C. Lair

During my four years of Army service, I led a very transient life. I moved from Illinois to Missouri to California to Texas to Massachusetts to Germany and back to Illinois again, never staying in one place for very long. Consequently, I had to live a very sparse lifestyle with few possessions, and those that I did try to keep fared poorly through all my relocation. (In the Army it is said that two or three moves have the same effect on one's belongings as does a house fire.) Therefore, when trying to think of a possession that has been significant to me personally, my choices are narrowed to only those items that I have been able to carry on my person. Of these items, I believe that my key chain says more about my self and my life than anything else does.

Upon entering the service I soon learned that my eventual duty station, after I completed training at various posts in the States, would be somewhere in Germany. At this time I bought a key chain decorated with an Imperial Eagle and the inscription "Deutschland" (which means Germany); it also came equipped with a handy bottle opener. This key chain was important because it came at a time when I was looking forward to being stationed in Germany. My training was long and mentally arduous, and the key chain served as a reminder of my goal. Whenever I felt discouraged, I pulled out my key chain and thought of traveling around Germany, learning the language, meeting the people, and drinking the beer, which I had heard great things about. I already had big plans for the bottle opener.

When I finally arrived in Germany, my outlook on life changed, and so did the "function" of my key chain. Now I lived life for the present. I traveled, learned the language, absorbed the culture, and sampled as many brands of beer as I could find. Along with this transition, the duties of my key chain became more based in the present. Now the keys on the chain represented my "home" in the city of Fulda as I wandered around the continent; now the inscription "Deutschland" made sense to me linguistically; and now the bottle opener was my most important tool. I will always look back on this time as a very happy period in my life.

My tour in Germany ended last December, and I returned to the States to begin my new life as a student. But the transition wasn't easy. I found that my mind often dwelled on my former lifestyle; I also found myself missing Germany. Once again, my key chain mirrored my state of mind. By this time the metal around the opener was rusted, the "Deutschland" insignia was scratched, and cracks had begun to form along the entire length of the chain. I frequently looked at my beloved belonging and remembered the fun I had had. As I sprung another cap from an imported beer, I realized that I was now living in the past. 4

Recently, while opening a beer, my key chain broke in half. The stress of opening all the beers finally drove the cracks completely through the key chain. This development caused me to reflect on my present situation. I decided that it was time to stop living in the past, and to start looking toward my future once again. 5

Over Christmas break my girlfriend and I will travel to Brazil to visit her parents, who live in Rio de Janiero. I am very excited about the trip. I am looking forward to exploring a new country once again and to meeting new people. When she heard that my key chain had broken, my girlfriend gave me a small present: a key chain with the Brazilian flag and the inscription "Brazil." Sure, there's no bottle opener, but we have "twist-tops" in the United States anyway. Now I can once again take my key chain out of my pocket and anticipate the future, while at the same time enjoying the present. 6

C h a p t e r

5

STRATEGIES FOR CLARIFYING MEANING

Definition and Explanation

"PowerTalk gives you a single mailbox icon for all incoming and outgoing mail—including fax, voice, electronic mail, and documents. Communication from on-line services and electronic mail from various sources are routed to your desktop mailbox when you install mail gateways supplied by the vendor," the manual for our new computer operating system cheerfully brags. Sounds great, but we have only the vaguest idea what PowerTalk *is!* How many of the terms in those two sentences would *you* need to have defined or explained? Moreover, how many terms would need definition and explanation for a reader in the 1970s?

THE POINT OF DEFINITION AND EXPLANATION

As suggested by the quotation from the computer manual and by the cartoon following this chapter introduction, the whole point of definition and explanation is to clarify things for people. Words are worse than unhelpful when they don't convey meaning but instead create confusion.

The special vocabulary of any group needs explanation when used to communicate with people outside that group. Some groups develop languages that are incredibly mysterious to outsiders. If you've ever been the outsider listening to a bunch of bridge players, computer gamers, or aerobic class addicts, you know the feeling of bafflement that grows quickly into boredom because you have no idea what they're discussing so enthusiastically. The same thing can happen when you read or write essays that don't define or explain as much material as necessary.

Some words can be defined briefly in parentheses, but complex ideas and terms need more than a phrase or sentence of explanation. In this chapter, you will read whole essays whose main purpose is to define and explain difficult or controversial concepts.

THE PRINCIPLES OF DEFINITION AND EXPLANATION

Definitions and explanations make use of a few basic techniques that can be found in almost all writing.

Descriptive Details

Can you imagine explaining anything without using descriptive details? "Why are you afraid you'll become a slave to your new silk shirt?" a friend might ask you. To explain, you would naturally give the details of caring for it: you must wash it in cold water by hand; then, instead of wringing it, you should wrap it in a clean towel to blot excess water; then it needs to hang dry on a padded hanger away from sun or electric light; when dry, it will be crinkled and must be ironed with a very cool iron; finally, on the day of wearing, it should be steamed while you shower and lightly re-ironed. In other words, you think you will be a slave to it.

Examples

Concepts are frequently defined or explained through examples. The classic Type A personality can be defined through examples of behavior: if Jake is Type A, he is extremely impatient in a long grocery line, he cannot find the time to go to a film starring his favorite actor, and he considers getting a promotion at work a life-or-death issue. He is also likely to slam doors and throw books when angry.

In this chapter, an essay by Dave Barry, a humorist, provides several comical examples of what different people mean by *fat-free* and *low fat*.

Narration

Aesop's fables, which you probably remember from childhood, make use of narratives, or stories, to explain basic truths about humans. A "sour grapes" attitude is explained by the story of the fox who sees a bunch of delicious-looking grapes but can't reach them; the fox therefore comforts itself by deciding that they were probably sour, anyway. A writer might define an abstract quality like heroism or courage by telling a story with a hero who acts out the virtue.

In this chapter, scientist Isaac Asimov uses a narrative to explore the meaning of the word *intelligent*.

Comparison

Sometimes we define a word by emphasizing its likeness to something else. A **fable** is a kind of story, for example. Writers use imaginative comparison to clarify meaning, too: "A true friend is a port in a storm," and "A true friend is as comfortable as an old shoe."

A comparison may be used for surprising effect. In this chapter, Barbara Ehrenreich shows how a "cultural heritage" may really be "cultural baggage."

Contrast

Sometimes the best way to define something is to contrast it with something different. This technique can be quite simple: *Dearth* is the opposite of *plenty.* Or the definition can consist of a comparison spiked with a contrast. As our friend heard her five-year-old explain to her four-year-old, "Death is like going to Omaha, only longer."

In some cases, contrast is needed to correct a common misconception about a term. *Schizophrenia,* contrary to popular belief, does not involve having more than one personality. And being *educated,* according to Asimov's garage mechanic, doesn't mean being "smart."

THE PITFALLS OF DEFINITION AND EXPLANATION

When you write a definition or explanation, you risk making certain characteristic mistakes.

Missing Your Audience

Would you explain what a control key is to a computer whiz? We hope not. But if you were writing directions for a beginning word processing course, you'd be a fool *not* to define what a control key is. Analyzing your intended audience is important in all writing. If you misjudge what your audience needs to have defined or explained, you will either insult or confuse them.

Going in Circles

Some definitions are called circular because they don't go anywhere. They restate rather than explain. "A *smooth operator* is a person who functions without roughness," for example, tells you nothing. The second part of that definition only rewords the first part. The definition must lead somewhere, like this: "A *smooth operator* is a person who takes advantage of others by using charm and persuasion."

Abstraction

The previous definition also demonstrates the flaw of abstraction. It includes nothing concrete to hang onto. A high-flown sentence like "Our ideal leader is the hope of the future" provides no helpful terms about qualities we can actually identify.

Leaving Information Out

To say merely that a fable is a story doesn't get across the whole idea, only part of it: a fable has special features, like talking animals and a moral lesson. Incompleteness is a pitfall especially of short definitions, such as "Love is never having to say you're sorry." In this chapter, the essay "Mommy, What Does 'Nigger' Mean?" shows that a sentence like "*Nigger* is a degrading label for an African American" is not a full definition.

Of course, an explanation is incomplete when your reader needs to ask for clarification. Sometimes it's hard to see the holes in what you have written yourself because you already know what you're trying to say. You need to enlist a good peer editor to point out whether you have omitted important information.

WHAT TO LOOK FOR IN DEFINITION AND EXPLANATION

Here are some guidelines to follow as you study the selections in this chapter:

1. *Focus on which term or concept is being defined or explained.* This focus will help you evaluate the essay's effectiveness.
2. *Identify the ways in which the writer develops the idea,* especially details, narration, example, comparison, and contrast.
3. *Figure out who the intended audience is.* Then think about how the essay would be different if written for a different audience. What definitions and explanations would be added or deleted?
4. *Ask yourself whether the definition or explanation is complete.* If it is not complete, does the writer tell you why?

How would you define the phrases "top drawer" and "bottom drawer"?

How does the cartoon redefine those terms?

Can you think of other phrases that might have two meanings, a serious one and a humorous one?

PREPARING TO READ

What word could be used to label you? Even consider labels that you do not think accurate. Might someone call you a jock? a nerd? an egghead? a bimbo? a tramp? a hero? a male chauvinist? a rabid feminist? a spoiled brat? a bully? a heartbreaker?

"Mommy, What Does 'Nigger' Mean?"

GLORIA NAYLOR

Gloria Naylor came from a rural, working-class southern background and did not enter college until she was twenty-five, after working as a missionary and a telephone operator. Naylor graduated from Brooklyn College in 1981, and in 1983 she won the American Book Award for best first novel for *The Women of Brewster Place*. In the essay we excerpt here, Naylor discusses the ways a word's meaning changes according to the context in which it is used.

TERMS TO RECOGNIZE

necrophiliac *(para. 1)*	someone attracted to corpses
verified *(para. 1)*	proven true
gravitated *(para. 2)*	tended to move
mecca *(para. 2)*	a place regarded as the center of interest or activity
inflections *(para. 3)*	tones of voice
trifling *(para. 8)*	shallow, unimportant
connotation *(para. 9)*	the idea suggested by a word or phrase, in addition to its surface meaning
stratum *(para. 12)*	level
internalization *(para. 12)*	making other people's attitudes a part of your own way of thinking

1 remember the first time I heard the word "nigger." In my third-grade class, our math tests were being passed down the rows, and as I handed the papers to a little boy in back of me, I remarked that once again he had received a much lower mark than I did. He snatched his test from me and

spit out that word. Had he called me a nymphomaniac or a necrophiliac, I couldn't have been more puzzled. I didn't know what a nigger was, but I knew that whatever it meant, it was something he shouldn't have called me. This was verified when I raised my hand, and in a loud voice repeated what he had said and watched the teacher scold him for using a "bad" word. I was later to go home and ask the inevitable question that every black parent must face—"Mommy, what does 'nigger' mean?"

And what exactly did it mean? Thinking back, I realize that this could not have been the first time the word was used in my presence. I was part of a large extended family that had migrated from the rural South after World War II and formed a close-knit network that gravitated around my maternal grandparents. Their ground-floor apartment in one of the buildings they owned in Harlem was a weekend mecca for my immediate family, along with countless aunts, uncles and cousins who brought along assorted friends. It was a bustling and open house with assorted neighbors and tenants popping in and out to exchange bits of gossip, pick up an old quarrel or referee the ongoing checkers game in which my grandmother cheated shamelessly. They were all there to let down their hair and put up their feet after a week of labor in the factories, laundries and shipyards of New York.

Amid the clamor, which could reach deafening proportions—two or three conversations going on simultaneously, punctuated by the sound of a baby's crying somewhere in the back rooms or out on the street—there was still a rigid set of rules about what was said and how. Older children were sent out of the living room when it was time to get into the juicy details about "you-know-who" up on the third floor who had gone and gotten herself "p-r-e-g-n-a-n-t!" But my parents, knowing that I could spell well beyond my years, always demanded that I follow the others out to play. Beyond sexual misconduct and death, everything else was considered harmless for our young ears. And so among the anecdotes of the triumphs and disappointments in the various workings of their lives, the word "nigger" was used in my presence, but it was set within contexts and inflections that caused it to register in my mind as something else.

In the singular, the word was always applied to a man who had distinguished himself in some situation that brought their approval for his strength, intelligence or drive:

"Did Johnny really do that?"

"I'm telling you, that nigger pulled in $6,000 of overtime last year. Said he got enough for a down payment on a house."

When used with a possessive adjective by a woman—"my nigger"—it became a term of endearment for husband or boyfriend. But it could be more than just a term applied to a man. In their mouths it became the pure essence of manhood—a disembodied force that channeled their past history

of struggle and present survival against the odds into a victorious statement of being: "Yeah, that old foreman found out quick enough—you
don't mess with a nigger."

In the plural, it became a description of some group within the commu-   8
nity that had overstepped the bounds of decency as my family defined it:
parents who neglected their children, a drunken couple who fought in
public, people who simply refused to look for work, those with excessively
dirty mouths or unkempt households were all "trifling niggers." This particular circle could forgive hard times, unemployment, the occasional bout of
depression—they had gone through all of that themselves—but the unfor-
givable sin was lack of self-respect.

A woman could never be a "nigger" in the singular, with its connotation   9
of confirming worth. The noun "girl" was its closest equivalent in that sense,
but only when used in direct address and regardless of the gender doing the
addressing. "Girl" was a token of respect for a woman. The one-syllable word
was drawn out to sound like three in recognition of the extra ounce of wit,
nerve, or daring that the woman had shown in the situation under discussion.

"G-i-r-l, stop. You mean you said that to his face?"   10

But if the word was used in a third-person reference or shortened so that   11
it almost snapped out of the mouth, it always involved some element of
communal disapproval. And age became an important factor in these
exchanges. It was only between individuals of the same generation, or from
an older person to a younger (but never the other way around), that "girl"
would be considered a compliment.

I don't agree with the argument that use of the word "nigger" at this   12
social stratum of the black community was an internalization of racism. The
dynamics were the exact opposite: the people in my grandmother's living
room took a word that whites used to signify worthlessness or degradation
and rendered it impotent. Gathering there together, they transformed
"nigger" to signify the varied and complex human beings they knew themselves to be. If the word was to disappear totally from the mouths of even
the most liberal of white society, no one in that room was naïve enough
to believe it would disappear from white minds. Meeting the word head-
on, they proved it had absolutely nothing to do with the way they were
determined to live their lives.

So there must have been dozens of times that the word "nigger" was   13
spoken in front of me before I reached the third grade. But I didn't "hear"
it until it was said by a small pair of lips that had already learned it could
be a way to humiliate me. That was the word I went home and asked my
mother about. And since she knew that I had to grow up in America, she
took me in her lap and explained.

RESPONDING TO READING

Do you agree that Naylor's relatives used the word *nigger* in a nonracist or counterracist way? Use your own reactions to the word to explain your answer.

GAINING WORD POWER

The following words appear in Gloria Naylor's essay. They have an ending, *-tion*, in common. This ending occurs frequently in our language, making nouns out of verbs: for example, the noun *conversation* comes from the verb *converse*, which means "to talk." Use your dictionary to find the verb behind each of the nouns in the following list, and give a brief definition of the verb. Begin each brief definition with the word *to*. We will show how the first one is done.

	VERB	**DEFINITION**
connotation	connote	to imply or suggest
conversation		
degradation		
description		
generation		
inflection		
internalization		
recognition		
situation		

Now see how it works the other way around. Here is a list of verbs used in Naylor's essay. Find the *-tion* noun that comes from each verb (some are obvious, but for others in the list you will need the dictionary). Be sure to copy the spelling of the noun exactly: sometimes the first part of the word will change. Then write a brief definition of the noun you have written. We will do the first one for you.

	NOUN	**DEFINITION**
apply	application	a form to be filled out
consider		
determine		
explain		
gravitate		
humiliate		
migrate		
punctuate		
realize		
receive		
repeat		
transform		
verify		

CONSIDERING CONTENT

1. What are Naylor's background and social class? How do you know? Why are they significant to the main point of the essay?
2. Why was the child puzzled when the boy called her *nigger,* even though she had heard the word before?
3. List the definitions of the word *nigger* that were used in the author's grandparents' apartment.
4. Reread paragraph 12. How did the black community's uses of *nigger* make it not racist, according to Naylor?
5. What does the last sentence suggest about the author's mother? What does it suggest about America?

CONSIDERING METHOD

1. What kind of third-grader was Gloria Naylor? Why do you think she presents her childhood self as no angel? What effect does this early presentation of self have on the reader?
2. Reread the description of the author's grandparents' apartment. List at least seven words or phrases that appeal to your senses.
3. How is paragraph 12 different from the rest of the essay? How does the appearance of the page prepare you for this difference?
4. The central part of the essay includes many direct quotations. Why do you think Naylor used people's exact words so often?

WRITING STEP BY STEP

Following Gloria Naylor's essay as an example, write a paper discussing a term that has various—even contradictory—meanings, depending on context: who says it, when it is used, and whether it is applied to men or women, young or old, individual or group, for example. Like Naylor, you might think of a term that holds more meaning than you once thought.

A. Before you start your essay, brainstorm and jot down the various ways you have heard your term used. Ask friends and classmates for help if you need it.
B. See whether your definitions fall into groups. For example, can you separate the negative meanings from the positive ones? Or do different meanings belong to different social, racial, or ethnic groups? Try at least to decide on a reasonable order in which to present your definitions. For example, the most widely used meanings might come first, with rarer and rarer meanings following it until the last one is the rarest.
C. Begin your essay with an anecdote, as Naylor does.

D. Launch into the body of your essay by looking back into your past. Write about how you used to think of the term, perhaps as a child.

E. Develop each meaning of the term with an explanation and examples of direct quotations using it. Keep looking at how Naylor develops her meanings.

F. Close the body of your essay with a speculation about why the term has such a variety of meanings. Look at Naylor's paragraph 12 for ideas about how to present your thoughts.

G. Use the last paragraph to reflect upon the anecdote you used in the opening of your essay. This is how Naylor concludes her piece. Your discussion of the term has, by now, added a new dimension to the anecdote.

OTHER WRITING IDEAS

1. What is the first memory you have of someone saying something purposely to hurt you? Or a memory of your saying something purposely to hurt someone else? Write an essay about your own and others' responses to the harsh words.

2. In paragraphs 2 and 3, Gloria Naylor describes the lively atmosphere in her grandparents' apartment. Write a description of the atmosphere in some family or social setting that you remember from childhood. Were there unwritten rules about conversation or about the roles of adults and children, as there were in Naylor's setting? Try to capture the scene vividly.

3. Think of a phrase or word that seems to be plain but is actually used to mean many different things; for example, "Just a minute," "Well," "I'm ready," and "I'll call you," are more slippery than they seem. A group of students in your class can have some fun discussing such sayings, developing ideas for your individual essays.

EDITING SKILLS: HYPHENS

Consider the use of the hyphen—the short dash—in these phrases from Gloria Naylor's essay:

third-grade class one-syllable word
close-knit network third-person reference
ground-floor apartment

The hyphenated adjectives, which modify the nouns that come after them, are called *temporary compounds*. They are compounds because they consist of two words; they are temporary because the two words usually exist separately. They are hyphenated because they make up a unit that seems more like one adjective than two. Sometimes you need to hyphenate in order to make your meaning clear. Think about these examples:

an Italian art specialist	an Italian-art specialist
a small auto dealer	a small-auto dealer
a comic book approach	a comic-book approach

In the second list, the hyphen shows which words go together—the specialist is not Italian, the dealer is not small, and the approach is not comic.

Sometimes, it is difficult to decide whether to hyphenate two words that frequently occur together (back-seat driver), whether to run them together as a compound word (backseat driver), or whether to leave them separate (back seat driver). There is not wide agreement even among professional writers about some of these blends. You will see "Thank you" and "Thank-you" about equally as often. Your dictionary should be your guide to making the decision.

EXERCISE

Look up the following combinations to see whether words are hyphenated, compound, or separate. Write out the form your dictionary endorses.

back seat driver	open and shut case
happily married couple	least restrictive environment
girl friend problems	part way finished
back door business deals	part time worker
child like expression	better fitting word
an easy pick up	half baked plan

Look back on the essay you have just written. Did you use any compound words that needed hyphens? Did you leave out any hyphens? Check a dictionary or with your instructor before making any corrections.

PREPARING TO READ

If you took an intelligence test and scored low, how would you feel? What might you say that the test failed to measure about you?

What Is Intelligence, Anyway?

ISAAC ASIMOV

Isaac Asimov was an American, born in Russia, who wrote more than 200 books, including children's stories, popular science, science fiction, fantasy, and scholarly science. With so many intellectual accomplishments, he was well qualified to wonder just what intelligence is—and is not.

TERMS TO RECOGNIZE

KP *(para. 1)*	kitchen patrol (working in the kitchen)
complacent *(para. 2)*	self-satisfied
bents *(para. 2)*	interests, tendencies
oracles *(para. 3)*	communications from God
devised *(para. 4)*	made up
foist *(para. 4)*	impose
arbiter *(para. 4)*	judge
indulgently *(para. 6)*	as if doing a favor
raucously *(para. 6)*	loudly, in a disorderly way
smugly *(para. 6)*	in a self-satisfied way

What is intelligence, anyway? When I was in the Army, I received a kind of aptitude test that all soldiers took and, against a normal of 100, scored 160. No one at the base had ever seen a figure like that, and for two hours they made a big fuss over me. (It didn't mean anything. The next day I was still a buck private with KP as my highest duty.) 1

All my life I've been registering scores like that, so that I have the complacent feeling that I'm highly intelligent, and I expect other people to think so, too. Actually, though, don't such scores simply mean that I am very good at answering the type of academic questions that are considered worthy of answers by the people who make up the intelligence tests— people with intellectual bents similar to mine? 2

For instance, I had an auto repairman once, who, on these intelligence tests, could not possibly have scored more than 80, by my estimate. I always 3 took it for granted that I was far more intelligent than he was. Yet, when anything went wrong with my car, I hastened to him with it, watched him anxiously as he explored its vitals, and listened to his pronouncements as though they were divine oracles—and he always fixed my car.

Well then, suppose my auto repairman devised questions for an intelli-   4
gence test. Or suppose a carpenter did, or a farmer, or, indeed, almost anyone but an academician. By every one of those tests, I'd prove myself a moron. And I'd *be* a moron, too. In a world where I could not use my academic training and my verbal talents but had to do something intricate or hard, working with my hands, I would do poorly. My intelligence, then, is not absolute but is a function of the society I live in and of the fact that a small subsection of that society has managed to foist itself on the rest as an arbiter of such matters.

Consider my auto repairman, again. He had a habit of telling me jokes   5
whenever he saw me. One time he raised his head from under the auto-mobile hood to say, "Doc, a deaf-and-dumb guy went into a hardware store to ask for some nails. He put two fingers together on the counter and made hammering motions with the other hand. The clerk brought him a hammer. He shook his head and pointed to the two fingers he was hammering. The clerk brought him nails. He picked out the sizes he wanted, and left. Well, doc, the next guy who came in was a blind man. He wanted scissors. How do you suppose he asked for them?"

Indulgently, I lifted my right hand and made scissoring motions with my   6
first two fingers. Whereupon my auto repairman laughed raucously and said, "Why, you dumb jerk, he used his *voice* and asked for them." Then he said, smugly, "I've been trying that on all my customers today." "Did you catch many?" I asked. "Quite a few," he said, "but I knew for sure I'd catch *you*." "Why is that?" I asked. "Because you're so goddamned educated, Doc, I *knew* you couldn't be very smart."

And I have an uneasy feeling he had something there.   7

RESPONDING TO READING

Do you think that people who are academically intelligent are often poor at nonacademic things? Why or why not?

GAINING WORD POWER

Complete these sentences in a reasonable way, showing that you under-stand the vocabulary words included.

1. Troy indulgently promised to take Rachel _____

_____.

2. Because he had a mechanical bent, Mark specialized in _____
   _____.

3. _____, the crowd cheered
   raucously.

4. Dr. Morse foisted her ideas on us when she _____
   _____.

5. By setting himself up as the arbiter of good taste in clothes, Shel-
   don _____.

CONSIDERING CONTENT

1. Why do you think that Asimov's high intelligence score "didn't
   mean anything" in the Army?
2. What is the basic conflict discussed in this essay?
3. Why was the repairman sure he would catch "Doc" Asimov with
   the joke? Was the repairman stereotyping college professors?
4. What might be included in an intelligence test written by auto
   mechanics? carpenters? farmers? mothers of preschoolers? portrait
   painters? What point is Asimov making with this type of suggestion?
5. Which "small subsection" (para. 4) of society has set itself up as the
   definers of intelligence?
6. What do you think about Asimov's "uneasy feeling"? Do you think
   the mechanic "had something there"? Or do you think the joke
   would fool most people, intelligent or not?

CONSIDERING METHOD

1. Asimov's essay contains two anecdotes (look up the word *anecdote*
   if you have not already done so). How do the anecdotes help you
   understand the conflict the writer is discussing?
2. In a fitting reflection of the content of the essay, Asimov uses both
   highly academic words (*oracles, bents, arbiter*) and common, informal
   words. Point out some of the informal words.
3. Count the number of words in each of the six sentences that make
   up paragraph 4. Notice the variety of lengths included. This variety in length makes writing lively to read instead of plodding. When
   you think your own writing sounds plodding, check to see whether
   you have a good range of sentence lengths. If they are too much
   alike, see whether there are sentences you can combine into longer
   ones or divide into shorter ones.
4. The last paragraph consists of just one sentence. What difference do
   you see between placing it this way and just adding it as a closing
   sentence on the paragraph before it?

WRITING STEP BY STEP

Write an essay that investigates the meaning of an abstract term—an idea that cannot be directly observed, such as intelligence. You can use some of Asimov's techniques. We will also suggest some other techniques for developing an extended definition. Use any combination of techniques to develop your definition. To get your thinking started, consider these abstractions:

common sense	humility	educated
optimism	professionalism	cool
courage	resourcefulness	simplicity
generosity	street smart	beauty
laziness	foolish	stubbornness

Choose your own term, but be sure your choice is an abstraction (not something concrete, like *submarine, pizza,* or *tennis*).

A. Begin with the question, "What is _____ , anyway?"

B. If you have an anecdote that will serve as an extended investigation of the term, include the story, as Asimov did.

C. Use examples of people you know who demonstrate the abstraction you are defining. Show how they behave or think, with specific details.

D. Use description. For example, an abstract feeling may have a counterpart in a certain type of landscape or weather that you could describe.

E. Point out differences. A good definition will make clear the difference between the word you are explaining and other words with similar meanings. You might tell how feeling peaceful is different from feeling happy or calm.

F. Provide a contrast. We often explain words by clarifying what they are *not*. For example, you could point out that laziness does not merely include lying around doing nothing, which could be depression instead.

G. In your closing, let the reader know how the abstraction is important in your own life.

OTHER WRITING IDEAS

1. Write an essay similar to Asimov's that questions the usual definition of a term. Challenge the term's usefulness or its usual interpretation or its everyday misuse.

2. Make up a word for a concept or item that doesn't have a name, as far as you know. These new words, called *sniglets,* are sometimes collected in humorous books. Here are some examples:

    BEAVO (*n.*): A pencil with teeth marks all over it.

    FICTATE (*v.*): To inform a television or screen character of impending danger under the assumption that he or she can hear you.

    OPUP (*v.*): To push one's glasses back up on the nose.

    You may need to make up a related group of words and explain how you came up with them in order to write a whole essay.

3. Instead of presenting a unified definition of a concept, try to write an essay presenting all the different, even contradictory, meanings a certain term could have. For example, if you asked a group of people to explain what *sex appeal* means to them, you would probably get some widely varying answers. You may call on a group of classmates to help you come up with meanings.

EDITING SKILLS: USING THE RIGHT TENSE

One of the trickiest skills we learn as we grow up is using the correct tense for verbs. If you have ever learned a foreign language, you are fully aware of the complications of verb tense. In your native language, as you speak, you almost always choose the right tense, but in writing you can get in a snarl.

Asimov's essay shows a combination of tenses. For things that occur in the present or are true in the present, he uses plain old present tense: "I *have* the complacent feeling that I'*m* highly intelligent, and I *expect* other people to think so, too" (para. 2). For the story about the mechanic, which happened in the past, Asimov uses past tense: "Indulgently, I *lifted* my right hand and *made* scissoring motions with my first two fingers" (para. 6).

In telling stories, speakers and writers sometimes get confused as they go along, and they switch from past to present and back within the same anecdote. Haven't you heard someone tell a story this way?

> You know, if you wait too long, you have to go in person to deal with the licensing bureau. Well, yesterday I went to get my driver's license renewed. So I have to wait in line for an hour. I finally get to the front, and the guy tells me I should have brought my form that I got in the mail. So now I had to go home, and it took my whole lunch hour. When I get back, I tell the guy that if I starve to death, it's his fault. I hate these heartless bureaucracies.

The speaker gives you a sense of being there by switching to present tense; however, in academic writing you have to stick to the past tense for everything that happened in the past. (When writing about what happened in a piece of literature or a film, though, you can summarize plot in the present tense.)

To make sure you get the idea, rewrite the anecdote above, correcting it so that everything in the past is written in past tense, and anything that is currently in force is in present tense.

Now look at the verb tenses in the essay you wrote in response to the Asimov article. Which tenses did you use? Are they consistent and logical? Check over your writing, and make any needed corrections in the verb tenses.

PREPARING TO READ

What do the terms "low-fat" and "fat-free" mean to you? Do you worry about the fat content of the foods you eat? Do you know people who do? Why do they?

When It Comes to Chewing the Fat, We're Obsessive

DAVE BARRY

Dave Barry, who was born in 1947 in Armonk, New York, is one of America's most popular humorists. A graduate of Haverford College, Barry began his career as a reporter for the Associated Press in Philadelphia. He is now a syndicated columnist for the *Miami Herald* and the author of more than twenty humorous books. He won the Pulitzer Prize for commentary in 1988. In the following essay, Barry brings his usual wit and irreverent humor to the subject of our national obsession with low-fat foods.

TERMS TO RECOGNIZE

virtually *(para. 2)*	nearly, for all practical purposes
edible *(para. 2)*	suitable for use as food
antibiotic *(para. 3)*	substance that kills bacteria and fights disease
notoriously *(para. 11)*	widely and unfavorably known
steroids *(para. 12)*	chemical compounds that promote growth and enhance performance

recently, a reader named Jim Cornell sent me a postcard with a picture   1
of insects on it, posing an interesting question. (No, the insects were not posing a question. As far as I know.)

Jim stated that he, like every other American above the age of 4, is on   2
a low-fat diet, and he noted that we have become basically a nonfat nation. This is true; virtually all edible substances, and many automotive products, are now marketed as being "low-fat" or "fat-free." Americans are OBSESSED with fat content.

DOCTOR: Mrs. Stoatbonker, you will die within hours unless you take   3
this antibiotic.

PATIENT: Is it fat-free?   4

115

DOCTOR: I don't know.   5

PATIENT: I'll just have a Diet Pepsi.   6

So anyway, Jim, after noting that "millions of pounds of formerly fat-rich   7
food is now defatted," asks: "What are they doing with all that fat?"

Jim, that is an excellent question, and I intend to answer it just as soon   8
as I have written enough words to make a column. (Don't you wish you
had a job like mine? All you have to do is think up a certain number of
words! And they don't even have to be true! Plus, you can repeat words!
And they don't even have to be true!)

First, however, we need to consider exactly what "fat" is. Just off the   9
top of my head, without glancing at a dictionary, I would define fat as
"any of various mixtures of solid or semisolid triglycerides found in adipose
animal tissue or in the seeds of plants." A "triglyceride," as I vaguely
recall from my high-school years, is "any of a group of esters,
$CH2(OOCR1)CH(OOCR2)CH2(O-OCR3)$, derived from glycerol and
three fatty acid radicals."

But what does this mean? One thing it means, of course, is that "Three   10
Fatty Acid Radicals" would be an excellent name for a rock band.

But it also means that fat is some kind of chemical item that nature puts   11
inside certain plants and animals to make them taste better. A good rule of
thumb is: the more fat something contains, the better it tastes. This is why
we eat hamburgers, but we do not eat ants. Ants have a very low fat
content, so nobody eats them except unfortunate animals such as birds,
who, because of a design flaw, cannot use drive-thru windows. Human
beings, on the other hand, enjoy hamburgers, because they (the hamburgers) come from cows, which are notoriously fat. You will never see a cow
voluntarily going anywhere near an Abdominizer.

Of course there have been efforts to make low-fat "hamburgers." In   12
researching this column I purchased a product called "Harvest Burgers,"
which are "All Vegetable Protein Patties" manufactured by the Green Giant
Corp. Upon examining the package, the first thing I noticed was that the
Jolly Green Giant has apparently had plastic surgery. He no longer looks
like the "Ho! Ho! Ho!" guy; he now looks like Paul McCartney on steroids.
Check it out.

The second thing I noticed is that the key ingredient in Harvest Burg-   13
ers is "soy." This ingredient is found in many low-fat foods, and I think it's
time that the Food and Drug Administration told us just what the hell it
is. A plant? A mineral? An animal?

Are there enormous soy ranches in Nebraska with vast herds of soys   14
bleating and suckling their young? As a consumer, I'd like some answers. I
don't want to discover years from now that "soy" is an oriental word meaning "compressed ant parts." This is not intended as a criticism of the

"Harvest Burger," which is a well constructed, extremely cylindrical frozen unit of brown foodlike substance.

The package states that it contains "83 percent less fat than ground beef"; I believe this because it also tastes exactly 83 percent less good than ground beef. Nevertheless I highly recommend it for anybody who needs more "soy" or a backup hockey puck.   15

Oh, sure, there will be people who will claim that soy patties taste "almost as good" as real hamburgers. These are the same people who have convinced themselves that rice cakes taste "almost as good" as potato chips, when in fact eating rice cakes is like chewing on a foam coffee cup, only less filling. You could fill a container with roofing shingles and put it in the supermarket with a sign that said "ZERO-FAT ROOFING SHINGLES," and these people would buy it and convince themselves it tasted "almost as good" as French toast.   16

Yes, we have become a low-fat society, which brings us back to the question posed by Jim Cornell. What's being done with all the fat? Jim offers this theory: "I suspect that they're dumping it in some small town in Texas or Mexico." No way, Jim. Our government would never allow a major fat-dumping facility in the same region where we're storing the dead UFO aliens.   17

No, the truth is that the fat is being loaded into giant tanker trucks, transported by night, and pumped into: my thighs. There was no choice; Marlon Brando was already full. But I'm happy to do my part for a lean America, so don't bother to thank me. Are you going to finish those fries?   18

POSTSCRIPT—After I wrote this column, my editor, Tom Shroder, sent me a note saying he thinks he read somewhere that ants DO contain fat. I think he's wrong, but since we're both professional journalists neither of us will look it up. I will say this: if ants DO contain fat, it's only a matter of time before somebody comes out with low-fat ants.   19

RESPONDING TO READING

Do you think Americans are obsessed with fat content? What examples can you cite to support your opinion?

GAINING WORD POWER

Dave Barry uses a number of -ly adverbs in his writing: recently, basically, virtually, formerly, exactly, vaguely, notoriously, voluntarily, apparently, extremely, highly. If you look carefully at how these words are used, you will notice that they occur in a number of different places in the sentence. Adverbs are often movable; you can put them at the beginning of the sentence or at the end, before the verb or after—in any number of spots.

Go back to Barry's essay and find six of the *-ly* words listed above. Which ones can be moved? Which ones cannot be moved? Rewrite two or three sentences to illustrate how the *-ly* adverb in it can be used in several different places. Here's an example:

Original sentence:	<u>Recently</u>, a reader named Jim Cornell sent me a postcard with a picture of insects on it, posing an interesting question.
Rewrites:	A reader named Jim Cornell <u>recently</u> sent me a postcard. . . .
	A reader named Jim Cornell sent me a postcard <u>recently</u>. . . .

Now use five of the *-ly* adverbs in sentences of your own. Experiment with several different versions to see where the adverb can be placed.

CONSIDERING CONTENT

1. Does Barry have a serious point to make? If so, what is it?
2. Barry says that "The more fat something contains, the better it tastes." Do you agree? Give several examples to support your opinion.
3. What is soy? Why is it used in many low-fat foods? (You may have to do some research to find the answers to these questions.)
4. Why do people say that soy patties taste "almost as good" as real hamburgers, or that rice cakes taste "almost as good" as potato chips?

CONSIDERING METHOD

1. Why does Barry begin with a comment from a reader? What role is he trying to establish for himself as a writer?
2. Why does Barry use the invented dialogue between a doctor and patient?
3. What is the effect of the comment in parentheses in paragraph 8? Why does Barry appear to make fun of himself? Can you find any other places where Barry mocks himself or his profession?
4. Why does Barry include the technical definitions of "fat" and "triglyceride" (para. 9)?
5. Barry says he does not intend to criticize the "Harvest Burger," but he then describes it as "a well-constructed, extremely cylindrical frozen unit of brown foodlike substance." How complimentary is that description? Why is it funny?
6. How would you describe Barry's humor?
7. What is the reason for adding a postscript?

WRITING STEP BY STEP

In his essay, Dave Barry takes some popular words and expressions and humorously redefines them to get at the truth of their meaning. He comically points out, for instance, that many low-fat foods taste pretty awful and don't make good substitutes for the fatty foods they're meant to replace. Think of some words or expressions that are misleading, and redefine them accurately or humorously the way Barry does. You might choose words used in TV commercials, personal ads, real estate descriptions, fast-food restaurants, or menu language. You can focus on a single expression (like "family values") or a group of related terms (like names for sandwiches or sizes of drinks or the names of real estate subdivisions).

A. Begin, as Barry does, by telling how the word or name came to your attention. Perhaps you have an amusing story to relate to explain your interest in the term.

B. Offer the accurate or dictionary definition.

C. Then explain what the advertisers or salespeople want it to mean. Use humorous examples and descriptions to make your point about how odd or misleading the term is.

D. As you explain the "true" meaning, explain why this expression was chosen. If the word or name caught on with the public (like "lite" or "fat-free"), speculate on why it became so popular.

E. Conclude by calling for action from your readers—perhaps to protest this transparent attempt to manipulate the public through the misuse of language.

OTHER WRITING IDEAS

1. Think of all the words used to describe fat people: large, chubby, full-figured, overweight, big-boned, portly, beefy, stout, heavyset, fleshy, chunky, burly, rotund. Write an essay explaining why there are so many of these terms.

2. Interview several foreign students on your campus, and ask them for examples of expressions (like "cramp my style" or "hit the hay") that surprised or confused them. How did they find out what the expressions really meant? Write up the results of your interviews.

3. Barry's essay makes fun of using language that hides or masks the truth. But sometimes it's a relief not to have to say exactly what you mean. Write an essay about times when you were glad you could use a word or expression (like "We have a personality conflict") instead of a more explicit description ("I can't stand the jerk, and he hates me too").

EDITING SKILLS: CAPITALIZATION

Barry's essay illustrates many of the conventions for using capital letters in English. The author, of course, capitalizes the first word in every sentence. He also capitalizes the pronoun *I* every time he uses it. Here are some of the other capitalization rules he follows:

1. Capitalize the names of people, even fictional ones: Jim Cornell, Paul McCartney, Jolly Green Giant, Marlon Brando, Tom Shroder.
2. Capitalize the names of nationalities, races, tribes, and languages: American, French.
3. Capitalize the names of organizations and governmental agencies: Food and Drug Administration.
2. Capitalize brand names of products: Diet Pepsi, Abdominizer, Harvest Burger.
3. Capitalize names of geographical locations, such as cities, states, and countries: Nebraska, Texas, Mexico.

Look over the essay you have just written, and check your use of capital letters. A college dictionary will give you a list of capitalization rules along with examples. Entries for specific words will also tell you when to use capitals.

PREPARING TO READ

What do you know about your ethnic heritage? Is your ethnic heritage reflected in your everyday life or your family traditions?

Cultural Baggage

BARBARA EHRENREICH

Barbara Ehrenreich is an outspoken leftist political leader whose writings are usually controversial. She regularly contributes to the magazines *Ms.* and *Mother Jones,* as well as to many other periodicals. In the piece we reprint here, Ehrenreich reconsiders the meaning of cultural heritage.

TERMS TO RECOGNIZE

chauvinism *(para. 2)*	unreasoning, boastful devotion to one's own kind
venerable *(para. 3)*	impressive and respectable
ecumenism *(para. 4)*	the practice of promoting understanding among all religions
sweetbreads *(para. 4)*	animal thymus or pancreas eaten as food
seder *(para. 7)*	a feast on the first day of Passover
secular *(para. 8)*	worldly rather than spiritual
epiphany *(para. 10)*	a flash of insight
spewed *(para. 11)*	gushed forth
maxim *(para. 11)*	a short statement of a general principle
inverted *(para. 11)*	turned upside down
progenitors *(para. 12)*	ancestors

1   An acquaintance was telling me about the joys of rediscovering her ethnic and religious heritage. "I know exactly what my ancestors were doing 2,000 years ago," she said, eyes gleaming with enthusiasm, "and *I can do the same things now.*" Then she leaned forward and inquired politely, "And what is your ethnic background, if I may ask?"

2   "None," I said, that being the first word in line to get out of my mouth. Well, not "none," I backtracked. Scottish, English, Irish—that was something, I supposed. Too much Irish to qualify as a WASP; too much of the hated English to warrant a "Kiss Me, I'm Irish" button; plus there are a number of dead ends in the family tree due to adoptions, missing records, failing memories and the like. I was blushing by this time. Did "none"

mean I was rejecting my heritage out of Anglo-Celtic self-hate? Or was I revealing a hidden ethnic chauvinism in which the Britannically derived served as a kind of neutral standard compared with the ethnic "others"?

Throughout the 60's and 70's, I watched one group after another— African-Americans, Latinos, Native Americans—stand up and proudly reclaim their roots while I just sank back ever deeper into my seat. All this excitement over ethnicity stemmed, I uneasily sensed, from a past in which *their* ancestors had been trampled upon by *my* ancestors, or at least by people who looked very much like them. In addition, it had begun to seem almost un-American not to have some sort of hyphen at hand, linking one to more venerable times and locales.

But the truth is, I was raised with none. We'd eaten ethnic foods in my childhood home, but these were all borrowed, like the pasties, or Cornish meat pies, my father had picked up from his fellow miners in Butte, Montana. If my mother had one rule, it was militant ecumenism in all matters of food and experience. "Try new things," she would say, meaning anything from sweetbreads to clams, with an emphasis on the "new."

As a child, I briefly nourished a craving for tradition and roots. I immersed myself in the works of Sir Walter Scott. I pretended to believe that the bagpipe was a musical instrument. I was fascinated to learn from a grandmother that we were descended from certain Highland clans and longed for a pleated skirt in one of their distinctive tartans.

But in *Ivanhoe*, it was the dark-eyed "Jewess" Rebecca I identified with, not the flaxen-haired bimbo Rowena. As for clans: Why not call them "tribes," those bands of half-clad peasants and warriors whose idea of cuisine was stuffed sheep gut washed down with whisky? And then there was the sting of Disraeli's remark—which I came across in my early teens— to the effect that his ancestors had been leading orderly, literate lives when my ancestors were still rampaging through the Highlands daubing themselves with blue paint.

Motherhood put the screws on me, ethnicity-wise. I had hoped that by marrying a man of Eastern European-Jewish ancestry I would acquire for my descendants the ethnic genes that my own forebears so sadly lacked. At one point, I even subjected the children to a seder of my own design, including a little talk about the flight from Egypt and its relevance to modern social issues. But the kids insisted on buttering their matzohs and snickering through my talk. "Give me a break, Mom," the older one said. "You don't even believe in God."

After the tiny pagans had been put to bed, I sat down to brood over Elijah's wine. What had I been thinking? The kids knew that their Jewish grandparents were secular folks who didn't hold seders themselves. And if ethnicity eluded me, how could I expect it to take root in my children, who are not only Scottish-English-Irish, but Hungarian-Polish-Russian to boot?

But, then, on the fumes of Manischewitz, a great insight took form in   9 my mind. It was true, as the kids said, that I didn't "believe in God." But this could be taken as something very different from an accusation—a reminder of a genuine heritage. My parents had not believed in God either, nor had my grandparents or any other progenitors going back to the great-great level. They had become disillusioned with Christianity generations ago—just as, on the in-law side, my children's other ancestors had shaken off their Orthodox Judaism. This insight did not exactly furnish me with an "identity," but it was at least something to work with: we are the kind of people, I realized—whatever our distant ancestors' religions—who do *not* believe, who do not carry on traditions, who do not do things just because someone has done them before.

The epiphany went on: I recalled that my mother never introduced a   10 procedure for cooking or cleaning by telling me, "Grandma did it this way." What did Grandma know, living in the days before vacuum cleaners and disposable toilet mops? In my parents' general view, new things were better than old, and the very fact that some ritual had been performed in the past was a good reason for abandoning it now. Because what was the past, as our forebears knew it? Nothing but poverty, superstition and grief. "Think for yourself," Dad used to say. "Always ask why."

In fact, this may have been the ideal cultural heritage for my particular   11 ethnic strain—bounced as it was from the Highlands of Scotland across the sea, out to the Rockies, down into the mines and finally spewed out into high-tech, suburban America. What better philosophy, for a race of migrants, than "Think for yourself"? What better maxim, for people whose whole world was rudely inverted every 30 years or so, than "Try new things"?

The more tradition-minded, the newly enthusiastic celebrants of Purim   12 and Kwanzaa and Solstice, may see little point to survival if the survivors carry no cultural freight—religion, for example, or ethnic tradition. To which I would say that skepticism, curiosity and wide-eyed ecumenical tolerance are also worthy elements of the human tradition and are at least as old as such notions as "Serbian" or "Croatian," "Scottish" or "Jewish." I make no claims for my personal line of progenitors except that they remained loyal to the values that may have induced all of our ancestors, long, long ago, to climb down from the trees and make their way into the open plains.

A few weeks ago, I cleared my throat and asked the children, now mostly   13 grown and fearsomely smart, whether they felt any stirrings of ethnic or religious identity, etc., which might have been, ahem, insufficiently nourished at home. "None," they said, adding firmly, "and the world would be a better place if nobody else did, either." My chest swelled with pride, as would my mother's, to know that the race of "none" marches on.

RESPONDING TO READING

Did you find Ehrenreich's pride in being an atheist shocking or disturbing or delightful? Write in your journal about your initial response; then analyze why you had this response.

GAINING WORD POWER

Proper nouns (and the words related to them) designate specific persons, places, languages, brands, titles, and so forth, rather than general categories. For example, *Episcopalian, Coca-Cola,* and *Othello* are proper nouns, unlike *religion, soda pop,* and *play,* which are the matching common nouns. Proper nouns are capitalized, whereas common nouns are not. Much of the reading you do in college will include proper nouns, expecting that you understand the references, like the Ehrenreich reading we reprint here. These words pose a special vocabulary-building problem because they may or may not be in your college dictionary. You have to branch out to find some of the definitions. An encyclopedia like *Funk & Wagnall's* or *Encarta* will help you in many cases. Sometimes, you need to go to the library for a more specialized reference book, like *The Reader's Encyclopedia* (specifically about authors and literary works) or *Webster's Biographical Dictionary* (specifically about notable people). Your librarian can help you look in the appropriate book. When you are really stuck, you may find it advisable to simply ask around among your friends and acquaintances: one of them may steer you to the right source for the definition.

Here, in the order in which they appear, are some proper nouns from Barbara Ehrenreich's essay. They are important if you want to get the full meaning of the reading. Find out what the words mean, and fit the definitions into the context of the essay. Write down your observations as well as the place you found each definition.

Anglo-Celtic

Britannically

Cornish

Sir Walter Scott

Ivanhoe

Rebecca

Rowena

Disraeli

Highlands

Manischewitz

Purim

Kwanzaa

Solstice

CONSIDERING CONTENT

1. Why does Ehrenreich report that she "just sank back ever deeper into [her] seat" when other groups celebrated their ethnicity? What made her feel strange?
2. At what times in life was it important to the author that she have a heritage? What did she do to try to acquire one? How did those efforts turn out?
3. When did Ehrenreich's ideas about heritage change? How did she broaden the definition of *heritage* from what other people meant?
4. What are some of the elements of Ehrenreich's cultural heritage?
5. Is tradition always good? What does Ehrenreich think? What are some traditions that are not so good?

CONSIDERING METHOD

1. Look closely at paragraphs 1 through 9, noticing particularly where the paragraphs divide. Can you explain some logic behind each division?
2. Consider the first sentence of each paragraph. What techniques are used to show how this paragraph is related to the paragraph before it?
3. How does the introduction catch the reader's attention? To what senses does it appeal?
4. Although the subject of this essay is quite abstract—the meaning of heritage—the writer includes many vivid specific details. Find at least three passages that are concrete and specific. What is their contribution to the essay?
5. Did you find any humor in the essay? If so, point out where, and tell why you found it funny.

WRITING STEP BY STEP

Barbara Ehrenreich writes about how she sometimes felt awkward and uneasy when everyone around her discussed their ethnic heritage because she was raised without one. Start your essay with a similar situation: think of something that makes you feel odd or out of place socially at times (or that used to make you feel this way). One of our friends, for example, was brought up without television; now, in conversations as an adult, she sometimes feels that her peer group shares a culture that she lacks. Another friend was brought up in an unusual family: she and her two sisters were raised by her mother and two aunts, and she sometimes feels that everyone else came from a more "normal" family. Like Ehrenreich, you will investigate the meaning of the difference you possess.

A. In the first section of your essay, set the scene. Show what situation makes (or made) you feel out of place. Briefly state why you feel (or felt) uneasy. Use first person ("I") because this is a personal essay. Consider starting out with a sample incident, as Ehrenreich does in paragraph 1.

B. In the next section, explain how you have tried to come to terms with your difference. You might go back to how you dealt with it as a child, as Ehrenreich does in paragraphs 5 and 6. You might discuss a time when the difference really gained importance, as Ehrenreich does in paragraphs 7 and 8.

C. In the third section of your essay, explain where you stand now on the subject. Perhaps you have had an epiphany, as Ehrenreich did, in which you see your difference as valuable. Maybe there was one experience that changed your thinking about being different. Maybe just writing about it brought you to some new conclusions. If you are still as uneasy as ever, say so. Do you expect any change in the future?

D. Divide each section of your essay into paragraphs. You can divide paragraphs according to a shift in time, a new turn of thought, or a switch of focus, or to introduce a new example.

E. Write a closing sentence that reinforces your current point of view about the difference you have explained.

OTHER WRITING IDEAS

1. Write an essay explaining your own cultural heritage and what it means. Be sure to clarify how you are defining *cultural heritage.*

2. Investigate some "great insight" (para. 9) or "epiphany" (para. 10) in which your thinking on a subject changed significantly. The experience need not concern cultural heritage, as Ehrenreich's did. Your essay will be similar only in that it focuses on a change in your point of view and how that change came to be.

3. Get together with some classmates to brainstorm about traditions that should be eliminated or at least revised. Think about holidays,

courtship, campus culture, and political campaigning to get you started. Choose one tradition, explain it, and explain how and why it should be altered.

EDITING SKILLS: USING QUESTIONS

Notice how Barbara Ehrenreich uses questions to help us see the thought processes that went on as she thought about cultural heritage. Here are a few of these questions:

Did "none" mean I was rejecting my heritage out of Anglo-Celtic self-hate? (para. 2)

As for clans: Why not call them "tribes," those bands of half-clad peasants and warriors whose idea of cuisine was stuffed sheep gut washed down with whisky? (para. 6)

What had I been thinking? (para. 8)

What did Grandma know, living in the days before vacuum cleaners and disposable toilet mops? (para. 10)

What better philosophy, for a race of migrants, than "Think for yourself"? (para. 11)

These questions make readers feel that they are witnessing the writer's mental struggle on the spot. We often pose questions to ourselves when we are thinking through an issue. When such musings are written in a personal essay, they are called **rhetorical questions,** since they are there only to achieve this effect of immediacy—no one expects the reader to try to answer them.

Look at the essay you have written. Add at least one rhetorical question that reflects your thought process. If you like the effect, try using a few more.

Student Essay Using Definition

Nothing to Be Scared Of

Kerri Mauger

For most of my life, I remember my mother being in and out of hospitals. No one was sure what was wrong with her, and it took many years to finally put a label on her. My mother has been diagnosed with schizophrenia. I am sorry to think about when my friends and I have passed a mental hospital on the street and made rude comments; but we, like most people, were very ignorant about mental illnesses. People may laugh and make jokes about it, but it is a reality to me. I live with it every day of my life. 1

It has taken me many years to understand what is wrong with my mother. My dad chose to be very secretive about anything that had to do with her. I think he tried to protect my sister and me, but in the long run ignorance hurt us even more. 2

Schizophrenia is a mental disorder that makes it hard for people who have it to distinguish between what is real and what is imagined. Therefore, schizophrenics also have trouble managing emotions, thinking clearly, and dealing with other people. They cannot tell what other people's talk and actions mean, and they respond strangely. People who have never encountered someone with schizophrenia may feel intimidated because of bizarre and socially unacceptable behavior. My mother may sit and listen to the voices she hears all day long, ignoring everything else. She explains that they are communicating to her through telepathy. She replies to these voices and denies that there is anything wrong with her. Some schizophrenics shout angrily at people on the street, believing that they have been insulted or threatened when they have not. 3

Early on the day of my eleventh birthday party, my sister and I were downstairs watching TV. My mom came down and told us to come up to my room. We followed her upstairs, where she told us to lie on the floor. She said that there was a man outside with 4 a gun and we had to hide so he would not come and get us. I was really scared and confused, and we stayed in my room for two hours in almost complete silence. Finally I got up and looked out the window. Our neighbors were outside gardening. When my father got home, he called the hospital, and I saw my mother taken away by force. My birthday party was canceled, and I was crushed. I realize now that my mother was hallucinating, having an experience that seemed real but was only in her imagination. Hallucinations can include all of the senses, and my mother had both seen and heard things that weren't there.

There is no cure for schizophrenia. Medication 5 may help some people with the symptoms, but no medicine has helped my mother yet. Psychotherapy can assist schizophrenics in controlling their thoughts. Along with drugs and therapy, family understanding can help. The person suffering from schizophrenia needs sympathy, compassion, and respect. It is best to stay calm and nonjudgmental. Getting excited or starting to argue with the person can worsen an episode. Schizophrenia is not the person's moral fault or rational choice.

It is sometimes easier to laugh at something we 6 fear and do not understand. But ignorance about something like schizophrenia can be hurtful. I love my mother dearly and after many years of being afraid and uninformed, I can finally say I am not scared of her at all. She still is not a "normal" mother, but I now know the facts and can deal with whatever comes my way.

STRATEGIES FOR SORTING IDEAS

Classification and Division

The next time you get ready to do your laundry, look on the back of the detergent box. There you will see directions for sorting your clothes according to the temperature of the water that you should use. The directions may read something like this:

FOR BEST CLEANING RESULTS

Sort and select temperature and begin filling washer with water.

Hot	Warm	Cold
White cottons	Bright colors	Dark colors
Colorfast pastels	Permanent press	Colors that could bleed
Diapers	Knits	Delicates
Heavily soiled items		Stains like blood and chocolate

Do you follow a procedure like this when you do your laundry? Why do you suppose the detergent makers put directions like this on the back of the box?

THE POINT OF CLASSIFICATION AND DIVISION

As the previous laundry example shows, separating and arranging things helps us to accomplish tasks more efficiently and more effectively. This process of "sorting things out" also helps us to clarify our thinking and understand our feelings.

Many writing tasks lend themselves to grouping information into categories. For example, you might write a paper for psychology class on the various ways people cope with the death of a loved one. For a course in economics, you might write about the three basic types of unemployment (*frictional, structural,* and *cyclical*). This approach—called **classification** and **division**—enables you to present a body of information in an orderly way.

Dividing and classifying also forces you to think clearly about your topic. By breaking a subject down into its distinct parts, or categories, you can look at it more closely and decide what you want to say about each part. For example, if you are writing an essay on effective teaching styles, you might begin by dividing the teachers you have had into the "good" ones and the "bad" ones. Then you could break those broad categories down further into more precise ones: teachers who held your interest, teachers who knew their subject, teachers who made you do busy work, and so forth. As you develop each category, you have to think about the qualities that impressed you, and this thought process leads you to a better understanding of the topic you are writing about. You may end up writing only about the good teachers, but dividing and classifying the examples will help you to organize your thinking.

THE PRINCIPLES OF CLASSIFICATION AND DIVISION

Most things can be classified or divided in more than one way, depending on the reason for making up the groups. In the laundry example, for instance, you are told to sort the clothes according to the temperature of the water. Putting bright colors with knits doesn't make any sense if you don't know the reason—or basis—for the category: *items to be washed in cold water.* When you divide and classify a topic, be sure to have a sound basis for formulating your categories. The following suggestions will help you develop a useful system of classification.

Give a Purpose to Your Classification

Merely putting facts or ideas into different groups isn't necessarily meaningful. Consider these sentences that classify for no apparent reason:

1. There are five kinds of friends in most of our lives.
2. People deal with their spare money in four basic ways.

How could you give a purpose to these ideas? You would have to add a *reason* or declare a *point* for the categories. Here are some revisions that give purpose to these two classifications:

1. a. There are five kinds of friends in most of our lives, and each kind is important in its own way.
   b. Most of us have five kinds of friends, and each one drives us crazy in a special way.

131

2. a. People deal with their spare money in four ways that reflect their overall attitudes toward life.

    b. People deal with their spare money in four ways, only one of which is truly constructive.

Establish a Clear Basis for Your Classification

If you are going to classify items or ideas, you have to decide which organizing principle you want to use to form your groups. For example, if you are classifying friends, you could group them according to how close you are to them, as Judith Viorst does in her essay in this chapter. Or you could group them according to other principles: how long you have known them, what you have in common with them, or how much time you spend with the people in each group. The important thing is to choose a workable principle and stick with it.

Make Your Groups Parallel and Equal

In a classification essay, you usually announce the groups or classes in the introduction: several ways to handle criticism, four kinds of friends, three types of stress, three levels of intelligence, and so forth. You then devote one section to each group of your classification. A section can be one paragraph or several, but the sections for the major categories should be about equal in length. In a classification essay about friendship, for instance, if you cover "childhood pals" in 150 words, then you should use approximately the same number of words for each of the other kinds of friends.

Experienced writers also present each section in a similar way. For example, in this chapter, psychologist David Elkind classifies the three basic types of stress that young people experience. He labels each one with a letter, describes it, and gives examples. He follows the same order—label, description, examples—in covering each type. He also mentions the same two conditions when explaining each type: if it's foreseeable and if it's avoidable. This parallel development helps the reader to recognize the similarities and identify the distinctions among the types.

THE PITFALLS OF CLASSIFICATION AND DIVISION

The following advice will help you to avoid some of the problems that writers sometimes encounter in developing an essay of classification.

1. *Know the difference between useful and useless ways of classifying.* Sorting your clothes by brand name probably won't help you get the best cleaning results when doing the laundry. And dividing teachers into those who

wear glasses and those who don't is not a very useful way to organize a paper on effective teaching styles. But classifying teachers into those who lecture, those who use a question–discussion format, and those who run small-group workshops might be significant, mainly because such groupings would allow you to discuss the teachers' philosophies, their attitudes toward students, and their effectiveness in the classroom.

2. *Be sure your classification covers everything you claim it covers.* If, for instance, you know some teachers who sometimes lecture and sometimes use small groups, you can't pretend these people don't exist just to make your classification tidy. At least mention exceptions, even if you don't give them as much space as the major categories.

3. *Don't let the basis of division shift.* If you can see a problem with the following classification system, you already understand this warning:

TYPES OF TEACHERS

   a. Teachers who lecture
   b. Teachers who lead discussions
   c. Teachers who have a sense of humor
   d. Teachers who run workshops
   e. Teachers who never hold office hours

Notice that three types of teachers (a, b, and d) are grouped according to the way they run their classes, but two types (c and e) are defined by some other standard. You can see the confusion these shifting groups cause: Can teachers who lecture have a sense of humor? Don't those who use workshops hold office hours?

4. *Be sure your groups are parallel or equal in rank.* The following classification illustrates a problem in rank:

KINDS OF POPULAR MUSIC

   1. Easy listening
   2. Country and western
   3. Rock 'n' roll
   4. Ice-T

Although Ice-T does represent a type of popular music distinct from easy listening, country, and rock, the category is not parallel with the others— it is far too small. It should be "rap," with Ice-T used as an example.

5. *Avoid stereotypes.* When you write about types of behavior or put people into groups, you run the risk of oversimplifying the material. The best way to avoid this problem is to use plenty of specific examples. You can also point out exceptions and describe variations; such honesty shows that you have been thinking carefully about the topic.

WHAT TO LOOK FOR IN A CLASSIFICATION

As you read the essays in this chapter, pay attention to these points:

1. *Figure out what the author is classifying.* Then identify the basis for making up the groups and the purpose of the classification.
2. *Look for the specific groups or classes* into which the author has sorted the material. Jot down a brief list of the major categories just to see if you can keep track of them.
3. *Ask yourself if the groups are clearly defined.* Do they shift? Do they cover what they claim to cover? Are they parallel?
4. *Be alert for stereotypes.* How does the author handle exceptions and variations?
5. *Identify the audience.* How do you know who the intended readers are?

| *Hanging Loose* | *Hanging Tough* | *Just Hanging In There* |

What are the three men in the cartoon doing? What type of jobs do they have? How can you tell?

How does this cartoon classify the approaches toward office work? What other labels could you use for the three types? Could you use the same classifications for people in other jobs? Might there be classifications within these groups—for example, could there be different types of workers who are "just hanging in there"?

Stereotypes make broad generalizations about groups; they lump individuals together on the basis of a few examples. What stereotypes do you see depicted in this cartoon?

PREPARING TO READ

How do you cope with all the notes, tests, handouts, forms, notices, and reports that you get in school or at work? Do you have a particular system? How would you describe your approach to organizing your paperwork?

It's Only a Paper World

KATHLEEN FURY

Born in New York and educated at Purdue University in Indiana, Kathleen Fury has been a writer and magazine editor for more than thirty years. She has held editorial positions at *Redbook, Ladies' Home Journal,* and *Savvy* and writes a regular column for *Working Woman,* where the following article first appeared (August 1986). In this essay Fury takes a humorous look at different types of office "paper pushers," classifying each kind as an animal that behaves in a similar way.

TERMS TO RECOGNIZE

advent *(para. 1)*	the coming or arrival, especially of something important
dictates *(para. 2)*	orders, commands
ecosystem *(para. 2)*	physical surroundings to which living creatures adapt to meet their needs
genetic *(para. 3)*	relating to the genes, the units controlling biological development
uncanny *(para. 5)*	amazing, mysteriously keen and perceptive
deft *(para. 5)*	quick and skillful
scavengers *(para. 11)*	animals that feed on dead and decaying matter
CEO *(para. 13)*	abbreviation for Chief Executive Officer
FYI *(para. 16)*	abbreviation that means "For Your Information"
marsupials *(para. 18)*	animals (like kangaroos, possums, and wombats) that carry their young in pouches
predators *(para. 20)*	creatures who live by feeding on others
raison d'être *(para. 21)*	reason or justification for existence, reason for being

Many experts claimed that the computer age heralded the advent of the paperless office. Clearly, this is not to be. If anything, offices are overwhelmed by even more paper, much of it now with sprocket holes.

Humankind is adapting, fortunately. According to the dictates of our 2
varied individual natures, we have developed ways of coping with our
changing ecosystem.

The beaver uses paper to build. It may not be exactly clear to observers 3
just what she's building, but deep in her genetic code she knows.

On one side of the typical beaver's desk leans a foot-high stack of papers. 4
Close by is a vertical file stuffed with bulging folders, some waving in the
air, unable to touch bottom. In between, the beaver constructs a clever
"dam" to prevent the entire structure from falling over: Her two-tier
In/Out box supports the pile and allows movement of papers from one
place to another.

Incredibly, to nonbeaver observers, the beaver has an uncanny ability to 5
locate a two-month-old report buried within the pile. With deft precision,
she can move her hand four millimeters down the pile and extract what
she's looking for, confident that the dam will hold.

In this way, the beaver has evolved a protective mechanism that makes 6
her invaluable within the organization, for nobody else, including her secretary, can find anything on her desk. When the beaver goes away on vacation, her department simply ceases work until she returns. She is thus
assured that the cliché "nobody's indispensable" doesn't apply to her.

The squirrel's desk, by contrast, is barren. Throughout the year, in all 7
kinds of weather, the squirrel energetically stores away what her brain tells
her she may need someday. In her many file cabinets, drawers and book-
cases she neatly stores memos, letters, printouts and receipts she believes will
nourish her in the months and years to come.

Unlike her co-worker the beaver, the squirrel does not always know 8
exactly where she has hidden a particular item. She knows she *has* it but
is not skilled at remembering the exact location.

Like the maple tree, which produces enough seeds to reforest a conti- 9
nent, the squirrel illustrates nature's method of "overkill." By saving and
storing everything, she increases her chance of retrieving something.

Of necessity, squirrels have developed the ability to move through a wide 10
territorial range. When a squirrel moves on to another job, as she tends to
do rather often due to lack of space, management must hire a special team
of search-and-destroy experts to go through her files.

Nature's scavengers, her "clean-up crew," crows are regarded with wary 11
admiration by squirrels and beavers, who recognize their contribution to
keeping the corporate ecosystem tidy.

Crows are responsible for such paper-management advice as "Act on 12
it—or throw it away." They are deeply drawn to paper shredders, trash
compactors and outsized waste receptacles and will buy them if they
happen to work in purchasing.

Crows belie the common epithet "birdbrained," for it has taken centuries   13
of evolution to create a mind disciplined enough to know with certainty
that it is OK to throw the CEO's Statement of Corporate Policy in the
wastebasket after a glance.

Other species, who must adapt to the corporate food chain, quickly   14
learn not to address any crow with a sentence that begins, "Do you have
a copy of . . . ?"

The clever bees are among the wonders of the corporate world. A bee   15
neither hoards nor destroys paper; she redistributes it, moving from office
to office as if between flowers.

Her methods are various and unpredictable, but there is no madness in   16
them. Sometimes she arrives in an office with paper in hand and, distract-
ing a colleague with conversation, simply leaves the paper inconspicuously
on her desk. Sometimes she moves paper through seemingly legitimate
channels, sending it through interoffice mail with ingenious notes like
"Please look into this when you get a chance." More often, she employs
the clever notation invented by bees, "FYI."

Whatever her methods, she ensures that paper floats outward and does not   17
return to her. Students of human behavior have come to call this cross-
pollination "delegation," though to the bee it is simply a genetic imperative.

While others of the species hoard, distribute and destroy paper, the   18
possum follows the evolutionary dictates of all marsupials and carries it
with her.

Instead of a pouch, the office possum has a briefcase—in some cases,   19
several. It is large and soft-sided to accommodate her needs. Some possums,
as an auxiliary system, carry handbags large enough to hold legal-size files.
When a possum needs to retrieve paper, she goes not to a file cabinet or
an In box but to her bags. She protects her paper by carrying it with her
at all times—to her home, to the health club, to lunch.

Though she has no natural predators, the possum's habits create special   20
risks. She must spend considerable time at the lost-and-found department
of theaters and restaurants and knows by heart the telephone number of
the taxi commissioner. One of her arms is longer than the other.

But in nature, all things serve a purpose. And if the office burned down,   21
the lowly possum would be the sole possessor of the paper that is the raison
d'être of all the other animals.

RESPONDING TO READING

Did you recognize anyone you know in the five types of paper pushers
described by Fury? Which animal do you resemble most in the way you

deal with paperwork? Write a journal entry giving an example of this behavior.

GAINING WORD POWER

In paragraph 8, Fury writes, "the squirrel does not always know *exactly* where she has hidden a particular item." In the next sentence, we read the phrase "the *exact* location." Both words share the meaning of being precise and accurate. *Exact* is an adjective, describing the noun *location*. *Exactly* is the adverb form of the same word; adverbs describe words other than nouns, in this case the verb *know*. Most adverbs are made by adding -*ly* to adjectives: for example, *clearly* comes from *clear, quickly* comes from *quick,* and *deeply* comes from *deep.*

This reading includes seven other adverbs that end in -*ly*. Find at least five of them. Then write their adjective forms, checking with the dictionary for spelling if necessary. Then express the shared meaning between the two forms, again using the dictionary. Here's an example to get you started:

Adverb: awkwardly

Adjective: awkward

Shared meaning: clumsiness, lacking in skill or grace

CONSIDERING CONTENT

1. Does this essay have a thesis statement? If so, where is it? If not, what is the main idea?
2. What does the term "sprocket holes" mean in paragraph 1?
3. Do the animal comparisons help clarify the categories of paper pushers? Is the author making fun of people by comparing them to animals? What is her purpose in using animals to set up her categories?
4. Why does Fury seem to admire the crows? Do you know people like this, who can defy authority without getting in trouble?
5. Paragraph 20 mentions three "risks." What are they, and why would they be a problem for the possum-type worker?
6. Are you a beaver, a squirrel, a crow, a bee, or a possum? Would you prefer to be in another group? Which group do you think Fury prefers?

CONSIDERING METHOD

1. Does the author tell you in the introduction that she's going to compare humans working in offices to animals working in nature? Do you think maybe she should have?

2. For what audience is the essay intended?

3. Fury's comparison of an office worker stacking files to a beaver building a dam is called an **analogy**—that is, a comparison that explains something new or unfamiliar by comparing it to something similar that's already understood. Explain the other human-animal analogies in this essay.

4. Fury uses a number of biological terms in developing her human-animal analogies. Explain the connection intended between human and animal in the following terms: *protective mechanism* (para. 6), *nature's overkill* (para. 9), and *genetic imperative* (para. 17).

5. Why are all the workers referred to as *she* or *her* (with no mention of a *he* or *him*)? Do you think this use of only female pronouns is sexist? Explain why or why not.

6. Point out the transitions that Fury uses to connect her categories.

7. Although the essay has no concluding paragraph, how does the author draw all her points together and provide a sense of completeness to the discussion?

8. What other strategies besides classification and comparison does Fury use to develop her ideas? Look for use of examples, description, narrative, and definition.

WRITING STEP BY STEP

Think about various ways that animal behavior is similar to human behavior. For a number of such comparisons, we have familiar sayings (once interesting similes but now grown into clichés from overuse): busy as a bee, working like a horse, contented as a cow, crazy as a loon, frisky as a colt, lazy as a slug, gentle as a lamb, ferocious as a lion, wise as an owl, faithful as a dog, sly as a fox, and so on. Choose an area of behavior that can be classified into types—for instance, the way different people walk to class or eat pizza or study for a test or move on a dance floor. Or consider the ways they approach their work, style their hair, arrange their closets, discipline their children, or buy their groceries.

A. Decide on a behavior that you find interesting and figure out three or four categories into which you can group the people who engage in that behavior. For example, say you want to write about spaghetti eaters. You could discuss those who cut and nibble small bites from the outside in, those who suck it up a few strands at a time, and those who wind it around a spoon and shovel it in.

B. Then, think of animals that typically behave in a way similar to the people in each category. The nibblers, for example, might be rabbits.

The strand-suckers could be anteaters (who suck food up through their long snouts). And the shovelers could be huge-mouthed hippos or hungry wolves.

C. Begin your essay, as Fury does in the first two paragraphs, with a general observation about your topic, but mention that you will be comparing humans to animals. Just a couple of sentences will do. Mention that people and animals eat in many different ways, some more polite than others, and that at your house, when spaghetti is served, you feel as if you're dining at the zoo.

D. Devote one or two paragraphs to each type. Fury gives each animal three or four brief paragraphs, but she is following the style of journalists who break their essays into short paragraphs to make them easier to read when they are printed in narrow columns in a magazine or newspaper. Since your essay won't be presented in narrow columns, you can use fewer and longer paragraphs.

E. Use lots of specific details to describe the behavior. Look again at the wealth of detail in Fury's article: *two-tier In/Out box; four millimeters down the pile; memos, letters, printouts and receipts; paper shredders, trash compactors and outsized waste receptacles; to her home, to the health club, to lunch;* and so on.

F. Use a transition between two of your types like the one Fury uses between paragraphs 6 and 7: "The squirrel's desk, *by contrast*, is barren." Other transitional terms to consider include *on the other hand, but, still, however, yet, although, nevertheless, unlike, in this way, another type,* and *in other groups.*

G. You can conclude without adding a final paragraph if you can think of a way to echo the important elements of your introduction (as Fury does with her mention of "the paper that is the raison d'être of all the other animals").

But you may find it easier to add a brief conclusion mentioning the usefulness of your categories. If your purpose is simply to entertain your readers, you might end, instead, with a summarizing comment on your topic. You could, for instance, conclude by saying that the styles of the spaghetti eaters in your household are fairly revolting, but you count your blessings that at least they don't eat this way in public.

OTHER WRITING IDEAS

1. Using a plan similar to the Step by Step essay (but omitting the animal analogies), classify the different ways people react to some uncomfortable situation: a car accident, a death in the family, a broken relationship, an unexpected pregnancy.

2. Get together with a group of classmates and discuss various ways that society stereotypes females and males. Think of labels to identify these types, like *the Super-Mom, the Nagging Wife, the Clinging Vine, the Liberated Woman, the Tramp*—or for males, *the Jock, the Mama's Boy, the Macho Man, the Ladies' Man, Mr. Sensitive*. Then write an essay describing three or four types (either males or females). You can draw your examples and specific details from movies, TV programs, comic strips, or videos. Your purpose could be to show how unfair or misleading these stereotypes are.

3. What different methods of managing money do you see among your friends and family members? Write an essay classifying a few types of money managers. Be sure to give plenty of specific details to identify each type. You might conclude by offering several tips of your own for managing money.

EDITING SKILLS: USING APOSTROPHES

Using apostrophes makes most writers at least a bit nervous. To get a grip on this slippery piece of punctuation, think about these basic rules:

1. Use an apostrophe to indicate that two words have been pushed together to form a contraction. Put the apostrophe where you leave the letters out.

would not = wouldn't	is not = isn't
you are = you're	he is = he's
they will = they'll	we have = we've

2. Use an apostrophe plus *s* with singular nouns to show possession.
   the heat of the sun = the sun's heat
   the rent for one year = one year's rent
   the wig belonging to Judy = Judy's wig
   cards from UNICEF = UNICEF's cards

3. Use an apostrophe with plurals to make them possessive.
   papers from three students = three students' papers
   alibis of four criminals = four criminals' alibis
   If the plural does not already end in *s,* add an *s* after the apostrophe.
   games for children = children's games
   poetry by men = men's poetry

In the Fury essay, there are eight separate words (besides the French expression *raison d'être*) that use apostrophes. Copy the eight words exactly. Don't count repeats. Next to each one, write whether the apostrophe makes the word a contraction or a possessive.

Now return to your classification essay, and make sure that you have used apostrophes correctly.

PREPARING TO READ

List five or ten of the people you call "friends." Are they all friends to an equal degree? Do you have a flexible meaning for the word *friend?*

Friends, Good Friends—and Such Good Friends

JUDITH VIORST

Judith Viorst is a popular humorist who writes essays and light verse for many well-known magazines. The following selection appeared in her regular column in *Redbook* magazine in 1977. Like much of her work, this essay focuses on dimensions of the female experience.

TERMS TO RECOGNIZE

ardor *(para. 2)*	enthusiasm, intensity
nonchalant *(para. 3)*	indifferent, offhand
Tuesday-doubles *(para. 11)*	tennis played by four people, in pairs, on Tuesdays
sibling rivalry *(para. 16)*	competition among children for parental favor
dormant *(para. 19)*	sleeping, inactive
revived *(para. 19)*	brought back to life
calibrated *(para. 29)*	adjusted, determined

Women are friends, I once would have said, when they totally love and support and trust each other, and bare to each other the secrets of their souls, and run—no questions asked—to help each other, and tell harsh truths to each other (no, you can't wear that dress unless you lose ten pounds first) when harsh truths must be told. 1

Women are friends, I once would have said, when they share the same affection for Ingmar Bergman, plus train rides, cats, warm rain, charades, Camus, and hate with equal ardor Newark and Brussels sprouts and Lawrence Welk and camping. 2

In other words, I once would have said that a friend is a friend all the way, but now I believe that's a narrow point of view. For the friendships I have and the friendships I see are conducted at many levels of intensity, 3 serve many different functions, meet different needs and range from those as all-the-way as the friendship of the soul sisters mentioned above to that of the most nonchalant and casual playmates.

Consider these varieties of friendship: 4

1. Convenience friends. These are the women with whom, if our paths 5 weren't crossing all the time, we'd have no particular reason to be friends: a next-door neighbor, a woman in our car pool, the mother of one of our children's closest friends or maybe some mommy with whom we serve juice and cookies each week at the Glenwood Co-op Nursery.

Convenience friends are convenient indeed. They'll lend us their cups 6 and silverware for a party. They'll drive our kids to soccer when we're sick. They'll take us to pick up our car when we need a lift to the garage. They'll even take our cats when we go on vacation. As we will for them.

But we don't, with convenience friends, ever come too close or tell too 7 much; we maintain our public face and emotional distance. "Which means," says Elaine, "that I'll talk about being overweight but not about being depressed. Which means I'll admit being mad but not blind with rage. Which means that I might say that we're pinched this month but never that I'm worried sick over money."

But which doesn't mean that there isn't sufficient value to be found in 8 these friendships of mutual aid, in convenience friends.

2. Special-interest friends. These friendships aren't intimate, and they 9 needn't involve kids or silverware or cats. Their value lies in some interest jointly shared. And so we may have an office friend or a yoga friend or a tennis friend or a friend from the Women's Democratic Club.

"I've got one woman friend," says Joyce, "who likes, as I do, to take 10 psychology courses. Which makes it nice for me—and nice for her. It's fun to go with someone you know and it's fun to discuss what you've learned, driving back from the classes." And for the most part, she says, that's all they discuss.

"I'd say that what we're doing is *doing* together, not being together," 11 Suzanne says of her Tuesday-doubles friends. "It's mainly a tennis relation-ship, but we play together well. And I guess we all need to have a couple of playmates."

I agree. 12

My playmate is a shopping friend, a woman of marvelous taste, a woman 13 who knows exactly *where* to buy *what,* and furthermore is a woman who always knows beyond a doubt what one ought to be buying. I don't have the time to keep up with what's new in eyeshadow, hemlines and shoes and whether the smock look is in or finished already. But since (oh, shame!) I care a lot about eyeshadow, hemlines and shoes, and since I don't *want* to wear smocks if the smock look is finished, I'm very glad to have a shopping friend.

3. Historical friends. We all have a friend who knew us when . . . maybe   14
way back in Miss Meltzer's second grade, when our family lived in that three-
room flat in Brooklyn, when our dad was out of work for seven months,
when our brother Allie got in that fight where they had to call the police,
when our sister married the endodontist from Yonkers, and when, the morning after we lost our virginity, she was the first, the only, friend we told.

The years have gone by and we've gone separate ways and we've little   15
in common now, but we're still an intimate part of each other's past. And
so whenever we go to Detroit we always go to visit this friend of our girlhood. Who knows how we looked before our teeth were straightened.
Who knows how we talked before our voice got unBrooklyned. Who
knows what we ate before we learned about artichokes. And who, by her
presence, puts us in touch with an earlier part of ourself, a part of ourself
it's important never to lose.

"What this friend means to me and what I mean to her," says Grace, "is   16
having a sister without sibling rivalry. We know the texture of each other's
lives. She remembers my grandmother's cabbage soup. I remember the way
her uncle played the piano. There's simply no other friend who remembers those things."

4. Crossroads friends. Like historical friends, our crossroads friends are   17
important for *what was*—for the friendship we shared at a crucial, now past,
time of life. A time, perhaps, when we roomed in college together; or
worked as eager young singles in the Big City together; or went together,
as my friend Elizabeth and I did, through pregnancy, birth and that scary
first year of new motherhood.

Crossroads friends forge powerful links, links strong enough to endure   18
with not much more contact than once-a-year letters at Christmas. And out
of respect for those crossroads years, for those dramas and dreams we once
shared, we will always be friends.

5. Cross-generational friends. Historical friends and crossroads friends   19
seem to maintain a special kind of intimacy—dormant but always ready to
be revived—and though we may rarely meet, whenever we do connect, it's
personal and intense. Another kind of intimacy exists in the friendships
that form across generations in what one woman calls her daughter-mother
and her mother-daughter relationships.

Evelyn's friend is her mother's age—"but I share so much more than I   20
ever could with my mother"—a woman she talks to of music, of books,
and of life. "What I get from her is the benefit of her experience. What she
gets—and enjoys—from me is a youthful perspective. It's a pleasure for
both of us."

I have in my own life a precious friend, a woman of 65 who has lived   21
very hard, who is wise, who listens well; who has been where I am and

can help me understand it; and who represents not only an ultimate ideal mother to me but also the person I'd like to be when I grow up.

In our daughter role we tend to do more than our share of self-revelation; in our mother role we tend to receive what's revealed. It's another kind of pleasure—playing a wise mother to a questing younger person. It's another very lovely kind of friendship. 22

6. Part-of-a-couple friends. Some of the women we call our friends we never see alone—we see them as part of a couple at couples' parties. And though we share interests in many things and respect each other's views, we aren't moved to deepen the relationship. Whatever the reason, a lack of time or—and this is more likely—a lack of chemistry, our friendship remains in the context of a group. But the fact that our feeling on seeing each other is always, "I'm *so* glad she's here" and the fact that we spend half the evening talking together says that this too, in its way, counts as a friendship. 23

(Other part-of-a-couple friends are the friends that came with the marriage, and some of these are friends we could live without. But sometimes, alas, she married our husband's best friend; and sometimes, alas, *she* is our husband's best friend. And so we find ourself dealing with her, somewhat against our will, in a spirit of what I'll call *reluctant* friendship.) 24

7. Men who are friends. I wanted to write just of women friends, but the women I've talked to won't let me—they say I must mention man-woman friendships too. For these friendships can be just as close and as dear as those that we form with women. Listen to Lucy's description of one such friendship: 25

"We've found we have things to talk about that are different from what he talks about with my husband and different from what I talk about with his wife. So sometimes we call on the phone or meet for lunch. There are similar intellectual interests—we always pass on to each other the books that we love—but there's also something tender and caring too." 26

In a couple of crises, Lucy says, "he offered himself, for talking and for helping. And when someone died in his family he wanted me there. The sexual, flirty part of our friendship is very small, but *some*—just enough to make it fun and different." She thinks—and I agree—that the sexual part, though small, is always *some*, is always there when a man and a woman are friends. 27

It's only in the past few years that I've made friends with men, in the sense of a friendship that's *mine*, not just part of two couples. And achieving with them the ease and the trust I've found with women friends has value indeed. Under the dryer at home last week, putting on mascara and rouge, I comfortably sat and talked with a fellow named Peter. Peter, I finally decided, could handle the shock of me minus mascara under the dryer. Because we care for each other. Because we're friends. 28

8. There are medium friends, and pretty good friends, and very good friends indeed, and these friendships are defined by their level of intimacy. And what we'll reveal at each of these levels of intimacy is calibrated with care. We might tell a medium friend, for example, that yesterday we had a fight with our husband. And we might tell a pretty good friend that this fight with our husband made us so mad that we slept on the couch. And we might tell a very good friend that the reason we got so mad in that fight that we slept on the couch had something to do with that girl who works in his office. But it's only to our very best friends that we're willing to tell all, to tell what's going on with that girl in his office.   29

The best of friends, I still believe, totally love and support and trust each other, and bare to each other the secrets of their souls, and run—no questions asked—to help each other, and tell harsh truths to each other when they must be told.   30

But we needn't agree about everything (only 12-year-old girl friends agree about *everything*) to tolerate each other's point of view. To accept without judgment. To give and to take without ever keeping score. And to *be* there, as I am for them and as they are for me, to comfort our sorrows, to celebrate our joys.   31

RESPONDING TO READING

What do you think about friends of the other sex? Is there always a sexual spark? Are cross-sex friendships different in quality than same-sex friendships? Would you try to restrict your sweetheart in his or her friendships?

GAINING WORD POWER

The following partial sentences include slightly different forms of the "Terms to Recognize." Complete each sentence in a reasonable way that shows you understand the word used. Use your dictionary to be sure you grasp the meaning.

1. Elena is an ardent hockey fan, but _____
   _____.

2. Stanley did not understand the fine calibrations of politeness: he
   often _____.

3. After _____, Jean's
   social life went into a period of dormancy.

4. The writer's nonchalance about spelling was clear when _____
   _____.

CONSIDERING CONTENT

1. What ideas is Viorst giving up, according to the beginning of the essay? Why does she begin with what she no longer believes?
2. Make a list of the different kinds of friends discussed in the essay. Which kind is the exception from the others?
3. What kind of person is the author of this essay? What kind of life does she lead? Look at paragraphs 5, 6, and 16 for evidence. How might the writer's point of view limit her audience? Did you feel included?
4. What are the functions friends perform, according to the essay? Are there underlying similarities among most of the types?
5. Why do you think the women Viorst interviewed insisted that she discuss man-woman friendships?

CONSIDERING METHOD

1. How do you know when Viorst is beginning a section about a new type of friend? What other method might she use to signal such a shift?
2. What is the relationship between the opening of the essay and the closing?
3. Look at the ways Viorst develops the explanation of each type. She uses narration, definition, example, comparison and contrast, and cause-and-effect reasoning. Identify instances showing at least three of these methods.
4. What do the direct quotations do for the essay? Are they from famous people? Think of at least two reasons why they are included.
5. In paragraph 10, you can see the repetition of similar sentence openings. What words are repeated? Find another example of repetition of phrases or structures. What purpose does this repetition serve?

WRITING STEP BY STEP

Using Viorst's essay for inspiration, write an essay that classifies several different types of intelligence.

A. Brainstorm, with help from friends or classmates if you want it, for ideas about the various kinds of "smart" you see around you. Jot down everything mentioned, even if it sounds silly or overlapping—you can sort it out later.
B. Choose three to six types to discuss in your essay. You might combine several different items from your brainstorming notes to make up one type, when the items seem closely related.

C. Make up a label for each type, as Viorst did in "Friends."

D. Develop a section explaining each type. Use examples of people who show each type of intelligence if you can—either people you know personally or public figures most of your readers will be able to identify. Interview your friends, as Viorst did, and use direct quotations from your interviews.

E. Be sure to show how the types are similar and different from each other by using comparisons and contrasts as you go along. Look at paragraphs 19 and 29 of Viorst's essay for samples of how to do this.

F. Use signals to show when you are shifting from one type to the next. You could use numbers and/or labels. Or you could use transitional words, like "The second type of intelligence is. . . ."

G. Write an introduction that discusses a misperception (of your own or of others) about intelligence. See Viorst's introduction for a model.

H. Close your essay with a statement that draws all the kinds of intelligence together, telling what they have in common. Alternatively, you may want to close, as Viorst did, by commenting on what you wrote in the introduction.

OTHER WRITING IDEAS

1. There are probably as many kinds of people you dislike as people you like. Write an essay categorizing the types that drive you crazy.

2. Classify the variations of a single emotion—anxiety, nervousness, love, anger, pleasure, embarrassment, confidence, or excitement, for example.

3. Judith Viorst wrote another essay in which she classifies the lies we tell. For example, she discusses lies we tell to save others' feelings, lies we tell to save our own pride, and so on. Write your own essay on this topic. You might get together with classmates to think of categories and examples.

EDITING SKILLS: PROOFREADING

Proofreading your essay should be a painstaking task. You need to look at every word and every piece of punctuation—and use your dictionary when you are not absolutely certain you have it all right. Remember that your dictionary includes a handbook for editing that gives you rules of punctuation and mechanics. If you are composing on a computer, your spelling checker will catch some of your errors, but not all. For example, if you typed *form* instead of *from,* your spelling checker will not flag it. Words that your checker does not know will also need to be looked up in the dictionary—the computer program knows only about half as many words as a dictionary holds.

EXERCISE

Here is a paragraph from another essay by Judith Viorst, "The Truth about Lying." We have put in errors for you to find and correct. Retype your corrected version and trade papers with a classmate. Discuss any differences you see, and refer again to your dictionary for points of clarification.

Protective lies are lies folks tell—often quite serious lies-because their convinced that the truth would be to dammaging. They lie because they feel their are certian human values that supercede the wrong of of having lied. They lie, not for personnel gain, but because they believe its for the good of the person they're lying to. They lie to those they love, to those who trust them most of all, on the grounds that braking this trust is justifyed.

If you are interested in how well your computer program does, you can try typing in the uncorrected version of the paragraph and running the spelling checker. You will find that quite a few errors slip right past.

PREPARING TO READ

For the next twenty-four hours, make a note every time you hear someone describe another person's behavior (or idea or talk) as weird or strange
or crazy. Also record your ideas about why the behavior was pointed out
as different from normal.

I'm OK; You're a Bit Odd

PAUL CHANCE

Paul Chance, a psychologist and teacher at Salisbury State University in
Maryland, sits on the advisory board for the Cambridge Center for Behavioral Studies. He writes frequently about human behavior for various
professional and educational journals. In this article, first published in 1988
in *Psychology Today* magazine, Chance investigates the ways we decide
whether other people are mentally healthy.

TERMS TO RECOGNIZE

quirk *(para. 1)*	minor oddity
Platonic ideal *(para. 2)*	the perfect form, according to the Greek philosopher Plato
emulate *(para. 2)*	imitate
psychopath *(para. 8)*	seriously disturbed person who has aggressive, criminal tendencies
flimflam *(para. 8)*	swindle
paragon *(para. 13)*	ideal example
phobias *(para. 13)*	unreasonable and bothersome fears
benchmark *(para. 14)*	a standard level for judging quality or quantity

the new groom was happy with his bride, and everything, he explained,   1
was fine. There was just this one peculiarity his wife had. During love-
making she insisted that he wear his motorcycle helmet. He found it
uncomfortable, and he felt just a tad foolish. Is it normal to want someone
to wear a helmet during amorous activities? Does a quirk of this sort keep
one off the rolls of the mentally fit? The answer depends on how you
define mental fitness. There are several ways of going about it.

One model calls to mind the Platonic ideal. Somewhere in the heavens   2
there exists a person who is the perfect specimen of psychological health.

(Or maybe there are two of them: the perfect man may be different from the perfect woman. At least, one would hope so.) We all fall short of this ideal, of course, but it provides a model that we can emulate. Unfortunately, the Platonic answer merely begs the question, since somebody has to describe what the ideal is like. And how do we do that?

The everyday way of defining mental health is more subjective: if I do   3
it, it's healthy; if I don't do it, it's sick. Is it crazy to spend Saturdays jumping out of airplanes or canoeing down rapids? Not to skydivers and white-water canoers. Is it sick to hear voices when no one is there? Not if you're the one who hears the voices—and you welcome their company.

This commonsense way of defining mental health sets ourselves up as   4
the standard against which to make comparisons. There's nothing wrong with this, except that it's just possible that some of us—not me, you understand—are a bit odd ourselves. And you can't measure accurately with a bent ruler.

The psychodynamic model of mental health suggests that psychological   5
fitness is a kind of balancing act. There are, according to this view, impulses in all of us that society cannot tolerate. The healthy person is not the one who always keeps these impulses under lock and key but the one who lets them out once in a while when nobody's looking. If you run around the house smashing delicate things with a hammer, for example, someone's apt to object. But if you hammer a nail into a board, and seem to have a good excuse for it, nobody minds. So the healthy person with violent impulses builds a deck behind the house.

The chief problem with the psychodynamic model is that it doesn't   6
define the standard by which balance is to be measured. Building a deck may be an acceptable outlet for violent impulses, but what if every time a person feels like slugging someone he adds on to the deck until his entire backyard is covered in redwood? He's directing his impulses constructively, but his family might find him easier to live with if he just broke something once in a while.

Behaviorists offer a different solution. They focus on behavior, naturally,   7
and decide whether behavior is healthy on the basis of its consequences. If the results are good, the behavior is good. In this view, there is nothing nuts about building a two-acre redwood deck so long as the person enjoys it and it doesn't get him or her into trouble. Normal behavior, then, is whatever works.

The behavioral approach appears to offer an objective and rational way   8
of defining mental health. Alas, appearances are deceiving. We may agree that a person enjoys an activity, but is that enough? A sadist and a masochist may work out a mutually rewarding relationship, but does that make them healthy? A psychopath may flimflam oldsters out of their life savings and

do it with such charm that they love him for it, but should the rest of us emulate the psychopath?

An alternative is to let society decide. What is healthy then becomes 9 what society finds acceptable; what is unhealthy is whatever society dislikes. Thus, aggression is abnormal among the gentle Tasaday of the Philippines but normal among the fierce Yanomamo of Venezuela.

The societal model has a lot of appeal, but it troubles some mental-health 10 workers. There is something about fixing mental health to a mailing address that they find unsettling. They think that there ought to be some sort of universal standard toward which we might all strive. Besides, does it really make sense to say that murder and cannibalism are OK just because some society has approved them? And if it is, then why not apply the same standards to communities within a society? Murder is a popular activity among Baltimore youth. Shall we say that, in that city, murder is healthy?

A similar problem exists with the statistical model of mental health. In 11 this case, being mentally healthy means falling close to average. Take the frequency of sexual activity among married couples, for example. Let's say that, on average, married people your age have intercourse about twice a week. That's the norm. If you indulge more or less often than that, you're abnormal—with or without a helmet.

There's some logic to this view. The further people deviate from the 12 average, the more likely they are to seem strange. You may think, for instance, that limiting sex to two times a week is a bit prudish, but almost everyone is likely to think that once an hour is excessive. Again, however, there are problems.

Does it really make sense to hold up the average person as the paragon 13 of mental health? This logic would have everyone cultivate a few phobias just because they happen to be commonplace, even the best students would strive to earn Cs, and all couples in the country would be frustrated by their inability to have exactly 1.8 children.

We can all agree that there are a lot of weirdos around, but there seems 14 no way for us to agree about who's weird. And so there's no way for us to agree about what mental health is. That's unfortunate, because it gives us no clear goal toward which to strive and no stable benchmark against which to gauge our progress. Even so, I'm damned if I'm gonna wear a helmet to bed.

RESPONDING TO READING

Return to your notes from Preparing to Read. What explanations for branding something as weird are covered in Chance's essay? Does the essay change your perspective on the incidents you noted?

GAINING WORD POWER

Weird is an overused and imprecise word. Some synonyms from the thesaurus are *uncanny, puzzling, inexplicable, bizarre, nightmarish, irrational,* and *freakish.* Look up each of these synonyms in the dictionary. Write one sentence for each of the six words. Make your sentences reflect the differences in meaning among the terms.

CONSIDERING CONTENT

1. Who is the audience for this essay? How do you know? Who is *not* the audience for the piece? Why?
2. How many approaches to defining mental health or normality does Chance cover? List them.
3. Give your own examples that fit at least two of the models of mental health.
4. Which model of mental health, in your opinion, would label you and your friends most mentally abnormal? Consider your family: what approach would label your family as strange?
5. In paragraph 2, Chance suggests that the ideal of psychological health would be different for men and women. Do you agree? Why or why not?
6. Where does the title of the essay come from? If you don't know, look up the first two words of the title in your library's online or card catalog. How is the essay related to the original source of the title?

CONSIDERING METHOD

1. Under each approach to defining mental health, how does Chance organize his discussion? As you were reading, when did this organization become clear to you?
2. Does each approach include a specific example? Why are the examples important? Would you have liked another example of one of the points?
3. Count how many questions Chance asks in the essay. Thinking of your other reading, is this an unusual number of questions? What purpose do you think they serve?
4. What is the tone of the piece? For example, what tone of voice would someone use to read it out loud? Give several words that describe the tone. What clues you in to the tone?
5. Reread the last sentence. What is your reaction to it? What technique does it employ to indicate that the essay is finished?

WRITING STEP BY STEP

When we are faced with one of life's problems, we often find ourselves brainstorming to discover approaches to the problem and then considering the strengths and weaknesses of each approach. We ponder, for example, the problem of how to make housemates or family members share cleaning duties, the problem of how to make scarce money go further, or the problem of how to break unwelcome news to someone. Choose a problem that could be considered in several ways, and write an essay using Chance's discussion of approaches to mental health as a model.

A. Identify three or four approaches to the problem. On a piece of scratch paper or on your computer screen, brainstorm for a few minutes, jotting down ideas about each approach. If you need help, ask your classmates for ideas about your topic.

B. Decide on a reasonable order to present your approaches—from weakest to strongest (or vice versa), from your first hunch to your last solution, from the most ordinary to the most bizarre, or along any range that seems reasonable.

C. Choose a tone that suits your purpose and your audience. In choosing a tone, you might also consider the severity of the problem— a serious treatise concerning approaches to bad hair days will provide a humorous mismatch, for example. Paul Chance, in a similar way, chose a light tone to discuss a serious topic. However, a match between the topic and the tone is the usual expectation, and you should feel free to align them if you want: a humorous tone for a light topic, and a serious tone for a weighty topic.

D. Begin the essay with a little story that highlights the problem, as Chance does. Lead into a general statement of the problem.

E. Write a one- or two-paragraph discussion of your first approach. Begin with a description of the approach.

F. Give the strengths of the approach, and provide an example of how it is (or would be) used.

G. Follow the strengths by discussing the weaknesses of the approach, along with an example of its failings. As Chance does, you can use the same example for both strengths and weaknesses, or, if you prefer, you can use different examples to show positive and negative elements.

H. Follow steps E, F, and G for the next two or three approaches you identified in the brainstorming stage.

I. In your closing paragraph, you might follow Chance's model and write about why no single approach is perfect. On the other hand, you might explain which approach you think is best, if there is one.

J. Write a closing sentence that relates back to the little story in your introduction.

OTHER WRITING IDEAS

1. Choose either school or a workplace you know well, and write about the different approaches people take toward their work. Consider using specific people you know as examples of the approaches. Be sure to give enough examples and details for your reader to get a clear picture.

2. Think of a quality that many people have but that they use in different ways—for example, power, beauty, charm, intelligence, or wealth. Develop an essay that explains three or four approaches to possessing this quality. "Some people use their power for good causes, some for control over others, and some to amass even more power." Consider evaluating each approach or explaining why people differ along these lines.

3. Classify people according to their attitudes toward their own backgrounds—ethnic, religious, cultural, racial, or class roots. For example, in what ways do people who come from poverty-stricken backgrounds relate to their past? What stances do people raised as Catholics take toward the religion in later life? To help you get ideas for your paper, get together with a group of classmates and discuss how each of you views your roots.

EDITING SKILLS: CHOOSING *THERE, THEIR,* OR *THEY'RE*

Words that sound alike, called *homophones,* can be treacherous. In speech, we don't think about which one to select, but in writing we have to make a choice. Because homophones are often common words, like *there, their,* and *they're,* we can't avoid using them. And because their meanings are quite different, we really do have to get them right or our readers will be confused.

First, look at the use of the word *there* in these sentences from "I'm OK; You're a Bit Odd":

There was just this one peculiarity his wife had.

There are, according to this view, impulses in all of us that society cannot tolerate.

In these sentences, *there* is just a fill-in word; it doesn't have much meaning. We use *there* to begin sentences like these when we want to say that something or someone exists. The same spelling goes for the use of the word to indicate a place:

Is it sick to hear voices when no one is *there?*

Now look at the use of *their* in these passages from the same essay:

Not if you're the one who hears the voices—and you welcome *their* company.

A psychopath may flimflam oldsters out of *their* life savings.

The word *their* is a possessive, showing ownership or belonging. In the first example it refers to voices; in the second example, it refers to oldsters.

Finally, take a look at this sentence:

Behaviorists would say that if people enjoy an action and it doesn't get them in trouble, *they're* normal.

In this example, *they're* sounds just like the others, but you can substitute the words *they are* for it. *They're* is a contraction, just like *don't* for *do not* and *she's* for *she is*. If you can substitute *they are,* you know you have the right word. If you can't, you need *there* or *their.*

All right, let's review:

There are numerous sound–alike words in English.

You have to know the differences in *their* meanings if you want to use them correctly.

They're often common words that we use a lot.

EXERCISE

Fill in the blanks in the following sentences with *there, their,* or *they're.*

1. _____ are no solutions to this problem.
2. Your cousins have arrived, and _____ going to stay for dinner.
3. When George Eliot and Jane Austen wrote _____ great novels, _____ were few creative opportunities for women besides writing.
4. The team members should have known that _____ luck wouldn't hold. But _____ definitely looking forward to next season.

5. Although it wasn't _____ fault, the twins are sure to get blamed, and _____ not happy about it.

Look over the essay you have just written to see if you used *there, their,* or *they're.* Did you choose the right one? Go over some past papers, too, to see how accurate you are in using these three homophones. Copy three to five sentences in which you use one, and justify your choice in each case. (For more about homophones, see Chapter 9, pp. 251–52.)

PREPARING TO READ

How can you tell when someone has high self-esteem? How do people with high self-esteem handle life's problems?

Types of Stress for Young People

DAVID ELKIND

David Elkind is a psychologist who specializes in child development and has written influential books on the subject. In this reading from his book *All Grown Up and No Place to Go* (1988), he describes three kinds of situations that we all face but that are especially stressful for teenagers.

TERMS TO RECOGNIZE

expenditure *(para. 3)*   cost
potential *(para. 4, 12)*   possible
foreseeable *(para. 4)*   seen ahead of time
transient *(para. 7)*   temporary, passing away with time
jeopardize *(para. 7)*   threaten
incorporates *(para. 10)*   combines
inevitable *(para. 12)*   certain to happen
introverted *(para. 14)*   withdrawn, not sociable
extroverted *(para. 14)*   outgoing
bouts *(para. 15)*   short periods

ost situations that produce psychological stress involve some sort of   1
conflict between self and society. So long as we satisfy a social demand at the expense of a personal need, or vice versa, the social or personal demand for action is a psychological stress. If, for example, we stay home from work because of a personal problem, we create a new demand (for an explanation, for made-up time) at our place of work. On the other hand, if we devote too much time to the demands of work, we create new demands on the part of family. If we don't manage our energy budgets well, we create more stress than is necessary.

The major task of psychological stress management is to find ways to   2
balance and coordinate the demands that come from within with those that come from without. This is where a healthy sense of self and identity

comes in. An integrated sense of identity . . . means bringing together into a working whole a set of attitudes, values, and habits that can serve both self and society. The attainment of such a sense of identity is accompanied by a feeling of self-esteem, of liking and respecting oneself and being liked and respected by others.

More than anything else, the attainment of a healthy sense of identity 3 and a feeling of self-esteem gives young people a perspective, a way of looking at themselves and others, which enables them to manage the majority of stress situations. Young people with high self-esteem look at situations from a single perspective that includes both themselves and others. They look at situations from the standpoint of what it means to their self-respect and to the respect others have for them. This integrated perspective enables them to manage the major types of stress efficiently and with a minimum expenditure of energy and personal distress.

The Three Stress Situations

There are three major types of stress situations that all of us encounter. 4 One of these occurs when the potential stress is both foreseeable and avoidable. This is a *Type A* stress situation. If we are thinking about going on a roller coaster or seeing a horror movie, the stress is both foreseeable and avoidable. We may choose to expose ourselves to the stress if we find such controlled danger situations exciting or stimulating. Likewise if we know that a particular neighborhood or park is dangerous at night, the danger is both foreseeable and avoidable, and we do avoid it, unless we are looking for trouble.

The situation becomes more complicated when the foreseeable and 5 avoidable danger is one for which there is much social approval and support, even though it entails much personal risk. Becoming a soldier in times of war is an example of this more complicated Type A danger. The young person who enlists wins social approval at the risk of personal harm. On the other hand, the young person who refuses to become a soldier protects himself or herself from danger at the cost of social disapproval.

Teenagers are often caught in this more difficult type of situation. If the 6 peer group uses alcohol or drugs, for example, there is considerable pressure on the young person to participate. But such participation often puts the teenager at risk with parents and teachers, and also with respect to themselves. They may not like the image of themselves as drinkers or drug abusers. It is at this point that a sense of identity and a positive feeling of self-esteem stand the teenager in good stead.

A young person with a healthy sense of identity will weigh the danger 7 to his or her hard-won feeling of self-esteem against the feelings associated with the loss of peer approval. When the teenager looks at the situation from this perspective, the choice is easy to make. By weighing the laboriously arrived-at feeling of self-esteem against the momentary approval of a transient peer group, the teenager with an integrated sense of self is able to avoid potentially stressful situations. It should be said, too, that the young person's ability to foresee and avoid is both an intellectual and an emotional achievement. The teenager must be able to foresee events . . . but also to place sufficient value upon his or her self-esteem and self-respect to avoid situations that would jeopardize these feelings.

A second type of stress situation involves those demands which are   8
neither foreseeable nor avoidable. These are *Type B* stress situations. Accidents are of this type, as when a youngster is hit by a baseball while watching a game, or when a teenager who happens to be at a place in school when a fight breaks out gets hurt even though he was not involved. The sudden, unexpected death of a loved one is another example of a stress that is both unforeseeable and unavoidable. Divorce of parents is unthinkable for many teenagers and therefore also unforeseeable and unavoidable.

Type B stress situations make the greatest demands upon young people.   9
. . . With this type of stress teenagers have to deal with the attitudes of their friends and teachers at the same time that they are struggling with their own feelings. Such stress situations put demands upon young people both from within and from without. A youngster who has been handicapped by an accident, like the teenager who has to deal with divorce, has to adjust to new ways of relating to others as well as new ways of thinking about himself or herself.

Again, the young person with a strong sense of identity and a feeling of   10
self-esteem has the best chance of managing these stress situations as well as they can be managed. In the case of divorce, for example, the teenager who incorporates other people's perspectives with his or her own is able to deal with the situation better than other teenagers who lack this perspective. For example, one young man, who went on to win honors at an Ivy League school, told his father when he and the mother divorced, "You are entitled to live your own life and to find happiness too."

This integrated perspective also helps young people deal with the death   11
of a loved one. If it was an elderly grandparent who had been suffering great pain, the young person can see that from the perspective of the grandparent, dying may have been preferable to living a life of agony with no hope of recovery. As one teenager told me with regard to his grandfather who had just died, "He was in such pain, he was so doped up he couldn't really recognize me. I loved him so much I just couldn't stand to see him that way." By enabling the young person to see death from the perspective of others, including that of the person who is dying, the young person is able to mourn the loss but also to get on with life.

The third type of stress situation is one in which the potential stress is foreseeable but not avoidable. This is a *Type C* stress situation. A teenager who has stayed out later than he or she was supposed to foresees an unavoidable storm at home. Likewise, exams are foreseeable but unavoidable stress situations. Being required to spend time with relatives one does not like is another stress situation that the teenager can foresee but not avoid. These are but a few examples of situations the teenager might wish to avoid but must learn to accept as inevitable. ¹²

To young people who have attained a solid sense of self and identity, foreseeable and unavoidable stress situations are manageable, again, because of self-esteem and the integrated perspective. They look at the situation from the perspective of themselves as well as that of the other people involved and try to prepare accordingly. They may decide, as one young man of my acquaintance did, that "with my folks, honesty is the best policy. I get into less trouble if I tell the truth than if I make up stories." In the case of visiting relatives they do not like, integrated teenagers see it from the perspective of what it means to others, such as their parents. And with respect to stress situations like exams, because they want to maintain their self-esteem, they prepare for the exam so that they will make a good showing for themselves as well as for others. ¹³

It is important to say, too, that integrated teenagers come in any and all personality types. Some are introverted and shy, others are extroverted and fun-loving. Some are preoccupied with intellectual concerns, others primarily with matters of the heart. Despite this diversity, they all share the prime characteristics of the integrated teenager: a set of attitudes, values, and habits that enable the young person to serve self and society, and a strong sense of self-esteem. ¹⁴

To be sure, life is complex and varied. Even the most integrated teenager, of whatever personality type, may occasionally be so overwhelmed by stress that he or she loses the integrated perspective and suffers bouts of low self-esteem. We need to remember that teenagers are new at the game of stress management and have just acquired the skills they need for this purpose. Nonetheless, the general principle holds true. The more integrated the teenager is with respect to self and identity, the better prepared he or she is to manage the basic stress situations. ¹⁵

RESPONDING TO READING

Identify a source of stress in your own life, and see whether you can classify it as Type A, Type B, or Type C. Write in your journal about the stress and whether self-esteem contributes to how you handle it.

GAINING WORD POWER

Elkind's essay on stress uses several words and their opposites, their
antonyms, such as *extroverted* and *introverted, inevitable* and *avoidable, foreseeable* and *unforeseeable.* Use your dictionary or a dictionary of synonyms
and antonyms to find the opposites of the following words from the reading. Be sure to choose opposites that are the same part of speech; in the
three previous examples, all the words can be used as adjectives. You may
need to use two or three words instead of one. Your dictionary will help
you determine parts of speech.

transient   jeopardize
expenditure   potential
incorporate

CONSIDERING CONTENT

1. According to Elkind, what overall conflict causes most stressful situations?
2. Give examples of each type of stress from your own or your friends'
   lives.
3. Which type of stress does Elkind think is most difficult for teens?
   Why is this type the worst?
4. Elkind concentrates on how a teenager with high self-esteem would
   deal with stressful situations. How would a teen with low self-
   esteem deal with some of these situations?
5. What is an "integrated perspective" (paras. 3, 11, 13, and 15)? Give
   an example. Can you think of a synonym for the term?
6. In paragraph 7, Elkind writes, "[T]he young person's ability to foresee and avoid is both an intellectual and an emotional achievement." Explain this statement.

CONSIDERING METHOD

1. How many times does Elkind repeat his main point? Why might a
   writer repeat the main point several times?
2. Divide the fifteen paragraphs into five main sections. What label
   could you put on each section?
3. How does Elkind let you know what to expect when you are reading his essay?
4. How do you know when a new paragraph takes up a new type of
   stress situation?
5. How does Elkind clarify what each type of stress situation is like?

WRITING STEP BY STEP

Using Elkind's classification of types of stress as a model, write an essay in which you investigate types of social pressure in your world. Think about what influences you to think and behave the way you do. Consider which influences you resist and which you accept.

A. Identify two to four types of social pressure you see at work in your environment.

B. Think of some general strength that people could develop that would help them deal with these types of social pressure. Discuss what you mean by this strength in the introduction to the essay.

C. Write a paragraph briefly presenting the types of social pressure you intend to discuss.

D. Explain each type of social pressure in its own section of the paper. Use examples and details to clarify what you mean.

E. For each type, include an explanation of how the basic strength you discussed early in the essay would apply to this type of social pressure.

F. Put in some kind of transitional material or signal when you switch from one type to another. See the editing section at the end of this selection for help.

G. Point out some circumstances in which the basic strength might fail to help a person deal with social pressure.

H. In your closing (one or two sentences), reaffirm the general principle you have developed.

OTHER WRITING IDEAS

1. Classify and explain the types of stress that distinguish a certain period of life other than the teenage years. Think about the first year of college, marriage, parenthood, or retirement, for example.

2. Instead of focusing on stress, focus on the types of strength that you see as especially important to develop in young people today.

3. Consider the types of stress that seem to be assigned by gender. What are the types of stress usually felt most by women? What types of stress are felt most by men? You might get together in a mixed-gender group to brainstorm for ideas before you write your paper. Write on either gender but not both.

EDITING SKILLS: TRANSITIONS

Good writers use transitions—words and phrases that help connect ideas—to show how one sentence is related, logically, to the sentence before it. Look at these examples from the Elkind essay:

On the other hand, the young person who refuses to become a soldier protects himself or herself from danger at the cost of social disapproval. [*On the other hand* is a transitional phrase indicating that a contrast is about to be made.]

It should be said, too, that the young person's ability to foresee and avoid is both an intellectual and an emotional achievement. [The word *too* indicates that this sentence adds material consistent with the sentence before it.]

Again, the young person with a strong sense of identity and a feeling of self-esteem has the best chance of managing these stress situations as well as they can be managed. [The word *again* lets you know that this sentence repeats something said earlier.]

Notice that the transitional words are separated from the main sentence with commas. Find at least two other sentences in Elkind's essay that include transitional words, and copy them exactly.

Now check your own essay to see whether you can provide more transitional "glue" to hold the thoughts together. Transitions can show several types of movement:

Addition: also, too, moreover, next, furthermore, again
Exemplification: for example, that is, for instance
Emphasis: especially, in fact, primarily, most importantly
Contrast: but, on the other hand, nevertheless, however
Comparison: likewise, similarly, also, too
Qualification: admittedly, of course, granted that
Causation: so, consequently, therefore, as a result
Conclusion: finally, in conclusion, in short, at last

Add at least one transitional word or phrase to your own essay.

Student Essay Using Division and Classification

Stats on *ER*

Megan Quick

Have you ever wondered why people watch the television shows they do? I decided to find out why people watch the popular weekly television show *ER*. *ER* is a television series that tries to portray a real-life emergency room as well as the personal lives of the doctors and staff. The show is set in Chicago, a city full of action, accidents, and drama, so the emergency room is always busy. People of all ages watch this show, including me. What draws us to the television set every Thursday night at 9:00 P.M.? Some people are so obsessive about not missing one episode that all other activities cease while *ER* is on. In my search for answers, I discovered people have many different reasons for watching *ER*. 1

I interviewed fourteen people, ranging in age from seventeen to forty-eight. I asked them questions such as, "How often do you watch *ER* and why do you watch it?" I also asked them if they thought the show was true to life. For comparison, I asked if they had seen the live episode of *ER*. So much publicity and hype was put into that episode that I wondered how they compared it to the regular episodes of *ER*. I wanted to know why they thought the show is popular. Finally, I asked them to rate the acting abilities of the actors on *ER*. 2

Most of the people I interviewed watch *ER* as often as they can, but Courtney, who is twenty years old, is fanatical about seeing the show every week. She's the one extremist in the group. If a patient dies, she cries. I asked her, "How did you react when Dr. Green [a doctor on the show] was beat up by gang members?" "I bawled and bawled," she replied. My best friend, Amanda, said her main reason for watching *ER* is that "George Clooney is cute!" But on a more intellectual note she said, "The show has to be true to life. Everything the actors say has to be what doctors in real life would really say. Or obviously, 3 the viewers of the show, especially doctors, would know whether the information and terminology was correct or not. If it wasn't the show would be discredited." A male friend of mine, age nineteen, had similar views. He watches *ER* "because of the drama and simulated real-life events. What they're performing is factual for the most part." He informed me that *ER* has "real doctors on the set to make sure [the actors] are behaving like real-life doctors and nurses. It's almost like a real emergency room." I asked him how he knew this information, and he said, "From watching a show about the production of *ER*."

Continuing on my quest for answers, I interviewed 4 my mother, age forty-eight. She likes it that things happen on *ER* that actually happen in real life: "It's not like a soap opera where the stories are far-fetched." When I asked her how she liked the live show, she said, "It drove me nuts. It was like a bad video." She went on to explain how the camera bounced around from scene to scene, almost making her dizzy. I got the point. However, Angie Mulligan, a twenty-two year old senior who watches *ER* because she's fascinated with medicine, liked the live *ER*. She "got to see how the actors perform before everything is perfected." Shelby Bivens, a college sophomore, provided me with a totally different reason for watching *ER*. In high school she wanted to be involved in the conversations around her, so she watched *ER* because that was all anyone talked about. Also, watching *ER* makes her feel smart. She knows what's going on because of what she learned in Advanced Biology.

One of my good friends, Nathan, has views very 5 similar to mine. When I asked him why he watches *ER*, he replied, "I watch it because I like the intensity, realism, and the acting. Not only does it provide entertainment but also substance." These would be my reasons for watching *ER*. The actors often make jokes and humorous remarks, providing laughter in the face of adversity. It's also interesting to observe how people react in the most critical situations. Will the doctors buckle under pressure? Will the patients be hysterical and threatening? The answers are never certain. The show is not fake or far-fetched. *ER* has substance in its plot, intensity in its scenes, and excellence in its acting. To say the least, I am never bored while watching *ER*.

All the people I interviewed said everyone should 6 watch *ER* at least once, and I agree. It's a show all its own; no other program tries to portray an emergency room. If you have never seen *ER*, try watching the show one time. Watch out, though--you may get hooked.

C h a p t e r

STRATEGIES FOR EXAMINING TWO SUBJECTS

Comparison and Contrast

Every day we use **comparison-and-contrast** thinking to make decisions in our personal lives. Should I wear the pink shirt or the teal? Should I take my lunch to work or eat out? Will it be Taco Bell or MacDonald's? Should I write a check or use my credit card? Often the factors influencing an everyday decision are weighed so quickly in our minds that we may not be aware of having examined both sides. But when faced with a major decision, we think longer and may even make a list of pros and cons: "Reasons for Getting a New Car" on the left side of the sheet, "Reasons for Keeping Old Blue" on the right side. Intelligent decision making helps keep our lives from lapsing into chaos. Comparing and contrasting serve as useful tools in the struggle.

THE POINT OF COMPARISON AND CONTRAST

Technically, we *compare* things that are similar and *contrast* things that are different. But in order to contrast things, we have to compare them. And a comparison will often point out the differences of items being compared. You can see how fuzzy the distinction gets, so don't worry about it.

Using Comparisons to Explain

Using comparisons is a dandy writing strategy for explaining something your readers don't know much about by comparing it to something they do know about. For instance, geologists like to explain the levels in the earth's crust by comparing them to the layers in an onion. Or if you want to explain something complicated, like the way our eyes work, you could compare the human eye to a camera, which is simpler and more easily understood.

Using Comparisons to Persuade

Comparisons can be used effectively in persuasive writing to help clarify and convince. People who believe that illegal drugs should be decriminalized often compare the current drug-related gang warfare to the alcohol-related crime wave during prohibition in the 1930s. When alcohol was made legal again, the gangsters were out of business and the violence subsided. The same thing would happen today, the argument goes, if drugs were legalized. Such a comparison, called an **analogy**, can be quite convincing if you can think of one that is sensible and clearly parallel.

Using Contrast to Decide

You can set up a contrast to help clarify differences—if, for instance, you are faced with a choice between products or people or pets or proposals (or whatever). You might want to make this investigation for your own benefit or to convince someone else that one thing is preferable to another. Say, your boss asks you to find out which photocopying machine would be the best buy for the office. Since the machines are all fairly similar, your report would focus on the differences in order to determine which one would give the best results for the least money. Or if you are trying to determine whether to borrow money or get a part-time job to help pay next year's tuition, you should consider carefully the advantages and disadvantages of each choice.

THE PRINCIPLES OF COMPARISON AND CONTRAST

Since the purpose of comparing and contrasting is to show similarities and/or differences, good organization is crucial to success. There are two standard ways of composing this kind of writing: the **block pattern** and the **point-by-point pattern.** These patterns can, of course, be expanded to include consideration of more than two elements.

Using the Block Plan

Particularly useful for responding to comparison or contrast essay examination topics is this simple method of organization:

1. State your purpose.
2. Present key features of the first part of your comparison.
3. Make a transition.

4. Present corresponding features of the second part of your comparison.

5. Draw your conclusions.

This simple plan serves perfectly for showing how something has changed or developed: your earliest views about AIDS compared to the way you think now; Madonna's first album compared to her latest one; Picasso's early work compared to his later paintings; hair styles ten years ago compared with hair styles today. You will see how effectively this plan works when you read the first two essays in this chapter.

Using the Point-by-Point Plan

When you have time to carefully organize your ideas, you may want to present the material in a way that highlights individual differences. In other words, you choose the points of comparison that best illustrate the similarities or differences and organize the material to contrast those features. If you want to discuss the differences between married life without children and married life with children, you would think of several important ways that parenthood alters lifestyle. You might come up with an outline something like this:

1. Intro.—having kids makes for major life changes
2. Sleep and lack of
   a. Before kids
   b. After kids
3. Household chores
   a. Before kids
   b. After kids
4. Expenses, present and future
   a. Before kids
   b. After kids
5. Leisure time activities
   a. Before kids
   b. After kids
6. Romance in the marriage
   a. Before kids
   b. After kids
7. Conclusion—parenthood involves sacrifices as well as joys

You could use exactly the same material in writing a block-style essay as you would with this point-by-point pattern. The differences lie in the way you arrange your material.

THE PITFALLS OF COMPARISON AND CONTRAST

If you are following a block pattern, be sure to follow the same order in making your comparison. If you are writing about the differences between waterbeds and airbeds, you could start out by explaining the main features of the waterbed—something like this:

1. fill it with a hose
2. adjusting for comfort tricky
3. needs a heater
4. heavy when full of water
5. reasonable in cost

Then, after switching to your discussion of airbeds, take up the same features in the same order:

1. inflate it with a button
2. adjusting for comfort easy
3. no need for a heater
4. light when full of air
5. expensive to buy

Keep the same order in your point-by-point organization, too. After grouping all of the previous information under headings something like these:

1. comfort
2. convenience
3. cost,

be careful to discuss waterbeds first, then airbeds; waterbeds, then airbeds; waterbeds, then airbeds—in presenting the material in each category. As you read Mark Twain's "Two Views of the Mississippi," notice that in his second viewing, he describes the same details in the same order as he did in his first.

Avoid Using Too Many Transitional Words

True, comparison-and-contrast writing involves making lots of transitions, but you won't necessarily need to signal each one with a transitional word. In the block pattern, you will need an obvious transition to let your readers know that you're going to shift to the second item or idea. You'll write a sentence like "Airbeds, *on the other hand,* are an excellent buy for several reasons," or "*On the contrary,* waterbeds can sometimes prove troublesome to maintain."

But when you follow the point-by-point pattern, you will probably not want to signal every shift back and forth with a transitional term. (Did you notice that the term *but* in the previous sentence provided a transition between paragraphs?) With the point-by-point method of organization, you will be making contrasts under each point. If you try to signal each one, your prose may get clunky. Once you have established the shifts back and forth, let your readers be guided by the pattern—and stick to it.

Avoid Repetition in Concluding

In a brief comparison or contrast essay, you need not summarize all your points at the end. Your readers can remember what you've said. Instead, draw a meaningful conclusion about the material. Maybe you'll want to assert that two apparently different religions are basically the same. Or instead, you might stress that the differences are so crucial that conflict will always exist. If you are comparing products, come out in favor of one over the other—or else declare that neither amounts to a hill of beans—or perhaps invite your readers to judge for themselves. Just be sure to make a point of some sort at the end.

WHAT TO LOOK FOR IN COMPARISON AND CONTRAST

As you study the essays in this chapter, pay particular attention to the organization and the *continuity*—what makes it flow.

1. Look for a pattern (or maybe a combination of patterns) that each writer uses in presenting the material. Decide whether you think the method of organization is effective or whether there might be a better way.
2. Underline the transitional terms (like *on the other hand, but, still, yet, on the contrary, nevertheless, however, contrary to, conversely, consequently, then, in other words, therefore, hence, thus, granted that, after all*). Notice what sort of links are provided between paragraphs when no purely transitional terms appear.
3. Look at the introductions and conclusions to see what strategies are used to set up the comparison and/or contrast at the beginning and to reinforce the writer's point at the end.

Source: Courtesy P.S. Muller.

The cartoon gives a visual illustration of a common contrast: two people seeing the same thing in different ways. Mark Twain, in the first essay in this chapter, offers a verbal description of this same behavior.

As you look at the cartoon, how do you see the situation? In other words, are you an optimist or a pessimist? Do you usually think things are going to work out for the best? Or do you always think nothing's going to come out right?

Have you ever felt sorry for someone who turned out to be satisfied with his or her situation? Have you ever envied someone who was actually dissatisfied?

PREPARING TO READ

Do you think it's possible for two people to look at the same thing and see it quite differently? Consider how a loving owner might view an overweight, bowlegged dog and how a neighbor might view the same animal. Can you think of other examples?

Two Views of the Mississippi

MARK TWAIN

Before becoming Mark Twain, America's most beloved humorist, Samuel Clemens (1830–1910) was a riverboat pilot, a journalist, and an unsuccessful gold miner. He said late in his life that those days on the river were the happiest he ever spent. In *Life on the Mississippi,* he explains in detail how he became a pilot—how he learned to "read" the river. In the following slightly edited passage, Twain tells of one drawback to that otherwise rewarding experience.

TERMS TO RECOGNIZE

trifling *(para. 1)*	small, a tiny detail
acquisition *(para. 1)*	something gained or acquired
solitary *(para. 2)*	all alone
conspicuous *(para. 2)*	obvious
opal *(para. 2)*	a gemstone showing many shades of pink, blue, lavender, and gold
radiating *(para. 2)*	spreading
somber *(para. 2)*	dark
unobstructed *(para. 2)*	not hidden or blocked from view
rapture *(para. 3)*	joy, delight
wrought *(para. 3)*	brought about, caused
bluff reef *(para. 3)*	steep ridge of sand just beneath the surface of the water
shoaling *(para. 3)*	building up mud and sand
compassing *(para. 4)*	guiding (as with a compass)

ow when I had mastered the language of this water, and had come to   1
know every trifling feature that bordered the great river as familiarly as I knew the letters of the alphabet, I had made a valuable acquisition. But

I had lost something, too. I had lost something which could never be restored to me while I lived. All the grace, the beauty, the poetry, had gone out of the majestic river!

I still keep in mind a certain wonderful sunset which I witnessed when   2
steamboating was new to me. A broad expanse of the river was turned to blood; in the middle distance the red hue brightened into gold, through which a solitary log came floating black and conspicuous; in one place a long, slanting mark lay sparkling upon the water; in another the surface was broken by boiling, tumbling rings, that were as many-tinted as an opal; where the ruddy flush was faintest was a smooth spot that was covered with graceful circles and radiating lines, ever so delicately traced; the shore on our left was densely wooded, and the somber shadow that fell from this forest was broken in one place by a long, ruffled trail that shone like silver; and high above the forest wall a clean-stemmed dead tree waved a single leafy bough that glowed like a flame in the unobstructed splendor that was flowing in the sun. There were graceful curves, reflected images, woody heights, soft distances; and over the whole scene, far and near, the dissolving lights drifted steadily, enriching it every passing moment with new marvels of coloring.

I stood like one bewitched. I drank it in, in a speechless rapture. The   3
world was new to me, and I had never seen anything like this at home. But as I have said, a day came when I began to cease from noting the glories and charms which the moon and sun and the twilight wrought upon the river's face; another day came when I ceased altogether to note them. Then, if that sunset scene had been repeated, I should have looked upon it without rapture, and should have commented upon it, inwardly, after this fashion: "This sun means that we are going to have wind to-morrow; that floating log means that the river is rising, small thanks to it; that slanting mark on the water refers to a bluff reef which is going to kill somebody's steamboat one of these nights, if it keeps on stretching out like that; those tumbling 'boils' show a dissolving bar and a changing channel there; the lines and circles in the slick water over yonder are a warning that that troublesome place is shoaling up dangerously; that silver streak in the shadow of the forest is the 'break' from a new snag, and he has located himself in the very best place he could have found to fish for steamboats; that tall dead tree, with a single living branch, is not going to last long, and then how is a body ever going to get through this blind place at night without the friendly old landmark?"

No, the romance and beauty were all gone from the river. All the value   4
any feature of it had for me now was the amount of usefulness it could furnish toward compassing the safe piloting of a steamboat.

RESPONDING TO READING

Do you agree with Twain that gaining knowledge can take some of the "romance" out of life? Have you ever had a similar experience—perhaps learning something that robbed you of a childish illusion or learning something that caused you to question your former understanding of history? If you have, tell briefly in your journal how the change occurred.

GAINING WORD POWER

Twain says the sunset put him in a state of "speechless rapture." The suffix *-less* means "without," "lacking," or "not able to." So, speechless means "without speech" or "unable to speak."

For the following list of words, write out brief definitions that show what the root word means with the suffix added. If you don't know the meaning of the root word, look it up in your trusty dictionary.

1. clueless
2. ruthless
3. mirthless
4. dauntless
5. meaningless
6. peerless

Now, use each word in a sentence that conveys the meaning—something beyond "I am clueless" or "She is clueless" or "Clyde is clueless."

CONSIDERING CONTENT

1. What two modes of writing does Twain use in this selection?
2. In the opening sentence, what does he mean by the "language" of the river?
3. What did he lose by learning to be a riverboat pilot? What did he gain?
4. What contrast does he present in paragraphs 2 and 3?
5. At the beginning of his description in the second paragraph, he says, "A broad expanse of the river was turned to blood. . . ." What does that mean? Do you know what that figure of speech is called?
6. Can you find a thesis statement? If so, where?

CONSIDERING METHOD

1. Point out two **similes** (comparisons using *like* or *as*) in paragraph 2.
2. The second sentence in paragraph 2 is extremely long. Reread this complicated sentence, and carefully decide where you would put in periods to create several shorter sentences.
3. What major transitions does Twain use—first in setting up the contrast, then in shifting from the before to the after?

4. In paragraph 3, Twain **personifies** the river—that is, he gives it human characteristics. Point out three examples of this technique. Why do you think he uses this figure of speech?

5. Does the contrast follow a point-by-point or a block pattern of organization? Make a brief outline of the way the comparison is arranged.

WRITING STEP BY STEP

Often we feel nostalgic (warm and sentimental) about the past—about favorite former recording groups, TV programs, friends, cars, houses, articles of clothing, and the like. Get together with several friends or classmates, and talk about what you liked best in "the good old days." Take notes when meaningful memories from your past come to mind.

Choose something long gone that you still feel a fondness for—something now replaced by a newer one, but not a better one. Then, using a block pattern, write an essay contrasting your lost prize with today's version.

A. Begin by letting your readers know that you have a fine, new whatever—fancy bicycle, designer jeans, sports car, neighborhood bakery, favorite restaurant, TV series, or rock group—but that the new version can't measure up to what you enjoyed before.

B. Then, describe your former favorite. Use plenty of precise descriptive details, as Mark Twain does in his opening paragraph. Show your reader what makes you feel the way you do about this treasure from the past.

C. Next, make a transition similar to Twain's—"But as I have said, . . ." Or write your own: "Then, after old Shep died, I bought an unbelievably dumb purebred Russian wolfhound," or "Finally I sent my faithful Ford to the junkyard and spent a fortune on a classic MG that gives me nothing but trouble."

D. Now describe your replacement, focusing on its shortcomings—the many ways in which it doesn't measure up to the one you loved. Follow the same order here in presenting the failings that you followed in describing the virtues. (Notice that Twain uses exactly the same order in telling the two ways he saw the river. In his third paragraph, he begins with the sunset, then mentions the log, then the slanting mark on the water, then the "tumbling boils," then the lines and circles, then the streak in the shadow, and finally the dead tree—just as he did in his second paragraph.)

E. In your final paragraph, express again the sorrow you feel at having to make do with this unsatisfactory replacement and your longing to have the old one back.

OTHER WRITING IDEAS

1. Write an essay following the step-by-step instructions in the previous section, but choose instead something that you replaced with a new one that you think is a great deal better.

2. People of different ages sometimes see things differently. Write about an attitude (toward work, religion, education, sports, television, the law, and so forth) that you think is different for people who are older or younger than you are. If you can, interview your peers as well as people from the other generation to see if your understanding of this difference is accurate.

3. Using a block-type organization, first describe a place you knew as a child. Then describe how the place looks to you as an adult. In your conclusion, discuss whether the changes are real or are only in your way of seeing.

EDITING SKILLS: QUOTATION MARKS INSIDE QUOTATIONS

Once in a while, when you have enclosed conversation or quoted material in quotation marks, you may need quotation marks around a word or phrase within the passage. You can't use regular quotation marks inside quotation marks because your reader would never be able to tell what ended where. So inside regular double quotation marks, you use single quotation marks around any words that also need quotation marks.

Notice that in his third paragraph, Twain puts a passage in quotation marks because, as he describes his second way of looking at the river, he is giving us a "conversation" with himself. Within that pretended speech, the word "boils" also needs quotation marks because it has an unusual meaning (as did the word "conversation" in the previous sentence). So, he puts "boils" in single quotation marks because it is already inside double-marks. Here is another example:

Mr. Blackwell observed, "Baggy clothes are definitely 'in' this season."

On your keyboard, you may have a left-hand single quotation mark. Check the keys beside the numbers at the top. The right-hand mark is one you use all the time: the apostrophe. It will also serve as the left-hand quotation mark if you don't have a special key.

Here are some other uses of quotation marks that sometimes end up with single marks inside double ones:

1. To enclose words used as words:

   It's all right to begin a sentence with "and" as long as you don't do it too often.

   [You can use italics or underlining to indicate words used as words, if you prefer.]

2. To enclose titles of short works—short stories, poems, essays, chapters of books, or song titles, for example:

   Edgar Allan Poe's story "The Pit and the Pendulum"

   Robert Frost's poem "The Road Not Taken"

   Richard Selzer's essay "The Discus Thrower"

   Bob Dylan's song "Mr. Tambourine Man"

   But underline or put in italics the titles of longer, separately published works:

   Alice Walker's novel <u>The Color Purple</u>

   Arthur Miller's play <u>Death of a Salesman</u>

   Steven Spielberg's movie <u>Jurassic Park</u>

   Georges Bizet's opera <u>Carmen</u>

3. To enclose quoted material within a quotation:

   "What did your instructor do when you didn't turn in your term paper?"

   "I went into her office with my paper in my hand, and she said, 'I hope you just got out of the hospital; otherwise, you just failed the course.' "

EXERCISE

In the following sentences, insert quotation marks and single quotation marks where needed. You may use italics in some cases if you prefer.

1. Proofread carefully to be sure you have not confused its and it's.
2. Reggie said to me, You be there on time or I'm leaving without you, Squirt.
3. Then I said to Reggie, You call me Squirt again and I'm not going anywhere with you ever again!
4. Serena wrote an analysis of Sandra Cisneros's short story, Woman Hollering Creek.

5. I liked this poem, Kesha observed, but when Frost says The woods are lovely, dark, and deep, what does deep mean?

Now go through your writing for this class (your essays and your journal entries), and see whether you've been using quotation marks correctly. Then make up a sentence of your own using single quotation marks inside regular quotation marks.

PREPARING TO READ

Are you the kind of person who gets fidgety if the socks aren't tidily arranged by color in your drawer? Or are you a casual type who seldom manages to get the socks from the laundry basket into the drawer? Have you tried to change? Or do you not feel any need to?

Neat People vs. Sloppy People

SUZANNE BRITT

Suzanne Britt is a freelance journalist who teaches English at Meredith College in Raleigh, North Carolina. She has written for the *New York Times,* the *Baltimore Sun,* and *Newsday.* In her collection of witty essays *Skinny People Are Dull and Crunchy Like Carrots* (1982), Britt clearly favors fat folks. In the following essay, which comes from her book *Show and Tell* (1983), she sides solidly with slobs, demonstrating that taking an unusual stand—even a not very reasonable stand—can be an effective strategy for humorous writing.

TERMS TO RECOGNIZE

vs. *(title)*	abbreviation of *versus,* meaning in contrast with or against
rectitude *(para. 2)*	uprightness, correctness
metier *(para. 3)*	a person's area of strength or expertise
excavation *(para. 5)*	digging out, uncovering and removing
meticulously *(para. 5)*	giving great attention to details
scrupulously *(para. 5)*	carefully doing the right thing
cavalier *(para. 6)*	free and easy
vicious *(para. 9)*	hateful, spiteful
salvaging *(para. 9)*	saving from destruction, rescuing
swath *(para. 12)*	a long strip
organic *(para. 12)*	having to do with living things

1 've finally figured out the difference between neat people and sloppy people. The distinction is, as always, moral. Neat people are lazier and meaner than sloppy people.

2 Sloppy people, you see, are not really sloppy. Their sloppiness is merely the unfortunate consequence of their extreme moral rectitude. Sloppy

people carry in their mind's eye a heavenly vision, a precise plan, that is so stupendous, so perfect, it can't be achieved in this world or the next.

Sloppy people live in Never-Never-Land. Someday is their metier. 3 Someday they are planning to alphabetize all their books and set up home catalogues. Someday they will go through their wardrobes and mark certain items for tentative mending and certain items for passing on to relatives of similar shape and size. Someday sloppy people will make family scrapbooks into which they will put newspaper clippings, postcards, locks of hair, and the dried corsage from their senior prom. Someday they will file everything on the surface of their desks, including the cash receipts from coffee purchases at the snack shop. Someday they will sit down and read all the back issues of *The New Yorker*.

For all these noble reasons and more, sloppy people never get neat. They 4 aim too high and wide. They save everything, planning someday to file, order, and straighten out the world. But while these ambitious plans take clearer and clearer shape in their heads, the books spill from the shelves onto the floor, the clothes pile up in the hamper and closet, the family mementos accumulate in every drawer, the surface of the desk is buried under mounds of paper, and the unread magazines threaten to reach the ceiling.

Sloppy people can't bear to part with anything. They give loving atten- 5 tion to every detail. When sloppy people say they're going to tackle the surface of the desk, they really mean it. Not a paper will go unturned; not a rubber band will go unboxed. Four hours or two weeks into the excavation, the desk looks exactly the same, primarily because the sloppy person is meticulously creating new piles of papers with new headings and scrupulously stopping to read all the old book catalogues before he throws them away. A neat person would just bulldoze the desk.

Neat people are bums and clods at heart. They have cavalier attitudes 6 toward possessions, including family heirlooms. Everything is just another dust-catcher to them. If anything collects dust, it's got to go and that's that. Neat people will toy with the idea of throwing the children out of the house just to cut down the clutter.

Neat people don't care about process. They like results. What they want 7 to do is get the whole thing over with so they can sit down and watch the rasslin' on TV. Neat people operate on two unvarying principles: Never handle any item twice, and throw everything away.

The only thing messy in a neat person's house is the trash can. The 8 minute something comes to a neat person's hand, he will look at it, try to decide if it has immediate use and, finding none, throw it in the trash.

Neat people are especially vicious with mail. They never go through 9 their mail unless they are standing directly over a trash can. If the trash can is beside the mailbox, even better. All ads, catalogues, pleas for charitable contributions, church bulletins, and money-saving coupons go straight into the trash can without being opened. All letters from home, postcards from Europe, bills and paychecks are opened, immediately responded to, then dropped in the trash can. Neat people keep their receipts only for tax purposes. That's it. No sentimental salvaging of birthday cards or the last letter a dying relative ever wrote. Into the trash it goes.

Neat people place neatness above everything, even economics. They are incredibly wasteful. Neat people throw away several toys every time they walk through the den. I knew a neat person once who threw away a perfectly good dish drainer because it had mold on it. The drainer was too much trouble to wash. And neat people sell their furniture when they move. They will sell a La-Z-Boy recliner while you are reclining in it.

Neat people are no good to borrow from. Neat people buy everything in expensive little single portions. They get their flour and sugar in two-pound bags. They wouldn't consider clipping a coupon, saving a leftover, reusing plastic non-dairy whipped cream containers, or rinsing off tin foil and draping it over the unmoldy dish drainer. You can never borrow a neat person's newspaper to see what's playing at the movies. Neat people have the paper all wadded up and in the trash by 7:05 A.M.

Neat people cut a clean swath through the organic as well as the inorganic world. People, animals, and things are all one to them. They are so insensitive. After they've finished with the pantry, the medicine cabinet, and the attic, they will throw out the red geranium (too many leaves), sell the dog (too many fleas), and send the children off to boarding school (too many scuff marks on the hardwood floors).

10

11

12

RESPONDING TO READING

Do you think that Britt is right in preferring sloppy people? In your journal, make a list of some advantages of being neat; then make a list of some disadvantages of being sloppy.

GAINING WORD POWER

In her last paragraph, Britt speaks of the "*organic* as well as the *inorganic* world." You know from the "Terms to Recognize" list that *organic* means "having to do with living things." So what does the same word mean when you add the prefix *in-?* That prefix commonly means "no," "not," or "without." Thus, in her sentence, *inorganic* means "not organic"—having to do with things that are *not* living.

This prefix is quite common, partly because it has several different meanings. Besides making a word negative, *in-* often means "in," "into," "within," or "toward," as in a baseball *infield,* an *inboard* motor, or to *instill* values.

Knowing these two meanings of this prefix can help you make sense of new words. For each of the following terms, write out the meaning of the prefix *in-,* followed by the meaning of the root word, as in this example using *indefinite:*

in- = not   *definite* = certain, precise, clear

Get help from your dictionary if you need it.

inhale	inhuman	insomnia
injustice	inland	inability
inroad	invisible	indigestion
indirect	inlay	insane

CONSIDERING CONTENT

1. In the first paragraph, what is the moral difference that Britt finds between neat and sloppy people? Is this the difference you would give? Is she serious about this moral difference? How can you tell?
2. Does the essay have a thesis statement? If so, where does it appear?
3. What is "Never-Never Land," mentioned at the beginning of paragraph 3? Do you know where the term comes from?
4. What kinds of things does Britt say messy people are always planning to do? Point out her exact details.
5. What faults does she find with neat people? Again, point out details from every paragraph.
6. Is she being fair? If not, can you explain why not?

CONSIDERING METHOD

1. How does Britt let you know in her opening paragraphs that she isn't entirely serious?
2. What pattern of organization does she use to present her contrast?
3. What other writing strategies does Britt use to develop her contrast?
4. Can you find a transitional sentence that leads smoothly into the second part of the contrast?
5. Point out several words that Britt uses for humorous exaggeration. Point out several humorous examples.
6. You probably noticed that this essay has no conclusion. Do you think it would be more effective if it had one? Try writing a brief concluding sentence and see whether it adds or detracts.

WRITING STEP BY STEP

Get together with a few friends or classmates to discuss various kinds of people who can be classified into types the way Britt does with neat versus sloppy (like *plump vs. thin, fun-loving vs. serious, perky vs. droopy,* or *exercise nuts vs. couch potatoes*). In this brainstorming session, jot down any details that might be useful to include in an essay comparing the two types you choose. You can make your contrast either humorous or serious. If you decide to be humorous, you will probably also decide to defend the less positive group—praising fat folks instead of thin people, for instance. Or you may decide to make fun of both sides by contrasting two negative types, like *eggheads vs. airheads.*

A. Begin with a two- or three-sentence introduction letting your readers know that you'll be contrasting two types of people and favoring one group (as Britt puts it, "Neat people are lazier and meaner than sloppy people").

B. Organize your contrast in a block pattern, first discussing the important characteristics of one type, then the same or similar characteristics of the other type.

C. Be sure to include plenty of examples that will let your readers see the behavior you're explaining. Take another look at Britt's essay, and notice the kinds of details she uses—how many of them and how specific: not just *a corsage* but *a dried corsage from their senior prom,* not just *a recliner* but *a La-Z-Boy recliner,* not just *the geranium* but *the red geranium.*

D. In the body of your essay, begin every paragraph (as Britt does) with the name of your type—*plump people,* for instance. Vary this system of deliberate repetition once or twice by adding a transition, like the one Britt adds at the start of her fourth paragraph: "*For all these noble reasons and more,* sloppy people never get neat." (Leave out the *noble* part unless you're being funny.) Consider transitions like these:

    —*Besides all these features,* plump people . . .

    —*In addition to these troubles,* plump people . . .

    —*Furthermore,* plump people . . .

    —*As a matter of fact,* plump people . . .

    —*Without question,* plump people . . .

E. When you finish discussing your first type, include a transitional sentence. Britt shifts smoothly from praising sloppy people to criticizing neat ones with this sentence: "A neat person would just bulldoze the desk" (end of para. 5).

    If you can't come up with a similar sentence that supplies a bridge from one type to the next, it's just fine to begin the second half of the contrast with a transitional term like one of these:

Thin people, *on the other hand,* . . .

Contrary to popular belief, thin people . . .

Conversely, thin people . . .

Thin people, *however,* . . .

On the contrary, thin people . . .

Yet thin people . . .

By contrast, thin people . . .

F. If you can think of some insight concerning your contrast, offer it as a conclusion. But don't just tack on something obvious. That's worse than no conclusion at all. Just be sure to end your last paragraph with an impressive sentence—either a short, forceful one or a nicely balanced one, like Britt's:

> After they've finished with the pantry, the medicine cabinet, and the attic, they will throw out the red geranium (too many leaves), sell the dog (too many fleas), and send the children off to boarding school (too many scuff marks on the hardwood floors).

Work on that final sentence. Make it one you're proud of. Make it one that leaves your readers feeling satisfied.

OTHER WRITING IDEAS

1. Starting with the lists you made in responding to Britt's essay, write one of your own organized like hers (but probably serious) showing how neatness makes life easier and sloppiness leads to problems. Include plenty of details and examples to show the advantages of being tidy and the folly of being a slob.

2. Using the block pattern, contrast two types of players in a sport or game like basketball, tennis, poker, chess, or some video game. In your conclusion, tell what you think causes the differences between the two types.

3. Get together with some friends or classmates, and discuss major life changes that you and the others have gone through. Talk about what your lives were like before and after the changes occurred. Consider situations like life before marriage and life after; life before parenthood and life after; life in your folks' home and life in the dorm or your own apartment; life at your previous job and life at your new one.

   Then write an essay about one of your life changes, telling first what your life was like before, then telling how things were after.

Focus on one factor of your experience that changed greatly, like the amount of freedom you had or the amount of responsibility.

EDITING SKILLS: USING APOSTROPHES

Apostrophes probably cause more problems than other marks of punctuation. Even experienced writers feel shaky about using them. If you study the following rules about using apostrophes, you should be able to use them more confidently.

1. *Use an apostrophe to indicate that a noun is possessive.* Possessive nouns usually indicate ownership, as in *Miguel's hat* or *the lawyer's briefcase.* But sometimes the ownership is only loosely suggested, as in *the rope's length* or *a week's wages.* If you are not sure whether a noun is possessive, try turning it into an *of* phrase: *the length of the rope, the wages of a week.*

   A. If the noun does not end in *s,* add *'s.*

   Rita climbed into the driver's seat.

   The women's lounge is being redecorated.

   B. If the noun is singular and ends in *s,* add *'s.*

   The boss's car is still in the parking lot.

   Have you met Lois's sister?

   C. If the noun is plural and ends in *s,* add only an apostrophe.

   The workers' lockers have been moved.

   A good doctor always listens to patients' complaints.

2. *Use an apostrophe with contractions.* Contractions are two-word combinations formed by omitting certain letters. The apostrophe goes where the letters are left out, not where the two words are joined.

does not = doesn't	he is or he has = he's
would not = wouldn't	let us = let's
you are = you're	I am = I'm

3. *Do not use an apostrophe to form the plural of a noun.* The letter *s* gets pressed into service in a number of ways; its most common use is to show that a noun is plural (more than one of whatever the noun names). No apostrophe is needed with a simple plural:

   Two *members* of the starting team are suspended for the next three *games* for repeated curfew *violations.*

EXERCISE

1. Examine this sentence from paragraph 11 in Suzanne Britt's essay: "You can never borrow a neat person's newspaper to see what's

playing at the movies." Two words in this sentence end in *'s;* one is possessive and one is a contraction. Do you see the difference? Explain how you can tell.

2. Find two other possessive nouns in Britt's essay, and explain what they mean by turning each into an *of* phrase.

3. Find two other contractions that end in *'s* in Britt's essay. What do these contractions stand for?

4. Find six other contractions in Britt's essay, and explain their meaning.

5. Find several examples of plural nouns that end in *s* (without an apostrophe).

Now go back over the essay you have just written, and check your use of apostrophes. Have you left an apostrophe out of a possessive? Have you put an unneeded apostrophe in a plural noun? Have you misplaced any apostrophes in contractions?

PREPARING TO READ

Do you think men have it easier than women? Or do women have it easier than men? What makes you think so?

Women and Men

SCOTT RUSSELL SANDERS

Scott Russell Sanders, who teaches writing at Indiana University at Bloomington, is the author of several books, including *Secrets of the Universe* and *The Paradise of Bombs.* In the following passage (taken from a longer essay), he explains his surprise upon reaching college to find women who felt discriminated against. He eventually discovered that living the good life has a lot to do with expectations and social class as well as gender.

TERMS TO RECOGNIZE

grievances *(para. 1)*	resentments; complaints of injustices
fretted *(para. 1)*	worried
baffled *(para. 2)*	puzzled
cornered *(para. 2)*	grabbed more than a fair share of
barrios *(para. 2)*	Hispanic neighborhoods
Third World *(para. 2)*	poor, nonindustrial countries
tedium *(para. 2)*	boredom
ally *(para. 4)*	someone who sides with you in a disagreement

1 was slow to understand the deep grievances of women. This was because, as a boy, I had envied them. Before college, the only people I had known who were interested in art or music or literature, the only ones who read books, the only ones who ever seemed to enjoy a sense of ease and grace were the mothers and daughters. Like the menfolk, they fretted about money, they scrimped and made-do. But when the pay stopped coming in, they were not the ones who had failed. Nor did they have to go to war, and that seemed to me a blessed fact. By comparison with the narrow, ironclad days of fathers, there was an expansiveness, I thought, in the days of mothers. They went to see neighbors, to shop in town, to run errands at school, at the library, at church. No doubt, had I looked harder at their

lives, I would have envied them less. It was not my fate to become a woman, so it was easier for me to see the graces. Few of them held jobs outside the home, and those who did filled thankless roles as clerks and waitresses. I didn't see, then, what a prison a house could be, since houses seemed to me brighter, handsomer places than any factory. I did not realize—because such things were never spoken of—how often women suffered from men's bullying. I did learn about the wretchedness of abandoned wives, single mothers, widows; but I also learned about the wretchedness of lone men. Even then I could see how exhausting it was for a mother to cater all day to the needs of young children. But if I had been asked, as a boy, to choose between tending a baby and tending a machine, I think I would have chosen the baby. (Having now tended both, I know I would choose the baby.)

So I was baffled when the women at college accused me and my sex of   2
having cornered the world's pleasures. I think something like my bafflement has been felt by other boys (and by girls as well) who grew up in dirt-poor farm country, in mining country, in black ghettos, in Hispanic barrios, in the shadows of factories, in Third World nations—any place where the fate of men is as grim and bleak as the fate of women. Toilers and warriors. I realize now how ancient these identities are, how deep the tug they exert on men, the undertow of a thousand generations. The miseries I saw, as a boy, in the lives of nearly all men I continue to see in the lives of many—the body-breaking toil, the tedium, the call to be tough, the humiliating powerlessness, the battle for a living and for territory.

When the women I met at college thought about the joys and privi   3
leges of men, they did not carry in their minds the sort of men I had known in my childhood. They thought of their fathers, who were bankers, physicians, architects, stockbrokers, the big wheels of the big cities. These fathers rode the train to work or drove cars that cost more than any of my childhood houses. They were attended from morning to night by female helpers, wives and nurses and secretaries. They were never laid off, never short of cash at the month's end, never lined up for welfare. The fathers made decisions that mattered. They ran the world.

The daughters of such men wanted to share in this power, this glory. So   4
did I. They yearned for a say over their future, for jobs worthy of their abilities, for the right to live at peace, unmolested, whole. Yes, I thought, yes yes. The difference between me and these daughters was that they saw me, because of my sex, as destined from birth to become like their fathers, and therefore as an enemy to their desires. But I knew better. I wasn't an enemy, in fact or in feeling. I was an ally. If I had known, then, how to tell them so, would they have believed me? Would they now?

RESPONDING TO READING

If you could choose your gender, which would you be—male or female? In your journal, explain the reasons for your choice.

GAINING WORD POWER

Decide whether the italicized words below are used correctly or not. Then, write *yes* or *no* beside each sentence. After you finish, look back at the "Terms to Recognize" definitions to check your work.

_____ 1. When the chips were down, my *ally* betrayed me.

_____ 2. At the funeral, the mourners expressed their *grievances* with tears and moaning.

_____ 3. In the late 1970s, a crooked stockbroker *cornered* the silver market.

_____ 4. The police were *baffled* by what seemed to be a clueless crime.

_____ 5. The soccer game was held in the new sports *tedium*.

CONSIDERING CONTENT

1. What were the lives of the men Sanders grew up with like? And the lives of the women?
2. About the women, Sanders admits, "No doubt, had I looked harder at their lives, I would have envied them less." What sort of hardships had he overlooked?
3. Would you rather tend a baby or a machine? How stressful is caring for young children?
4. What other groups besides factory workers does Sanders say suffer lives that are equally grim for men and women?
5. What is being contrasted in this essay besides the roles of women and men?
6. Sanders wonders at the end of his essay whether women would consider him an ally, even though he considers himself on their side. What details does he use that show he is sympathetic to their cause?
7. Respond to his final question: would they accept him now?

CONSIDERING METHOD

1. Because this selection is an excerpt from a longer essay, it plunges right into the topic. Did you find it difficult to get interested in the material as a result? Why or why not?

2. How is the comparison between women and men organized? Does the author tell first about women's roles and then about men's? Or does he shift back and forth, point by point?

3. Does he mention any similarities shared by men and women?

4. Does he give equal space to both genders?

5. In the first paragraph, Sanders speaks of "the narrow, ironclad days of fathers." Write out the same idea in your own words. Which version do you like better? Which is clearer?

6. Does he ever state his thesis? If so, where? If not, what is the implied thesis—the main idea of the piece?

WRITING STEP BY STEP

Think of a situation, place, object, or person *then* and *now.* Choose something that has changed a lot: wedding receptions years ago and today, your desk before and after cleaning, your clunky typewriter and your smart computer, your childhood tennis shoes and your new athletic shoes, your granny then and now.

Write a comparison focusing mainly on the *now,* but mentioning the *then* occasionally to show the contrast. If you can get your friends to help, brainstorm with them to think of good points you can use in drawing the comparison. You need qualities that fit both *then* and *now,* but think of a lot more details about the *now.*

A. Begin by giving the subject of your comparison in a sentence or two. Don't state it directly but imply it: "I had no idea that wedding receptions were not always elaborate productions until my mom told me about her wedding thirty years ago," or "I was slow to appreciate the benefits of my new computer because it took so much effort to learn to use it. My trusty typewriter was easy by comparison."

B. As you discuss the *now,* remind your readers, whenever you take up a new point, how it was *then.* Use transitional words when you need them: *by comparison, on the other hand, on the contrary, but, still, after all, like, nevertheless, contrary to, however, granted that.*

C. Mention at least one similarity. For instance, while discussing women's behavior, Sanders mentions a trait they share with males: "Like the menfolk, they fretted about money, they scrimped and made-do."

D. In your last paragraph, tell how you feel about the change. Would you rather have the *then* instead of the *now*—or do you find the *now* a great improvement?

E. If you're stuck for an ending, try concluding with a question and then answering it: "If I had known then how much easier my computer would make writing, would I have complained so loudly? Maybe not," or "If I could go back to planning a reception that cost less than $10,000, would I? You bet I would!"

OTHER WRITING IDEAS

1. In a small group discuss gender stereotypes—the way society expects women and men to behave. From the notes you take, choose three or four categories—like manner of speaking, walking, dressing, and showing emotion; or typical careers, leisure activities, and taste in movies. Organize your essay using the point-by-point method, first doing the women's role, then the men's (or the reverse). At the end, draw a conclusion about how society treats people who do not conform to these roles and expectations.

2. Think of two possible views on one of these aspects of life: work, family, or sports. Write a paper comparing and contrasting two people who represent the two views.

3. Compare or contrast your mother's or father's life with your own— or the way you want your own life to turn out, once you get it under control.

EDITING SKILLS: USING PARENTHESES

When you want to include an idea that is interesting but not crucial to your discussion, put it in parentheses. Here's an example from the end of Sanders's first paragraph:

> But if I had been asked, as a boy, to choose between tending a baby and tending a machine, I think I would have chosen the baby. (Having now tended both, I know I would choose the baby.)

His statement about preferring baby tending (stereotypical women's work) to machine tending (stereotypical men's work) is quite to the point. But when, in the next sentence, he comments on that statement, the parentheses tell the reader that the remark is just added reinforcement of the same idea.

Parentheses are also used in these ways:

(1) To enclose numbers in a list (like the parentheses at the left of this list).

(2) To enclose brief definitions within a sentence (like the examples in the previous paragraph):

> . . . machine-tending (stereotypical men's work) . . .

> Writers use transitions to improve *continuity* (the flow of their ideas).

Notice that the period goes after the parenthesis at the end of a sentence.

(3) To enclose examples and brief explanations (like the ones in items 1 and 2 and this one you are presently reading).

(4) To enclose dates within a sentence:

> John Stuart Mill (1806–1873) favored women's equality with men.

Find five examples of parentheses in this chapter, and explain which of the uses previously discussed applies to each example.

Then look at the essay you just finished. Is there any material that should be enclosed in parentheses? Consider adding a definition, a date, a comment, or a brief explanation within parentheses that would add to the reader's understanding of your ideas.

PREPARING TO READ

Before looking at the following essay, consider whether you think children are born smart or whether they get smart by studying hard in school. Jot down your response in your journal.

The Trouble with Talent: Are We Born Smart or Do We Get Smart?

KATHY SEAL

A California-based freelance journalist, Kathy Seal frequently writes about children and education in such popular magazines as *Parents* and *Family Circle*. In the essay we reprint here, first published in *Lear's* magazine in July 1993, she examines an attitude that may help to explain why math scores of American children have fallen far behind those of children in Japan.

TERMS TO RECOGNIZE

rote *(para. 4)*	routine, mechanical repetition
efficacy *(para. 12)*	ability to bring about an effect
rampant *(para. 12)*	widespread, out of control
per se *(para. 16)*	in and of itself
mammoth *(para. 19)*	huge
conviction *(para. 19)*	firmly held belief

Jim Stigler was in an awkward position. Fascinated by the fact that Asian students routinely do better than American kids at elementary math, the UCLA psychologist wanted to test whether persistence might be the key factor. So he designed and administered an experiment in which he gave the same insolvable math problem to separate small groups of Japanese and American children.

Sure enough, most American kids attacked the problem, struggled briefly—then gave up. The Japanese kids, however, worked on and on and on. Eventually, Stigler stopped the experiment when it began to feel inhumane: If the Japanese kids were uninterrupted, they seemed willing to plow on indefinitely.

"The Japanese kids assumed that if they kept working, they'd eventually get it," Stigler recalls. "The Americans thought 'Either you get it or you don't.' " 3

Stigler's work, detailed in his 1992 book *The Learning Gap*, shatters our 4 stereotypical notion that Asian education relies on rote and drill. In fact, Japanese and Chinese elementary schoolteachers believe that their chief task is to stimulate thinking. They tell their students that anyone who thinks long enough about a problem can move toward its solution.

Stigler concludes that the Asian belief in hard work as the key to success 5 is one reason why Asians outperform us academically. Americans are persuaded that success in school requires inborn talent. "If you believe that achievement is mostly caused by ability," Stigler says, "at some fundamental level you don't believe in education. You believe education is sorting kids, and that kids in some categories can't learn. The Japanese believe *everybody* can master the curriculum if you give them the time."

Stigler and his coauthor, Harold W. Stevenson of the University of 6 Michigan, are among a growing number of educational psychologists who argue that the American fixation on innate ability causes us to waste the potential of many of our children. He says that this national focus on the importance of natural talent is producing kids who give up easily and artful dodgers who would rather look smart than actually learn something.

Cross-cultural achievement tests show how wide the gap is: In a series 7 of studies spanning a ten-year period, Stigler and Stevenson compared math-test scores at more than 75 elementary schools in Sendai, Japan; T'aipei, Taiwan; Beijing, China; Minneapolis; and Chicago. In each study, the scores of fifth graders in the best-performing American school were lower than the scores of their counterparts in the worst-performing Asian school. In other studies, Stigler and Stevenson found significant gaps in reading tests as well.

Respect for hard work pervades Asian culture. Many folk tales make the 8 point that diligence can achieve any goal—for example, the poet Li Po's story of the woman who grinds a piece of iron into a needle, and Mao Tse-tung's recounting of an old man who removes a mountain with just a hoe. The accent on academic effort in Asian countries demonstrates how expectations for children are both higher and more democratic there than in America. "If learning is gradual and proceeds step by step," says Stigler, "anyone can gain knowledge."

To illustrate this emphasis, Stigler videotaped a Japanese teacher at work. 9 The first image on screen is that of a young woman standing in front of a class of fifth graders. She bows quickly. "Today," she says, "we will be studying triangles." The teacher reminds the children that they already know how to find the area of a rectangle. Then she distributes a quantity of large paper triangles—some equilateral, others right or isosceles—and asks the class to think about "the best way to find the area of a triangle." For the next $14^1/_2$ minutes, 44 children cut, paste, fold, draw, and talk to each other. Eventually nine kids come to the blackboard and take turns explaining how they have arranged the triangles into shapes for which they can find the areas. Finally, the teacher helps the children to see that all nine solutions boil down to the same formula: $a = (b \times h) \div 2$ (the area equals the product of the base multiplied by the height, divided by two).

Stigler says that the snaillike pace of the lesson—52 minutes from start to finish—allows the brighter students enough time to understand the concept in depth, as they think through nine different ways to find the areas of the three kinds of triangles. Meanwhile, slower students—even learning-disabled students—benefit from hearing one concept explained in many different ways. Thus children of varied abilities have the same learning opportunity; and the result is that a large number of Japanese children advance relatively far in math. 10

Americans, on the other hand, group children by ability throughout their school careers. Assigning students to curricular tracks according to ability is common, but it happens even in schools where formal tracking is not practiced. 11

So kids always know who the teacher thinks is "very smart, sorta smart, and kinda dumb," says social psychologist Jeff Howard, president of the Efficacy Institute, a nonprofit consulting firm in Lexington, Massachusetts, that specializes in education issues. "The idea of genetic intellectual inferiority is rampant in [American] society, especially as applied to African-American kids." 12

A consequence is that many kids face lower expectations and a watered-down curriculum. "A student who is bright is expected just to 'get it,' " Stigler says. "Duller kids are assumed to lack the necessary ability for ever learning certain material." 13

Our national mania for positive self-esteem too often leads us to puff up kids' confidence, and we may forget to tell them that genius is 98 percent perspiration. In fact, our reverence for innate intelligence has gone so far that many Americans believe people who work hard in school must lack ability. "Our idealization of a gifted person is someone so smart they don't have to try," says Sandra Graham of UCLA's Graduate School of Education. 14

Columbia University psychologist Carol Dweck has conducted a fascinating series of studies over the past decade documenting the dangers of believing that geniuses are born rather than made. In one study, Dweck and 15

UCLA researcher Valanne Henderson asked 229 seventh graders whether people are "born smart" or "get smart" by working hard. Then they compared the students' sixth and seventh grade achievement scores. The scores of kids with the get-smart beliefs stayed high or improved, and those of the kids subscribing to the born-smart assumption stayed low or declined. Surprisingly, even kids who believed in working hard but who had low confidence in their abilities did very well. And the kids whose scores dropped the most were the born-smart believers with high confidence.

Dweck's conclusion: "If we want our kids to succeed, we should empha-   16
size effort and steer away from praising or blaming intelligence per se."

Psychologist Ellen Leggett, a former student of Dweck's at Harvard, has   17
found that bright girls are more likely than boys to believe that people are born smart. That finding could help to explain why many American girls stop taking high school math and science before boys do.

Seeing intelligence as an inborn trait also turns children into quitters,   18
says Dweck. "Kids who believe you're born smart or not are always worried about their intelligence, so they're afraid to take risks," Dweck explains. "But kids who think you can get smart aren't threatened by a difficult task or by failures, and find it kind of exciting to figure out what went wrong and to keep at it." Or, in Jeff Howard's words, "If I know I'm too stupid to learn, why should I bang my head against the wall trying to learn?"

Getting Americans to give up their worship of natural ability and to   19
replace it with the Asian belief in effort seems a mammoth undertaking. But Dweck maintains that it's possible to train kids to believe in hard work. The key to bringing kids around, says Dweck, is for the adults close to them to talk and act upon a conviction that effort is what counts.

The Efficacy Institute is working on exactly that. The institute's work is   20
based on theories that Howard developed as a doctoral candidate at Harvard, as he investigated why black students weren't performing in school as well as whites and Asians. Using the slogan "Think you can; work hard; get smart," the institute conducts a seminar for teachers that weans them from the born-smart belief system.

"We tell teachers to talk to kids with the presumption that they can all   21
get A's in their tests," explains project specialist Kim Taylor. Most kids respond immediately to their teachers' changed expectations, Howard says. As proof, he cites achievement-test scores of 137 third grade students from six Detroit public schools who were enrolled in the Efficacy Institute program during 1989 and 1990. The students' scores rose 2.4 grade levels (from 2.8 to 5.2) in one year, compared with a control group of peers whose scores only went up by less than half a grade level.

Institute trainers now work in approximately 55 school districts, from   22
Baltimore to St. Louis to Sacramento. In five cities, they're working to train
every teacher and administrator in the school district.

While current efforts for change are modest, no less a force than the   23
Clinton administration is weaving this new thinking into its education
agenda. During a talk this past spring to the California Teachers Association, U.S. Secretary of Education Richard Riley pledged to work on setting
national standards in education. "These standards," he says, "must be for all
of our young people, regardless of their economic background. We must
convince people that children aren't born smart. They get smart."

RESPONDING TO READING

Did reading the essay change your mind about kids being born smart
or getting smart through hard work? In your journal, explain how you
think the problem of Americans' attitudes on the subject could be changed,
especially if the government or the National Education Association decided
to spend money on the effort.

GAINING WORD POWER

In paragraph 10, Kathy Seal uses the interesting word *snaillike* to describe
the slow pace of the Japanese teacher's math instruction. The term *-like* is
a combining form meaning "resembling or characteristic of." By adding
-like to other words (many of them names for animals), you can produce
useful new descriptive terms. You could write, for instance, of a child's shell-
like ear, and your readers would be able to picture the delicate curve of
the ear. Notice that you hyphenate *shell-like,* when there are three *l*s
together, but not *snaillike,* when there are only two.

1. Add *-like* to the end of each of the following words:
war	child	bird	barn	ostrich
bell	lady	cat	flower	cow

2. Then write a definition that includes the characteristic conveyed by
   that new word: *slow as a snail, curved like a shell.*

3. Finally, write a sentence for each new word that makes use of the
   descriptive characteristic: The *snaillike* traffic on the freeway resulted
   from an accident.

CONSIDERING CONTENT

1. According to researchers, what happened when groups of American kids and groups of Japanese kids were given insolvable math
   problems to work on?

2. How do most Americans think Asian students are taught? According to researchers quoted by Seal, is this impression true?
3. How did the Japanese instructor teach about triangles in the example given in paragraph 9? What are the advantages of this method of teaching?
4. What is the typical American attitude about learning—that kids are born smart or that they get smart by working hard? What is the Japanese attitude?
5. Do you know what Seal means by "our national mania for positive self-esteem" (para. 14)? What problems do researchers think it causes?
6. How is the Efficacy Institute trying to change the American attitude and instead "train kids to believe in hard work" (para. 19)?

CONSIDERING METHOD

1. How does Seal's opening sentence help get you interested in her material?
2. Find two specific examples that help readers understand why the Japanese kids beat the American kids on achievement tests. How helpful are these examples?
3. What other method of providing evidence and explaining ideas does the author use in the second part of her article about Americans' attitudes?
4. Seal employs the block organization for her contrast. Find the sentence in which she makes the transition from explaining how Japanese kids learn to considering how American kids learn. What transitional term does she use?
5. The essay has a brief concluding section following the contrast of the two educational systems. What is the purpose of these final paragraphs (19–22)?
6. The essay concludes with a direct quotation (para. 23). What makes this ending effective?

WRITING STEP BY STEP

Think of an issue on which you and your parents—or you and your spouse—strongly disagree. With your parents, for instance, you might differ in your attitudes toward premarital sex; or they might disapprove of your taste in music, clothing, or hairstyles. With your spouse, you might disagree about household chores, child care, financial matters, or vacation plans. Choose an issue that you feel confident you are right about, but be sure that you are also quite familiar with the evidence for the opposing point of view.

A. Begin your essay by presenting the problem, as Kathy Seal does in her introduction when she states the "fact that Asian students routinely do better than American kids at elementary math" (para. 1). You can start by admitting that you have this heated disagreement in your immediate family about whatever it is.

B. Next, explain how your parents or your spouse views this matter, just as Seal explains how Japanese schoolchildren are taught math (paras. 2–10). Try to include brief specific examples, as Seal does in paragraphs 8 and 9. And be fair. Give as much space to presenting this opposing view as you will give to your own viewpoint in the second part of the essay.

C. Write a transitional sentence similar to the one that Seal uses at the start of paragraph 11: "Americans, on the other hand, group children by ability throughout their school careers."

D. Now, present your side of the issue. Offer plenty of specific examples. The evidence that Seal uses in analyzing the attitudes of Americans about how children learn are mainly quotations from researchers, but these quotations are full of specifics—problems, beliefs, research studies, and testing results.

E. If possible, include a final section similar to Seal's paragraphs 19–22, in which she tells what the Efficacy Institute is doing to encourage American kids to work harder in school. Try to think of a way to resolve the problem you described in your essay. It's possible that focusing on the opposing viewpoint (as you did in the first part of your essay) may reveal a middle ground. Look for a compromise. If you find a solution that stops short of involving the law and justice system, present it here.

F. If you can't think of a way to resolve the problem, conclude by admitting that you and your family will just have to agree to disagree. But consider the final quotation in Seal's essay. Modeling the deliberate repetition of a word, try to end with two forceful sentences similar to these: "We must convince people that children aren't born smart. They get smart" (para. 23).

OTHER WRITING IDEAS

1. Using a block pattern of organization, write a comparison of two sports. At the end, explain which one is easier to play or more fun to watch, and tell why you think so.

2. Contrast two movies that present a decidedly different treatment of similar subject matter, like *The Green Berets* with *The Saving of Private Ryan; Titanic* and *A Night to Remember; Scream* and *Psycho; Buffy the Vampire Slayer* and *Dracula; Unforgiven* and *She Wore a Yellow Ribbon*.

3. Compare a novel and the film made from it—*Pride and Prejudice, The Scarlet Letter, The Great Gatsby, The Color Purple, North Dallas Forty, Like Water for Chocolate, The Joy Luck Club, The Bridges of Madison County, Midnight in the Garden of Good and Evil, The Horse Whisperer, The Diary of Bridget Jones, Misery, The Rainmaker, Get Shorty, Interview with the Vampire.*

EDITING SKILLS: USING DASHES

The dash is a handy mark of punctuation that gives emphasis to whatever follows it—as long as you don't use it too often. Notice how the dash works in this sentence from Seal's essay:

> Sure enough, most American kids attacked the problem, struggled briefly—and then gave up.

Seal could have used a comma after *briefly,* but she chose the dash because readers pay more attention to what follows a dash than to what follows a comma. Using the dash is unusual, unexpected—thus emphatic.

You can also use two dashes to set off a few words in the middle of a sentence if you want to emphasize them, as Seal does here:

> Meanwhile, slower students—even learning-disabled students—benefit from hearing one concept explained in many different ways.

Commas would be quite correct there, but dashes give emphasis to the words enclosed.

There's another handy use for the dash—to avoid comma clutter. Look at this sentence from Seal's essay:

> Then she distributes a quantity of large paper triangles—some equilateral, others right or isosceles—and asks the class to think about "the best way to find the area of a triangle."

Again, commas would be correct before and after that phrase, but when the group of words set off contains one or more commas, putting dashes around it makes the whole sentence easier to read.

Finally, you can use a dash instead of a colon to introduce an example, as Seal does here:

> Many folk tales make the point that diligence can achieve any goal— for example, the poet Li Po's story of . . . and Mao Tse-tung's recounting of . . .

When typing, use two hyphens to form a dash (--); but if you are writing on a word processor, you may find that it has a separate key for the dash. In either case, don't put a space before or after the dash. And remember not to use dashes too often, or they will lose their good effect.

EXERCISE

Insert a dash or replace a comma with a dash whenever you think it would improve the following sentences:

1. My friend Yolanda said she just turned twenty-nine for the third time.
2. It's time I started saving for a Florida vacation, for a cruise to the Bahamas, for a new Lexus, for my retirement.
3. All kinds of spices, even pepper, garlic, and onion, give Eddie indigestion.
4. Madonna's costume, what there was of it, shocked even broad-minded me.
5. Marvin had only one chance and a slim one at that.

Now examine the sentences in the essay you just wrote. Can you improve any of them by inserting dashes? Try to revise at least two of your sentences using dashes.

Student Essay Using Comparison and Contrast

Four Eyes

David A. Dean

Among people with less than perfect eyesight, there exists a long-standing, sometimes heated argument between those who prefer to wear glasses and those who favor contact lenses. Both glasses and contacts are essential in improving the vision of millions of people. But setting aside these benefits, I want to argue that glasses are in several ways superior to those tiny bowl-shaped discs inserted into your eyes. 1

Glasses begin to show their advantages from the very moment the alarm wakes you. As you lift your head from your feather pillow, wiping the sleep from your eyes, the contact lens wearer will greet the new day as one great blur. Your impaired vision will continue to trouble you as you dodge fuzzy objects while struggling to find the place where your lenses are stored. Take the beginning of the same day for the glasses wearer. The alarm wakes you; you lift your head from your comfortable pillow, rub the sleep from your eyes, and reach for your custom-fitted glasses. Instantly the world is crisp and clear. You walk toward the bathroom in confidence, knowing you will not stub your toe on invisible obstacles. Those first few moments of the day are critical, for they can set the mood for the remainder of your waking hours. You can either choose a bleak beginning, fogged in by blurred surroundings, or you can select a bright new day free from floundering. Only glasses can provide this positive outlook for the vision impaired. 2

Another way in which glasses make life easier than contacts for the wearer involves their care. Maintaining a pair of glasses requires a minimum of upkeep. To keep them sparkling clean, all you need is tap water and a soft cloth. It need not even be a fancy cloth--a worn-out T-shirt or holey handkerchief works just fine. But with contact lenses the maintenance is time-consuming and costly. You need to 3 clean them daily in an expensive solution, then store them in a disinfecting solution (also expensive). Before putting the lenses in your eyes, you must rinse off those chemicals in a saline bath. After wearing them a week, your lenses need to be soaked in an enzymatic solution (incredibly costly) to remove the protein build-up secreted from your eyes. With the time and money you save by wearing glasses, you can enjoy the finer things which make living worthwhile.

For many people, another reason for preferring glasses to contacts is summed up by Olympia Dukakis, who wisely observes in *Steel Magnolias*, "The difference between us and the animals is our ability to accessorize." Just so. The person who wears glasses may select a variety of styles and colors to suit the occasion or complement the costume. With contact lenses, though, the wearer is hard pressed to create an image. Even a person of rich imagination and rare creativity is left with no possibility for flair or originality, having only two tiny, totally transparent lenses to work with. 4

The final reason why glasses are preferable to contact lenses is, for me, the most persuasive, for it is based on human vanity. Each and every one of us faces the unpleasant prospect of aging--the old biological clock, constantly ticking. Most of us struggle to keep a youthful appearance as long as possible. But if you choose to wear contacts, you will find yourself squinting a lot more than if you wore glasses. It's a known fact. And, of course, one result of squinting is the formation of those unsightly crow's feet around the eyes. Squinting adds undue stress to the delicate tissues. By wearing glasses, you can retard those wrinkles and retain that youthful glow for years longer. 5

Considering all these factors, you will surely agree that if you need to improve your vision, the choice between glasses and contact lenses is an easy one. Next time you find yourself at your local Lens Crafters, demand the very best for your eyes. Cast your lot on the sensible side: insist on glasses. 6

C h a p t e r

8

STRATEGIES FOR EXPLAINING HOW THINGS WORK

Process and Directions

Listen to our rural relatives explaining how to get to the family reunion: "Just follow the hard road down to where the Snivelys' cow barn used to stand before the fire; then turn off on the gravel track and go a piece until you get to the top of the second big rise after the creek. Look for Rabbithash's old pickup." All eighty-six first cousins find these directions perfectly clear, but anyone from farther away than Clay City is going to have some difficulty getting there before the potato salad goes funny.

THE POINT OF WRITING ABOUT PROCESS AND DIRECTIONS

When you want to include second-cousins-once-removed and even complete strangers in your audience, you will try to write out directions that don't rely on so much in-group information (such as where the Snivelys' barn *used* to be). Communicating directions so that almost anyone can understand them is a difficult task, as you know if you have ever tried to do it. Explaining a process is quite similar: after you've performed a certain job over and over, it's hard to explain to someone else exactly how it's done. And when a child asks, "Where does the rain come from?" most people would rather come up with a cute story than really grapple with the workings of nature.

But sometimes, frequently on the job, you must come up with an orderly, step-by-step explanation of how something is done or how it works. The explanation may be just part of a larger report or essay; for example, proposing a solution to the company's mail problems must include

207

an account of how the current mail system works. This chapter includes models of several types of process and direction writing.

THE PRINCIPLES OF PROCESS AND DIRECTIONS

The basic organizing principle behind process and direction writing involves time. You are usually concerned with a series of events, and these events may not float through your mind in the same order they should appear in your written work. Your readers will be frustrated and confused by flashbacks or detours to supply information that you should have covered earlier. Therefore, the scratch outline takes on great importance in this type of writing effort. A blank piece of unlined paper will help you to get started. On this page, you will list the steps or stages of the process as you first think of them—only be sure to space the items widely apart. In the spaces you can add points you forgot the first time through: these can be major steps ("Collect the dog shampoo and old towels before you attempt to collect the dog"), substeps ("Pile up more old towels than you think you will possibly need"), or warnings ("Don't speak to your beast in a tone of panicky sweetness; he'll know you're up to something"). Once you consider your notes complete, read through them while visualizing the process to pinpoint anything you have forgotten.

"How to Wash Your Dog" doesn't represent the only angle you can take on process writing, although it is a useful one. Garrison Keillor's directions on "How to Write a Personal Letter" combine practical and emotional features of the process—not only showing us how to do it but persuading us that it is worth doing. And Gary Larson's explanation of how he developed the idea for a cartoon also includes, in Larson's words, "an examination of what went wrong, what went right, and how rarely any two people seem to agree on which is which." On the other hand, "Flea Facts" does not concern a process that will be performed by the readers, but it explains chronologically the life cycle of the flea as an aid to exterminating fleas. Readings in the natural and behavioral sciences often follow this pattern. "How to Make Your Dendrites Grow and Grow" demonstrates another strategy. It starts from a desirable goal—keeping your brain in top shape—and describes several different methods for reaching that goal (rather than presenting a single process). In your future writing projects, all these techniques for explaining a process and giving directions will be useful.

THE PITFALLS OF PROCESS AND DIRECTIONS

The problems you encounter in process writing usually have their roots in understanding your audience. If you look at the issue from your point of view as a reader, you can see what we mean. Recently, for instance, we joined the Internet, the worldwide communications network that lets us send messages over our computer modems. We were assured that the printed directions we received were quite complete. They began, "Once you are connected to the CCSO Terminal, follow these steps to log on." Once we were *what?* To *what?* Obviously, the directions were written for people much more "connected" than we are. You have no doubt had similar experiences; hundreds of cartoons around Christmas time portray frantic parents trying to follow "easy" assembly instructions for their children's toys.

Reviewing Your Process

When you revise your process writing, think about the people who will be reading it. Ask yourself these questions:

1. Have I chosen the best starting point? Think about how much your audience already knows before you decide where to begin describing the process. Don't assume your readers have background knowledge that they may not have.
2. Have I provided enough definitions of terms? See Chapter 5 for help in writing definitions and deciding when they are needed.
3. Have I been specific enough in the details? "Dig a trench" is more specific than "Dig a hole," but how deep should the trench be? How wide? How long?

Addressing Your Audience

Another decision you will need to face in your process writing concerns not only who your audience is but how you intend to speak to them. In this book, we address you, our readers, as "you." This straightforward, informal voice is desirable in much writing. Sometimes, you can keep the informality yet leave out the "you," using imperative sentences (or commands) like "Gather the towels before catching the dog," or "Dig a trench two feet wide." You may also choose to describe a third person performing or observing the process: "The experienced water colorist works quickly," or "The first feature a palm reader examines is the life line, running from between the thumb and first finger in a curve down to the wrist." However you decide to deal with addressing your audience, you should be careful not to mix these approaches accidentally.

WHAT TO LOOK FOR IN PROCESS AND DIRECTIONS

The readings in this chapter differ greatly in their treatment of topics, even though they have process and directions in common. As you read, consider these questions:

1. What are the differences among the introductions? Can you account for these differences by looking at the purpose of each author?
2. How does each author signal where a new step, stage, or part begins?
3. How does each author address the readers? Is this way of addressing the readers suitable?
4. Are there any points at which you would like further details or explanation? Where, what, and why?
5. What strategies other than process and directions appear within these readings—for example, narration, description, or comparison and contrast?

"Oh, wait! Wait, Cory! ... Add the cereal *first* and *then* the milk!"

Why is this Gary Larson cartoon humorous?

Do you know anyone who follows directions to a humorous degree of exactness? How about someone who does the opposite, who doesn't bother with directions at all?

What other kinds of humor have you seen or heard concerning giving and following directions?

PREPARING TO READ

Who is the smartest person you know? What makes this individual smart? List some of the activities the person enjoys.

How to Make Your Dendrites Grow and Grow

DANIEL GOLDEN

Daniel Golden writes on a variety of topics for *Life* magazine. The reading we reprint here accompanied an article about research on what keeps people intellectually active into old age. Although people used to believe that mental powers declined naturally in old age, scientists now think that developing and exercising brain cell connections can keep us sharp. Golden suggests several ways to enrich the connections, which are called dendrites.

TERMS TO RECOGNIZE

UCLA *(para. 1)*	University of California at Los Angeles
computational *(para. 1)*	operating like a computer
reserves *(para. 1)*	supplies kept available for future uses
diverting *(para. 2)*	amusing
neuroscientist *(para. 3)*	scientist specializing in study of the brain
spatial *(para. 3)*	having to do with arrangement in space
cognitive *(para. 7)*	relating to mental processes; intellectual
provocative *(para. 8)*	stimulating, interesting
dendrites *(para. 8)*	the branched parts of brain cells that transmit impulses toward the cell body

What can the average person do to strengthen his or her mind? "The important thing is to be actively involved in areas unfamiliar to you," says Arnold Scheibel, head of UCLA's Brain Research Institute. "Anything that's intellectually challenging can probably serve as a kind of stimulus for dendritic growth, which means it adds to the computational reserves in your brain." 1

So pick something that's diverting, and most important, unfamiliar. A computer programmer might try sculpture; a ballerina might try marine 2 navigation. Here are some other stimulating suggestions from brain researchers:

- Do puzzles. "I can't stand crosswords," says neuroscientist Antonio   3
  Damasio of the University of Iowa, "but they're a good idea." Psychologist Sherry Willis of Pennsylvania State University says, "People who do jigsaw puzzles show greater spatial ability, which you use when you look at a map."
- Try a musical instrument. "As soon as you decide to take up the   4
  violin, your brain has a whole new group of muscle-control problems to solve. But that's nothing compared with what the brain has to do before the violinist can begin to read notes on a page and correlate them with his or her fingers to create tones. This is a remarkable, high-level type of activity," says Scheibel.
- Fix something. Learn to reline your car's brakes or repair a shaver,   5
  suggests Zaven Khachaturian, a brain expert at the National Institute of Aging. "My basement is full of electronic gadgets, waiting to be repaired. The solution is not the important thing. It's the challenge."
- Try the arts. If your verbal skills are good, buy a set of watercolors and   6
  take a course. If your drawing skills are good, start a journal or write poetry.
- Dance. "We keep seeing a relationship between physical activity and   7
  cognitive maintenance," says Harvard brain researcher Marilyn Albert. "We suspect that moderately strenuous exercise leads to the development of small blood vessels. Blood carries oxygen, and oxygen nourishes the brain." But be sure the activity is new and requires thinking. Square dancing, ballet or tap is preferable to twisting the night away.
- Date provocative people. Better yet, marry one of them. Willis suggests   8
  that the most pleasant and rewarding way to increase your dendrites is to "meet and interact with intelligent, interesting people." Try tournament bridge, chess, even sailboat racing.

And remember, researchers agree that it's never too late. Says Scheibel: 9
"All of life should be a learning experience, not just for the trivial reasons but because by continuing the learning process, we are challenging our brain and therefore building brain circuitry. Literally. This is the way the brain operates."

RESPONDING TO READING

Jot down in your journal the activities that you perform on an average weekday and on an average weekend day. Does one type of activity seem to dominate? For example, are you usually doing something verbal or nonverbal? Passive or active? Solitary or social? Artistic or practical? If you had time to add some activity to help your dendrites grow, what would it be?

GAINING WORD POWER

cognitive   dendritic   provocative

computational   spatial

These words are all used as *adjectives* in the reading. That is, they describe or modify other words (nouns) to make their meaning more specific and vivid. Look back through the reading to find the adjective-plus-noun combinations. We have done the first example for you.

cognitive   maintenance

computational   _____

dendritic   _____

provocative   _____

spatial   _____

The adjective *dendritic* obviously comes from the noun *dendrite,* which is also used in the reading. Using your dictionary, find the nouns that are related to these other four adjectives:

adj.: cognitive   noun: _____

adj.: computational   noun: _____

adj.: provocative   noun: _____

adj.: spatial   noun: _____

Now list one other related word, its meaning, and its part of speech for the five adjectives. Use your dictionary for help. For example, *cognitive* is related to the verb *cogitate,* which means "to think about." Both have to do with mental processes. Choose one set of three related words and try using them in three sentences of your own.

CONSIDERING CONTENT

1. Who is the audience for this reading—the "you" that the writer addresses? How do you know?

2. Why is it important that activity to strengthen your brain should be unfamiliar?

3. Why are some dances better than others to develop your dendrites?

4. The closing paragraph says that the brain operates by building "circuitry." What does this statement mean? How is developing your brain comparable to strengthening electrical circuits?
5. How could leisure activities help you with work activities?
6. If the experts quoted here are right, what lifestyle would cause a person's brain to deteriorate rather than grow over time?
7. Where in your own hometown could you meet "intelligent, interesting people" (para. 8)? What activities other than bridge, chess, or sailboat racing might such people be involved in?

CONSIDERING METHOD

1. How does the introductory paragraph catch the reader's interest?
2. Who are the people quoted in this reading? What do they have in common? Why are they quoted directly?
3. Give another example that could be added to the short paragraph "Try the arts" (para. 6).
4. How is each new suggestion introduced? What other ways could they be introduced?
5. What is the thesis of the reading? How does the conclusion reinforce the main point?

WRITING STEP BY STEP

You probably have ideas about how friendships are formed, maintained, and preserved. Write an essay called "How to Make Your Friendships Grow and Grow." You will be following the form of "How to Make Your Dendrites Grow and Grow."

A. Start by asking a question that will catch your readers' interests.
B. Give an overall statement that covers most of the specific points of advice you are going to make. What, in general, do you think makes good friendships?
C. Use the informal "you" to communicate directly to your readers.
D. Give five or six specific suggestions. Include specific details or examples to explain each suggestion.
E. Begin each of the five or six specific suggestions with an imperative sentence. Imperative sentences give commands and begin with a verb, like this: "Do puzzles" and "Try the arts." If you want, use a bullet (a symbol, like a box or circle) at the beginning of each suggestion.
F. Interview one or two people whom you consider experts on friendship. Use direct quotations from your interviews to support

one or more of your suggestions or to conclude your essay. Or look up some quotations about friends and friendship in a reference book like *Bartlett's Familiar Quotations.*

G. Whether you use a quotation or not, write a closing that reinforces your general statement about friendship.

OTHER WRITING IDEAS

1. Take some of the advice in "How to Make Your Dendrites Grow and Grow." Try an unfamiliar activity one day soon, and write notes in your journal directly afterward. Write an essay reporting on the experience.
2. Choose an activity that you do, and explain to your readers how they would benefit from doing it, too.
3. Explain a few basic principles of training a dog or child to behave.
4. Write a humorous essay on "How to Lose Your Dendrite Power." For fun, before you write, you might brainstorm with a small group of classmates for ideas about how to get mentally duller.

EDITING SKILLS: PUNCTUATING QUOTATIONS

Quotations from experts and from your reading will often enhance your writing. Most people find the punctuation of quotations tricky, though. This exercise will help you put the periods, commas, and quotation marks in the right places. (For advice on using single quotation marks inside regular double quotation marks, see pp. 179–80.)

Copy the following statements from "How to Make Your Dendrites Grow and Grow" *exactly:*

Psychologist Sherry Willis of Pennsylvania State University says, "People who do jigsaw puzzles show greater spatial ability, which you use when you look at a map."

"We keep seeing a relationship between physical activity and cognitive maintenance," says Harvard brain researcher Marilyn Albert.

"I can't stand crosswords," says neuroscientist Antonio Damasio of the University of Iowa, "but they're a good idea."

Notice that you can put the tag line (the part that tells who is being quoted) before the quotation, after the quotation, or in the middle of the quotation. Exchange your copies with a classmate and check each other's writing for exact, accurate placement of all the punctuation. Then look at your essay on "How to Make Your Friendships Grow and Grow" to make sure that you have punctuated the quotations correctly.

PREPARING TO READ

How do you feel when you receive a letter? Does anyone regularly write to you? To whom do you write, and why? Did you ever read letters written long ago?

How to Write a Personal Letter

GARRISON KEILLOR

Garrison Keillor is a famous radio program host. His show, *A Prairie Home Companion,* is especially popular because of Keillor's spoken essays about the Minnesota town of Lake Wobegon, a make-believe place where "all the men are strong, all the women are good-looking, and all the children are above average." Listeners are delighted by the charming quirkiness of Lake Wobegon citizens and their everyday lives. In the essay we reprint here, Keillor's neighborly style comes through as he gives advice and support to letter writers.

TERMS TO RECOGNIZE

wahoo *(para. 2)*	probably a type of *yahoo,* which is a coarse, crude person
anonymity *(para. 4)*	namelessness, being unknown
obligatory *(para. 6)*	required by custom or etiquette
sensate *(para. 6)*	filled with feelings
sensuous *(para. 8)*	pleasing to the senses
salutation *(para. 10)*	the greeting that opens a letter
declarative *(para. 10)*	making a statement
episode *(para. 13)*	an incident or event; a unit of a longer story
urinary tract *(para. 13)*	the system relating to the kidneys and their function
means *(para. 14)*	mode or process

W e shy persons need to write a letter now and then, or else we'll dry up and blow away. It's true. And I speak as one who loves to reach for the phone, dial the number, and talk. The telephone is to shyness what Hawaii is to February; it's a way out of the woods. *And yet:* a letter is better.

Such a sweet gift—a piece of handmade writing, in an envelope that is not a bill, sitting in our friend's path when she trudges home from a long day spent among wahoos and savages, a day our words will help repair. They don't need to be immortal, just sincere. She can read them twice and again tomorrow: *You're someone I care about, Corinne, and think of often, and every time I do, you make me smile.*

We need to write; otherwise nobody will know who we are. They will   3
have only a vague impression of us as A Nice Person, because, frankly, we don't shine at conversation, we lack the confidence to thrust our faces forward and say, "Hi, I'm Heather Hooten; let me tell you about my week." Mostly we say "Uh-huh" and "Oh really." People smile and look over our shoulder, looking for someone else to meet.

So a shy person sits down and writes a letter. To be known by another   4
person—to meet and talk freely on the page—to be close despite distance. To escape from anonymity and be our own sweet selves and express the music of our souls.

Same thing that moves a giant rock star to sing his heart out in front of   5
123,000 people moves us to take ballpoint in hand and write a few lines to our dear Aunt Eleanor. *We want to be known.* We want her to know that we have fallen in love, that we quit our job, that we're moving to New York, and we want to say a few things that might not get said in casual conversation: *Thank you for what you've meant to me. I am very happy right now.*

The first step in writing letters is to get over the guilt of *not* writing. You   6
don't "owe" anybody a letter. Letters are a gift. The burning shame you feel when you see unanswered mail makes it harder to pick up a pen and makes for a cheerless letter when you finally do. *I feel bad about not writing, but I've been so busy,* etc. Skip this. Few letters are obligatory, and they are *Thanks for the wonderful gift* and *I am terribly sorry to hear about George's death* and *Yes, you're welcome to stay with us next month.* Write these promptly if you want to keep your friends. Don't worry about the others, except love letters, of course. When your true love writes *Dear Light of My Life, Joy of My Heart, O Lovely Pulsating Core of My Sensate Life,* some response is called for.

Some of the best letters are tossed off in a burst of inspiration, so keep   7
your writing stuff in one place where you can sit down for a few minutes and—*Dear Roy, I am in the middle of an essay but thought I'd drop you a line. Hi to your sweetie too*—dash off a note to a pal. Envelopes, stamps, address book, everything in a drawer so you can write fast when the pen is hot.

A blank white 8" x 11" sheet can look as big as Montana if the pen's   8
not so hot—try a smaller page and write boldly. Get a pen that makes a sensuous line, get a comfortable typewriter, a friendly word processor— whichever feels easy to the hand.

Sit for a few minutes with the blank sheet of paper in front of you, and   9
meditate on the person you will write to, let your friend come to mind until you can almost see her or him in the room with you. Remember the

last time you saw each other and how your friend looked and what you said and what perhaps was unsaid between you, and when your friend becomes real to you, start to write.

Write the salutation—*Dear You*—and take a deep breath and plunge in. 10 A simple declarative sentence will do, followed by another and another. Tell us what you're doing and tell it like you were talking to us. Don't think about grammar, don't think about style, don't try to write dramatically, just give us your news. Where did you go, who did you see, what did they say, what do you think?

If you don't know where to begin, start with the present: *I'm sitting at* 11 *the kitchen table on a rainy Saturday morning. Everyone is gone and the house is quiet.* Let your simple description of the present moment lead to something else; let the letter drift gently along.

The toughest letter to crank out is one that is meant to impress, as we 12 all know from writing job applications; if it's hard work to slip off a letter to a friend, maybe you're trying too hard to be terrific. A letter is only a report to someone who already likes you for reasons other than your brilliance. Take it easy.

Don't worry about form. It's not a term paper. When you come to the 13 end of one episode, just start a new paragraph. You can go from a few lines about the sad state of pro football to the fight with your mother to your fond memories of Mexico to your cat's urinary-tract infection to a few thoughts on personal indebtedness and on to the kitchen sink and what's in it. The more you write, the easier it gets, and when you have a True True Friend to write to, a *compadre,* a soul sibling, then it's like driving a car; you just press on the gas.

Don't tear up the page and start over when you write a bad line—try 14 to write your way out of it. Make mistakes and plunge on. Let the letter cook along and let yourself be bold. Outrage, confusion, love—whatever is in your mind, let it find a way to the page. Writing is a means of discovery, always, and when you come to the end and write *Yours ever* or *Hugs and Kisses,* you'll know something you didn't when you wrote *Dear Pal.*

Probably your friend will put your letter away, and it'll be read again a 15 few years from now—and it will improve with age. And forty years from now, your friend's grandkids will dig it out of the attic and read it, a sweet and precious relic of the ancient Eighties that gives them a sudden clear glimpse of you and her and the world we old-timers knew. You will have then created an object of art. Your simple lines about where you went, who you saw, what they said, will speak to those children, and they will feel in their hearts the humanity of our times.

You can't pick up a phone and call the future and tell them about our 16 times. You have to pick up a piece of paper.

RESPONDING TO READING

After reading Keillor's essay, are you encouraged to try writing a letter to a friend? Why or why not? Answer these questions in your journal.

GAINING WORD POWER

Add to the following fragments, making them into reasonable sentences. Be sure that your additions show your understanding of the terms from the reading.

1. President Weber began his after-dinner speech with an obligatory _____.
2. To protect her anonymity, the writer _____.
3. Preparing _____ is more sensuous than _____.
4. Henry sat down and wrote this salutation: _____.
5. An office memo usually begins with a plain declarative statement, like "_____."

CONSIDERING CONTENT

1. Why are letters preferable to face-to-face communication for shy people? What other reasons might make letters preferable to conversation, according to Keillor?
2. What are some differences between Keillor's advice and other writing instructions or rules you have heard? Why do you think these differences exist?
3. Did you ever have to write a letter or essay "meant to impress" (para. 12)? What was the experience like? How did you feel about the writing you produced?
4. Note two or three spots where Keillor deals with the emotions a letter writer might have. Why is it important to give advice about these?
5. What does Keillor mean by "an object of art" in paragraph 15? What has changed the ordinary letter into art? Do you think this claim makes sense or exaggerates?
6. What about writing letters electronically, through media like e-mail? Does Keillor's essay have any relevance to electronic letters? Do you think he would see them as similar to or different from postal letters?

CONSIDERING METHOD

1. Make a brief list of Keillor's pieces of advice. What is the reasoning behind the order he uses?

2. Who is the "we" Keillor refers to in the essay? Who is the "you"? What kinds of people might feel the essay did not appeal to them?

3. Does this writing strike you as formal or informal? Point out words and phrases that influenced your decision. Why do you think Keillor made this choice about level of formality?

4. What are the lines and phrases printed in italics? Can you identify their purpose?

WRITING STEP BY STEP

In the reading, Keillor advocates writing a letter, even when a phone call is possible. Write an essay in which you promote doing something in the old-fashioned way even though new ways are available. Think about writing by hand rather than on a word processor, baking bread, sewing clothes, building furniture, doing math without a calculator, reading a novel rather than watching the movie, conducting a courtship, or raising children, for possible inspiration.

A. In the beginning of your essay, suggest one or two reasons why the old way might be better than the new way.

B. Use "I," "we," and "you" to refer to yourself, yourself and your readers, and your readers.

C. Use everyday language and familiar examples to get your points across to a wide audience.

D. Explain why some people feel hesitant about doing things the old way.

E. Suggest ways that the reader can overcome this reluctance. Look at paragraphs 6 through 13 for examples of how Keillor does this.

F. Include, if relevant, some "don'ts" to help your reader avoid problems, as Keillor does in paragraphs 10, 13, and 14.

G. In your closing, reinforce your main point by looking at the positive effect(s) the actions you promote could have. You might look into the future, as Keillor does.

OTHER WRITING IDEAS

1. Try writing a letter to a friend, using Keillor's advice if you want. At the same time, take notes about how you go about performing the task. Record the thoughts and feelings that you experience along the way as well as the techniques you use. Write an essay describing the experience of writing the letter. Use direct quotations from the letter in italics to illustrate your points.

2. Keillor asserts that "writing is a means of discovery" (para. 14). What does this mean? Write an essay about a piece of writing you once

did (or tried to do) that led you to an unexpected discovery. The discovery could be about yourself, about the writing process, about the subject matter, about school, about the intended audience, or about a combination of things.

3. The reading emphasizes writing letters as an outlet for shy people. Another form of communication, public speaking, brings out the shy side of almost everyone. Write an essay modeled on Keillor's in which you give emotional and practical advice to a person who reluctantly must make a speech or give a presentation. To develop ideas, you and a group of classmates may want to brainstorm before you each write.

EDITING SKILLS: BUSINESS LETTERS

Although Keillor gives good advice about writing personal letters, you will also be faced with writing business letters—applications for jobs, requests for action or information from people you don't know personally, or explanations of your proposals or ideas to other people in your workplace. The following diagram explains the format of a business letter. After studying the form, type a brief letter from Dr. Fisher to Susan Lee, telling her that she is sending the requested bibliography and also another list of books that Susan may find interesting.

7012 E. Front St.
Bloomington, IL 61701-5413
December 11, 1999

Your address: Provide your own address in case the letter gets separated from the envelope. Use letterhead stationery instead if you have it.

Dr. Gina Fisher
Department of Communications
Illinois Valley Community College
Oglesby, IL 61348

Today's date: Your reader will know exactly when you wrote the letter.

Inside address: Give the address where you are sending the letter. If the envelope gets ruined in the mail, the letter can still be delivered.

Dear Dr. Fisher:

I was your student in a Communications 211 course two years ago, and I am writing to ask you a favor.

Salutation: Use a colon after the greeting. If you do not know the exact name of the person you are writing to, use a title: Dear Director of Admissions.

The course was extremely interesting for me, and on the basis of some of the readings you assigned, I decided to major in psychology here at Illinois State.

Since taking your course, I have moved twice and have lost the bibliography about helping behavior which you gave us. This list of articles would be helpful to me again in my present courses. If you still have copies of it, I would greatly appreciate your sending me one.

Thank you for your trouble, and thank you, too, for starting me on a rewarding course of study. I am enclosing an SASE for your reply.

Sincerely,

Susan Lee

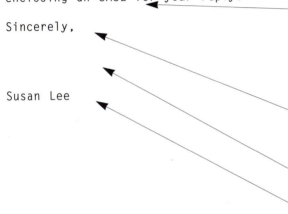

Ending: Say something positive if at all possible. "Thank you for your attention" is a good all-purpose ending.

SASE: Stands for self-addressed stamped envelope. Enclosing one of these, addressed to yourself with postage already attached, will increase your chance of a quick reply.

Complimentary close: *Sincerely* is fine for almost any case. Save cute closings for personal friends.

Leave four blank lines for your signature.

Type your full name.

PREPARING TO READ

Have you ever done battle with natural pests—fleas, cockroaches, mildew, cabbage worms, mosquitoes, or moths, for example? Who won?

Flea Facts

R I C H A R D   G R A Y ,   J R .

Richard Gray, Jr., is a contributor to *Cats* magazine. In this June 1994 essay about the flea, he uses a combination of process and explanation techniques. You will also see that he knows his audience well.

TERMS TO RECOGNIZE

bubonic plague, typhus *(para. 3)*	deadly infectious diseases
affliction *(para. 4)*	source of pain and suffering
host *(para. 4)*	the target of a parasite
voracious *(para. 9)*	greedy in eating
millimeter *(para. 10)*	one-thousandth of a meter, or 0.0394 inch
transmit *(para. 13)*	pass along
dermatitis *(para. 13)*	inflamed skin
lesions *(para. 13)*	sores
anemia *(para. 13)*	serious blood disease
persistent *(para. 14)*	not giving up

•← What's this? A period at the beginning of a sentence? Or is it a period? Maybe it's . . . a flea? 1

You brushed at it, I know you did. OK, it's a period, but if it had suddenly disappeared, the chances are quite good it was a flea. Chances are it would probably also have a lot of company. In other words, you have a flea problem. 2

Once upon a time, people didn't worry too much about fleas on their pets. They were too busy with more important things, like bubonic plague and typhus. Historians estimate that up to one-quarter of the population of Europe died from the Black Death in the fourteenth century. The plague was transmitted to humans by a flea that rode a rat that rode a boat that visited ocean-side city after city. Now this was a flea problem. 3

Typhus is another affliction that has been given to humanity by fleas   4
although, to be fair, the body louse has played a bigger role. The body louse
is the host to epidemic typhus, one of the biggest killers, second only to
war, during the first half of this century. Rat fleas, on the other hand, are
carriers of murine typhus, a much less contagious and lethal form of the
disease. Though once quite common in the American Southeast, it is a
fairly rare affliction today.

Both diseases were carried by rat fleas, but rat fleas are certainly not the   5
only player in the flea game. There's the human flea, cat flea, dog flea, horse
flea, rabbit flea, bird flea, poultry flea . . . the list goes on. With some 2,000
flea species identified in the world, one can choose what their "least
favorite" flea is. For those of us with infested pets, our least favorite would
be the cat flea.

The cat flea is the flea commonly found on both cats and dogs.   6
However, it has no problem moving from one species to another in search
of a host if it can't find its favorite. Did I say moving? Try jumping. Their
powerful back legs enable them to leap distances over a foot, creating a very
credible illusion that they simply disappear. (Is that a period?)

One of the most difficult aspects of combating a flea problem in the   7
home is understanding the four stages of the flea life cycle: adult, egg, larva
and pupa.

The adult flea, obviously, is at the end of the life cycle. It is also the sole   8
source of irritation for both you and your pet. Adults are the parasitic stage
of the flea, the only stage that actually lives and feeds on your pet. In the past
it was believed that they lived primarily in the environment and only jumped
on an animal to feed, but this is now considered inaccurate. Unless forced
off the pet (through scratching, etc.), they prefer to be on their food source.

The adult flea is quite voracious and can consume up to 15 times its   9
body weight in blood a day. All this blood fuels a very healthy 16 ovaries,
enabling the female flea to lay up to 50 eggs a day if temperature and
humidity are favorable. This can add up to 2,000 eggs per female over the
course of her life.

The eggs (white, oval and about one-half millimeter in length) will then   10
fall off the animal into the environment. As such, any area that your pet
frequents, such as a pet bed or under a chair, will tend to have a fairly large
amount of eggs around it. The eggs will usually hatch into the larvae stage
within 10 days of being laid.

Flea larvae resemble maggots more than anything else. They tend to live   11
in dark areas, such as deep in carpeting, where they feed on organic matter.
Their favorite food is flea dirt, a rather glamorous term for blood-rich flea
feces. They molt twice in a 5- to 11-day period and can reach five millimeters before they spin a cocoon and enter the pupae stage.

It is when the flea is in the pupae stage that controlling it is the hard- 12
est. The cocoons, about three millimeters in length, are sticky and blend in
with the environment. They are extremely weather resistant. Most troubling,
the flea can remain in the cocoon for up to a year. If you were to leave for
an extended period of time and come back expecting to find a flea-less
house, you would be in for a nasty surprise! The fleas wait for you. Or, more
accurately, wait for the right conditions that trigger them to hatch, such as
a change in temperature or the vibrations/carbon dioxide that indicates
the presence of a host. At this stage, they are adults and can live up to a
month without a blood meal.

Fleas are a nuisance, but they can also be quite harmful to your pet. 13
They transmit parasites such as tapeworm. Flea-allergy dermatitis is
common in animals with fleas and can range from simple, one-bite inflammation to more severe reactions that are characterized by hair loss, hot
spots and lesions. Smaller animals, particularly cats, can suffer from anemia
if enough fleas feed on them. Too many fleas on a kitten can kill it.

Fleas. Rhymes with please, which is probably the look in your pet's eyes 14
when he's scratching away at one of the little beasts. Controlling fleas is
merely a matter of understanding them and being persistent in your flea-
ridding efforts. And of course, it all starts with one question . . .

• ← Is that a flea? 15

_____

RESPONDING TO READING

After reading "Flea Facts," do you believe that "controlling fleas is merely
a matter of understanding them and being persistent"? If not, write another
sentence that would be more practical in paragraph 14.

GAINING WORD POWER

The vocabulary word *dermatitis* is an example of a root, *derma,* and a suffix,
-itis. **Roots** and **suffixes** that are very common, like these, are listed in your
dictionary. Look up *derma* and *-itis* to see how the two parts combine to
make the meaning of "skin inflammation." Now list at least three other
diseases that end with the Greek suffix *-itis.* This suffix is not only used seriously but also playfully, as when we make up words like *senioritis* to describe
the itch to get out felt by students in their final year of high school or college.
Make up or record three other playful *-itis* words, and write their definitions.

CONSIDERING CONTENT

1. How have fleas been harmful in the past? How are they harmful
   in the present?
2. What are the four stages of the flea life cycle?

3. What conditions cause the pupae to hatch out of their cocoons?
4. How does Gray explain the remarkable staying power of a flea problem? Name at least two factors that contribute to their endurance.
5. What detail did you find most disgusting?

CONSIDERING METHOD

1. What audience would be especially interested in this essay? How does Gray's introduction make a targeted appeal to these people?
2. Paragraph 7 is an unusually short one. Why do you think it stands alone instead of being combined with another paragraph?
3. Look at the transitions between paragraphs 9, 10, 11, and 12. What repetition is used to show the connection between one paragraph and the previous paragraph?
4. How are the opening and the closing of the essay unified or drawn together? Find another essay in this book or elsewhere that uses a similar technique of unifying the introduction and conclusion.
5. You are probably used to seeing technical information presented in an academic or formal style, but Gray chooses an informal style. Point out three features that let you know the writing is informal. How is the informality appropriate for the subject and the audience?

WRITING STEP BY STEP

Write an essay, in imitation of Gray's essay, about some common pest. Within your essay, you will be giving basic information about the pest. Think about insects, animals, weeds, and even minor ailments (like athlete's foot or acne), to get started on a topic.

A. Look in at least two reference books (two different encyclopedias, for example) to help you gather factual information about the pest or problem. Information that is widely shared among reference books is considered general knowledge, and you can use the facts without giving credit. Be sure that you do not use the same wording as the reference book, though. Doing so is considered plagiarism. Even copying several words in a row exactly from a source puts you in danger of plagiarism.
B. Direct your writing to people who may be bothered by the pest or problem you are considering. Use "you" to refer to the reader.
C. Catch the readers' attention at the beginning of your essay by appealing to their experiences with the pest.
D. Begin the body of the essay by telling about some of the damage the pest or problem has caused. Gray goes back into past centuries for this purpose. You may not have information about distant

history, so you might concentrate on recent history. (Describe the summer all your tomatoes expired from cutworms, for example.)

E. Identify some process that the pest or problem goes through. Gray, for example, explains the life cycle of the flea. If the life cycle of your topic is not important, you could explain some other process, like how a severe outbreak happens. On the other hand, you could explain the process of getting rid of the pest or problem. Notice that Gray introduces his process in paragraph 7, getting the reader prepared for the upcoming discussion.

F. Devote a section of your essay to each stage of the process you choose to explain. In paragraphs 9, 10, 11, and 12, Gray develops the four stages of the flea life cycle, devoting one paragraph to each stage. You may decide to devote two paragraphs to each stage instead, if you have a lot to say.

G. Close your essay with further warnings about the pest or problem and/or encouragement about dealing with it.

OTHER WRITING IDEAS

1. Write another essay modeled on Gray's, this time explaining a blessing instead of a pest. Bats, ladybugs, garlic, and some types of bacteria and molds, for example, come to mind as desirable natural aids.

2. Describe the life cycle of something that is not really alive: a fad, a turn of speech, a trendy toy, a new technological innovation, a fashion, a television series, a way of thinking, the identity of a group of people (yuppies, groupies, superstars).

3. Identify and explain the stages of an emotional process like falling in love (or falling out of love). You may want to work in a group to come up with emotional processes and ideas about their stages before you write your individual essay.

EDITING SKILLS: CHOOSING *ITS* OR *IT'S*

Look at the uses of the words *it's* and *its* in these sentences from "Flea Facts":

Maybe it's . . . a flea?

OK, it's a period, but if it had suddenly disappeared, the chances are quite good it was a flea.

However, it has no problem moving from one species to another in search of a host if it can't find its favorite.

The adult flea is quite voracious and can consume up to 15 times its body weight in blood a day.

Notice that in the first two instances, the words *it is* can be substituted for *it's*. This substitution would not work in the last two instances. Sometimes *it's* stands for *it has:*

It's been an exciting trip.

You can use the substitution test to see whether you have used the right form. If you have written *it's,* you should be able to read the sentence with *it is* or *it has* instead. *It's* is a contraction, like *don't* for *do not* and *there's* for *there is.*

Its is a possessive, carrying a sense of ownership or belonging:

The whale made its usual noises.

The plan failed due to its flaws.

I liked this novel in spite of its nasty main character.

Many writers are tempted to put an apostrophe in the possessive *its* just because so many other possessives require apostrophes: the professor's book, the whale's noise, the novel's plot. No wonder it's confusing. Try to put the possessive *its* in a mental list with the other possessives *his, hers,* and *ours,* which also have no apostrophes. This mental grouping will help you choose the correct form.

EXERCISE

Fill in the blanks in the following sentences with *its* or *it's.* Be prepared to explain your choices.

1. You proposal has much in _____ favor, but _____ unlikely that the committee will vote for it.
2. _____ an old car, but _____ paint job is new.
3. The dog bit _____ own tail; _____ not an exceptionally smart dog.

Go back over your past writings, and check to see whether you have used the correct form, *its* or *it's.*

PREPARING TO READ

Think of a time when you told a joke or laughed at a movie that no one else thought was funny. Why did you laugh? What makes something funny? Do you think your sense of humor is sometimes weird or unusual?

Cow Tools

GARY LARSON

From 1979 to 1995, Gary Larson's cartoon feature, "The Far Side," was syndicated in hundreds of newspapers across the United States. His quirky, sometimes downright insane sense of humor has earned him a loyal following of readers and admirers, and collections of his previously printed cartoons continue to be published. The following selection is taken from *The Prehistory of the Far Side* (1989), in which Larson looked back at the first ten years of his career and analyzed his work, both his successes and his failures.

TERMS TO RECOGNIZE

quintessentially *(para. 1)*	basically, fundamentally
intrinsically *(para. 1)*	naturally, essentially, built-in
primates *(para. 2)*	an order of animals—including humans, apes, and monkeys—with flexible hands and feet
inevitably *(para. 3)*	bound to happen, unavoidably
artifacts *(para. 4)*	objects made by human work, like tools, weapons, vessels
deciphering *(para. 5)*	figuring out, decoding
mortified *(para. 6)*	ashamed, embarrassed
obtuse *(para. 8)*	difficult to understand
paralytic *(para. 10)*	having paralysis, unable to move or function
constituents *(para. 15)*	group of clients, supporters, fans

Cow tools

the "Cow tools" episode is one that will probably haunt me for the rest of my life. A week after it was published back in 1982, I wanted to crawl into a hole somewhere and die. Cows, as some Far Side readers know, are a favorite subject of mine. I've always found them to be the quintessentially absurd animal for situations even more absurd. Even the name "cow," to me, is intrinsically funny.

And so one day I started thinking back on an anthropology course I had in college and how we learned that man used to be defined as "the only animal that made and shaped tools." Unfortunately, researchers discovered that certain primates and even some bird species did the same thing—so the definition had to be extended somewhat to avoid awkward situations such as someone hiring a crew of chimpanzees to remodel their kitchen.

Inevitably, I began thinking about cows, and what if they, too, were discovered as toolmakers. What would they make? Primitive tools are always, well, primitive-looking—appearing rather nondescript to the lay person. So, it seemed to me, whatever a *cow* would make would have to be even a couple notches further down the "skill-o-meter."

I imagined, and subsequently drew, a cow standing next to her work- 4 bench, proudly displaying her handiwork (hoofiwork?). The "cow tools" were supposed to be just meaningless artifacts—only the cow or a cowthro- pologist is supposed to know what they're used for.

The first mistake I made was in thinking this was funny. The second was 5 making one of the tools resemble a crude handsaw—which made already confused people decide that their only hope in understanding the cartoon meant deciphering what the *other* tools were as well. Of course, they didn't have a chance in hell.

But, for the first time, "Cow tools" awakened me to the fact that my 6 profession was not just an isolated exercise in the corner of my apartment. The day after its release, my phone began to ring with inquiries from reporters and radio stations from regions in the country where The Far Side was published. Everyone, it seemed, wanted to know what in the world this cartoon *meant!* My syndicate was equally bombarded, and I was ultimately asked to write a press release explaining "Cow tools." Someone sent me the front page of one newspaper which, down in one corner, ran the tease, "Cow Tools: What does it mean?" I was mortified.

In the first year or two of drawing The Far Side, I always believed my 7 career perpetually hung by a thread. And this time I was convinced it had been finally severed. Ironically, when the dust had finally settled and as a result of all the "noise" it made, "Cow tools" became more of a boost to The Far Side than anything else.

So, in summary, I drew a really weird, obtuse cartoon that no one under- 8 stood and wasn't funny and therefore I went on to even greater success and recognition.

Yeah—I like this country. 9

Responses to the cartoon:

"The Far Side, a single-panel cartoon by Gary Larson, obviously went 10 too far to the side some time ago and threw great chunks of the populace into paralytic confusion."—Newspaper Columnist, Chicago

"I asked 37 people to explain the 'Cow tools' (cartoon) of last week but 11 with no luck. Could you help?"—Reader, California

"Enclosed is a copy of the 'Cow Tools' cartoon. I have passed it around. 12 I have posted it on the wall. Conservatively, some 40-odd professionals with doctoral degrees in disparate disciplines have examined it. No one understands it. Even my 6-year-old cannot figure it out. . . . We are going bonkers. Please help. What is the meaning of 'Cow Tools'? What is the meaning of life?"—Reader, Texas

"We give up. Being intelligent, hard-working men, we don't often say 13 this, but your cartoon has proven to be beyond any of our intellectual capabilities. Is there some significance to this cartoon that eludes us, or have we been completely foolish in our attempts to unravel the mystery behind 'Cow Tools'?"—Reader, California

"I represent a small band of Fellows from every walk of American Life, 14 who have been drawn together by a need to know, a need to understand and a certain perplexity about what to do with this decade. We are a special interest group under the umbrella organization of The Fellowship of the Unexplained. . . . The Cow Tools Fellows have been brought together by the absolute certainty that your cartoon captioned 'Cow Tools' means something. But, as this letter signifies, just what it might mean has escaped us."— Reader, California

"Allow us to introduce ourselves: two humble and dedicated civil 15 servants who begin every working day with a one-hour review of the funnies. Mister Larson, please write us and let us know the message that this comic drawing is intended to portray. As an artist, you have a professional responsibility to your constituents, especially those whose mental health hinges upon the comic relief provided by your work."—Readers, Alabama

---

RESPONDING TO READING

Do you think the "Cow Tools" cartoon is funny? Look at the other Larson cartoons in this book (p. 33 and p. 211), and describe your reactions. Can you explain why so many people love The Far Side cartoons? Or why others are merely puzzled by them?

GAINING WORD POWER

Larson uses the word "anthropologist," which is made up of a combining form and two suffixes. The combining form *anthro-* means "human," and the first suffix, *-logy*, means a science or study of something. So *anthropology* is the science or study of humans. It's easy to make a word for the person specializing in the science named by the combining form. Just add *-ist* to *-logy* and, after dropping the *y*, you get *anthropologist*. Larson follows this word-building procedure to invent the humorous word *cowthropologist*, which evidently means a person who studies cows.

In your dictionary, look up the meaning of the combining forms that follow. Add *-logist,* and then write a definition of that word, like this:

psycho—mind or mental processes
psychologist—a specialist in the study of human emotional and mental states

1. socio-
2. bio-
3. ethno-
4. cardio-
5. eco-
6. patho-
7. zoo-
8. geo-
9. entomo-
10. meteor-

CONSIDERING CONTENT

1. What inspired Gary Larson to create this particular cartoon?
2. What line of reasoning led Larson to decide that cows would have primitive tools?
3. What mistakes did he make in carrying out his creative plans for the cartoon?
4. At first what did Larson think would happen to his career because of all the fuss over "Cow Tools"? What was ironic about what eventually happened?
5. What did Larson learn about his profession from this experience?
6. Why does Larson say, "Yeah—I like this country"?

CONSIDERING METHOD

1. What effect do the first two sentences create? How is this effect resolved in the end?
2. What organization does Larson follow in presenting his experience?
3. How does Larson tie his points together? What words and phrases act as transitions? Which ones do you think are most effective? (For a discussion of transitions, see pp. 164–65.)
4. Larson invented several new words in this piece: *skill-o-meter, hoofi-work, cowthropologist.* Why did he do that? Find other examples of lively, expressive language in Larson's writing.

5. How does Larson end his portion of this article? Why does he add the responses from some readers? What do the readers' comments tell us about Larson's fans?

WRITING STEP BY STEP

Gary Larson's article explains the process of creating a cartoon and describes what happened to that creation. In this essay, you will describe the steps of something you created that didn't turn out as planned and tell its outcome. Perhaps you devised a scheme or plan that backfired. Or maybe you fouled up a project at work or school.

A. First, think of something you invented, planned, arranged, or came up with. It could be a scheme to get someone to notice you or a surprise birthday party or a weekend trip or a gift that you made for a loved one—something that didn't work out the way you wanted it to.

B. Make a list of steps that went into your creation. Do some freewriting or brainstorming to tap into your memory and bring back all the important details.

C. Begin your essay with a statement that foreshadows the final outcome. Don't give away the ending; just hint at what happened. See the first two sentences in Larson's article.

D. Then sketch in the background of your creation process. Tell what prompted or inspired you to come up with this project.

E. Next, trace the steps of your process, as Larson does in paragraphs 2 through 4 of his essay.

F. Once you've completed explaining the creative process, then describe the aftermath. You might begin by pointing out any mistakes you made, as Larson does in paragraph 5. Why didn't your attempted plan succeed?

G. Give the specific reactions that people had to your creation. Use direct quotations and detailed descriptions to give your readers a feeling of what actually happened. See paragraph 6 of Larson's essay.

H. Draw any conclusions you can from this experience, as Larson does in paragraphs 7 and 8. What, if anything, did you learn from this failed attempt? How do you feel about it now?

I. If you can, write a clincher sentence that leaves your readers with a final thought. You might try to imitate Larson's sentence in paragraph 9: "Yeah—I like this country."

OTHER WRITING IDEAS

1. Write the paper outlined in the previous section, but instead focus on something you did or made that turned out well. Perhaps you assembled a complicated toy or a piece of furniture, or planned a successful party, or lost a good deal of weight.

2. Write a humorous essay in which you explain how *not* to do something: the wrong way to study for a test, the wrong way to impress a first date, the wrong way to make lasagna, and so on.

3. Get together with a group of classmates, and discuss some procedure or process that you would like to change or do away with, such as courting rituals, the first day of class, applying for credit, shopping for groceries (or some other type of shopping), registering for classes, or doing a certain job or chore. Then write an essay explaining the process and giving your objections to it.

EDITING SKILLS: USING COMMAS

Writers put a comma after a word or group of words that comes in front of the main part of the sentence. That main part is called the **independent clause** because it can stand alone as a sentence. Look at these examples from Larson's essay:

> A week after it was published back in 1982, I wanted to crawl into a hole somewhere and die.
>
> Unfortunately, researchers discovered that certain primates and even some bird species did the same thing. . . .
>
> Inevitably, I began thinking about cows. . . .
>
> In the first year or two of drawing The Far Side, I always believed my career perpetually hung by a thread.

The words and groups of words that come before the commas are called **dependent elements:** they cannot stand alone as sentences and are not really necessary to the meaning of the sentences.

Writers also put commas before and after dependent elements when they come in the middle of an independent sentence. Here are some examples from Larson's essay:

> Cows, as some Far Side readers know, are a favorite subject of mine.
>
> Even the name "cow," to me, is intrinsically funny.
>
> I imagined, and subsequently drew, a cow standing next to her workbench. . . .

Everyone, it seemed, wanted to know what in the world this cartoon *meant!*

These dependent elements are called **interrupters:** they break up the flow of the sentence and are not really necessary to the meaning of the sentence.

EXERCISE

In Larson's essay, find three more examples of introductory words or groups of words that are separated from the independent clause by a comma. Then find five more examples of interrupters that are set off by commas.

Now copy these sentences, putting in commas where needed:

1. The rabbit nevertheless does shed fur.
2. Like most people Ralph does not know the name of his Congressional representative.
3. Speaking of travel would you like to go to Seattle next week?
4. Jazz some people believe is America's greatest contribution to the arts.
5. Incidentally you forgot to pay me for your share of the expenses.
6. The result as we have seen is not a pretty one.

Finally, check the essay you have just written to be sure you have used commas to separate dependent elements from the rest of the sentence.

Student Essay Using Process and Directions

A Graceful Stride

Ann Moroney

A common misconception about hurdle races is that the runner "jumps" over the hurdle. This observation is completely false. A hurdle runner does just that-- runs. The hurdler takes long steps, or strides, over the hurdle and sprints on to the next one. As simple as this process may sound, running hurdles is complicated. For one thing, the hurdle itself is thirty-three inches high, which comes to about the hip. "Stepping" over something this high is really quite difficult, as I found out my freshman year in high school. I also had to master a number of other skills to run hurdles efficiently. [1]

The first problem to tackle when it comes to running hurdles is the fear. At every one of my races, I sat in my blocks looking at the line of hurdles in front of me with fear in my heart. No matter how good I became or how long I'd been running, I always felt *fear:* fear that I'd trip over the hurdle and fall on the track, fear that I'd knock the hurdle over in front of everybody, and fear that I'd actually get over the first hurdle with no problem and become a hurdler for four years. Throughout my experience, I found only one way to get over the fear: stop thinking and start running. [2]

The main thing to concentrate on is form. Form is the way the runner carries him or herself over the hurdles. The better the form is, the faster the run will be. Form includes many elements. The runner must coordinate legs, arms, torso, and eyes into a fluid sprint through 10 hurdles on 100 meters of track. [3]

The lead leg, the one to go over the hurdle first, should be slightly bent, but more or less straight in front of the body. The toe should be pointing toward the sky and the heel should line up with the middle of the hurdle. (As my former track coach Ms. Tolefree always said, "Heel to the Gill," referring to the brand name printed directly in the [4]

middle of the hurdle.) Just as the body comes over
the hurdle, the lead leg should snap down to the
ground. The goal is to bring the leg down as close to
the back of the hurdle as possible without actually
hitting it. The sooner the feet are on the ground,
the faster the runner can continue running.

The runner must also concentrate on the trail   5
leg--the one that comes second over the hurdle. The
knee should be bent with the leg at the side, the
thigh parallel to the hurdle. (Imagine sitting on the
ground with one leg bent at the side, mimicking a
frog.) As the lead leg snaps down, the trail leg will
be following over the hurdle. The hip will rotate so
the leg is once again perpendicular to the ground.
The knee should snap up to the chest as close as
possible, as this will help the runner stretch out
the stride. (As Ms. Tolefree was fond of saying,
"Your knee is like the scope on a rifle. It directs
where your stride will go. If your knee is high, your
stride will be long. If it's low, your stride will be
short.") After clearing the hurdle, the runner must
continue striding through the rest of the hurdles.

Another important part of form is arms; they not   6
only keep balance, but they also keep the form tight.
The arm opposite the lead leg is the lead arm. It
should be reaching out in front of the body toward
the toe of the lead leg. The other arm, the one
opposite the trail leg, is the trail arm. It should
come back in a biceps-flexing fashion and stay at the
side until the body is clear of the hurdle. It's
usually a good idea to keep the hands open; a closed
fist takes up energy and tenses the muscles in the
rest of the body.

The final elements of form have to do with small,   7
yet significant mechanics. Air time is a major factor
when running hurdles. The goal is to remain in the
air for as little time as possible; the faster the
feet return to the track, the faster the runner can
continue running. So the body should be as low to the
hurdle as possible without hitting it. Also, the
torso should lean slightly forward--but not bent,
since taking the time to straighten up will slow the

runner down. A slight lean forward will get the
runner over the hurdle and on to the next one. The
final point involves the eyes. Hurdlers should not
look at the hurdle they are about to step over.
Looking further down the track instead of directly in
front of them keeps runners running.

Running hurdles takes time, practice, and 8
commitment. During the split second it takes to clear
a hurdle, the runner must take into account a wide
variety of movements to run the race successfully. A
good, hard practice schedule is the only way to
acquire a productive hurdling technique. And
developing a graceful stride is not as easy as it
looks.

STRATEGIES FOR ANALYZING WHY THINGS HAPPEN

Cause and Effect

Human beings are naturally curious. We all want to know why. Why does the car keep stalling? Why are some people better at math than others? Why does a leaf change color? Why did Lisa Marie Presley marry Michael Jackson? This common human impulse to understand why things happen provides a powerful motive for reading and writing.

THE POINT OF CAUSE-AND-EFFECT WRITING

We study **causes** and their **effects** in order to understand events and solve problems. If we can find out why the car keeps stalling, we can fix it. If we can figure out why some people are good at math, maybe we can help those who aren't. If we know why a leaf changes color, we'll have a greater appreciation for nature and its processes. If we know why Lisa Marie married Michael, we might get on *Oprah*. A lot of the writing done in college courses requires cause–and–effect thinking; students are frequently asked to explain things like the origins of the Russian Revolution, the roots of prejudice, the causes of volcanic eruptions, the effects of hunger on learning, the reasons for Hamlet's delay. The good news about this kind of writing is that it feeds off the natural curiosity of both reader and writer. Inquiring minds want to know why, and you get to tell them.

When you develop an essay by analyzing causes, you are explaining to your readers *why* something happened. If you go on to explore the effects, you are analyzing *what* happened—the consequences. For example, if your topic is divorce and you write "Why Teenage Marriages Fail," that's primarily a cause paper. But if you write "What Divorce Does to Young Children," that's primarily an effect paper. You will probably stick to one purpose in a single essay, but you might take up both causes and effects if you have the time and the assignment allows you to.

THE PRINCIPLES OF CAUSE-AND-EFFECT WRITING

Analyzing cause-effect relationships is one of the primary methods of reasoning. It requires careful thinking and planning.

Types of Causes and Effects

When you think about causes and effects, you need to realize that they can be *immediate* or *remote*. The immediate causes are usually the obvious ones; they occur just before a result appears. An immediate cause for breaking up with your boyfriend might be that he didn't call you last night to tell you he'd be two hours late. But you also know there are deeper, more important reasons for the breakup: like his habit of forgetting to call and his general lack of concern for your feelings. These are the remote causes, the ones further removed from the effect they produce. They are also called *underlying causes* because they are often more difficult to see.

Effects can also be immediate or remote. The immediate effect of failing to get gas is that your car stops running. But the remote effects can stretch out for quite a while: you block traffic and cause an accident; you're late for class and miss an important lecture; you do poorly on the next exam and get a lower grade in the class; your car insurance goes up because of the accident; you have to change majors because you don't have the required grade-point average to be admitted into advanced courses. Remote effects are also called *long-term effects*.

Patterns of Cause and Effect

1. If you want to focus on causes, begin by describing a condition or problem or result (like breaking up with your boyfriend), and then fully explain the causes or reasons (for the breakup). With this approach, you may be able to use chronological order (according to time) if you can trace the causes from the earliest to the most recent. More likely, though, your organization will fall into some logical pattern that reflects the relative importance of the causes: from the least significant to the most critical or from personal reasons to more general ones.

2. If you want to focus on effects, start with some condition or event and explain the consequences. For example, you might begin by describing the breakup with your girlfriend and then go on to show how it affected you. Again, you can present the effects chronologically: at first you

were depressed; then you began to spend more time with your friends; you also had more time to study, so your grades improved; finally, you began to date again and found a much better girlfriend. Or you can arrange the effects according to importance: from a fairly obvious result to the most subtle, from effects on yourself to the effects on other people.

3. Since causes and effects are closely related, you might find that tracing a chain or sequence of events, including both causes and effects, is the best way to approach your topic. In a causal chain the first cause produces an effect, which becomes the cause of the next effect, and so on. In the example about running out of gas, there were two chains. First, running out of gas caused a blocked intersection, which led to an accident, which resulted (some time later) in higher insurance costs. Also, running out of gas caused you to be late and to miss an important lecture, which contributed to a lower grade, which affected your grade-point average, which prevented you from getting into the program, which caused you to change majors. If you decide to describe a chain of causes and effects, be sure to outline it carefully.

THE PITFALLS OF CAUSE-AND-EFFECT WRITING

An explanation of causes and effects won't be successful if your readers find your thinking fuzzy or flawed. Here are some ways to avoid the most common faults of cause-effect reasoning:

1. *Don't mix causes and effects.* When talking informally about why things happen, you may shuttle back and forth between causes and their effects. But in writing, you need to follow a clear pattern: focus on causes, focus on effects, or describe an orderly chain of causes and effects.

2. *Don't settle for obvious causes and immediate effects.* Your explanations will be much more convincing if you look for underlying causes and long-term effects. As Jade Snow Wong shows in her essay in this chapter, her date with a fellow student provided an opportunity to stand up to her parents, but it was not the cause of her rebellion. The "real" causes ran much deeper. It is, of course, possible to go too far back in searching for causes. You'll need to exercise some judgment in deciding which reasons are still valid and relevant.

3. *Don't oversimplify.* Most conditions and events are complex, involving multiple causes and numerous effects. In a short essay, you may have to concentrate on the primary reasons, but be sure to let your readers know that's what you are doing.

4. *Don't omit any key links in a chain of causes and effects.* You don't have to spell out every single step in a sequence of events, but be certain that your readers will be able to follow and make all the right connections themselves.

5. *Don't worry about absolute proof.* In explaining causes and effects, you can't always prove conclusively why something happened. But offer as much evidence as you can to help the reader see the connections that you see. You always need to support your causes and effects with specific details—examples drawn from personal experience, statistics, and statements by experts. You may want to conduct interviews and collect your own information or visit the library to find material on your topic.

WHAT TO LOOK FOR IN CAUSE-AND-EFFECT WRITING

As you read the selections in this chapter, ask yourself these questions:

1. Does the writer focus on causes or effects, or does the essay consider both? Make a list of the causes and/or the effects as you read.
2. Look for the point or purpose of the author's explanation of causes and effects.
3. Decide what kind of causes or effects the author presents—immediate, remote, or both. Does the writer follow a chain of causal relationships?
4. Does the author have a particular audience in mind? How can you tell?
5. What is the tone of the essay? Does the author sound serious, humorous, angry, irritated, sad, regretful, or something else? How does that tone relate to the author's purpose and audience?
6. Notice what writing strategies the author uses to develop the explanations. Take note of examples, descriptions, narratives, comparisons, definitions, and so on.

What appeals of advertising is this cartoon making fun of? Think of some ads that would fit this cartoon.

How is the cartoon making fun of consumers?

What do the man's words tell us about him?

Do you think you're affected by TV ads the way this cartoon humorously suggests?

PREPARING TO READ

Do you tell your parents and your best friends everything? What do you keep to yourself? Is revealing the truth always the best policy?

Ignorance Is Not Bliss

ERIC MARCUS

A graduate of Vassar College and Columbia University, Eric Marcus works as an associate producer for ABC's "Good Morning America." He also publishes articles and book reviews and is the co-author of *Breaking the Surface,* the biography of Olympic diver Greg Louganis. In this selection, which first appeared in the "My Turn" section of *Newsweek* in 1993, Marcus relates the effects of telling his grandmother about his sexual orientation to the "don't ask, don't tell" policy regarding gay people in the U.S. military.

TERMS TO RECOGNIZE

bliss *(title)*	extreme happiness, joy
Sam Nunn *(para. 1)*	Georgia senator and former chair of the Armed Services Committee
policy *(para. 1)*	a plan for making decisions and taking actions
charade *(para. 2)*	a pretense, a disguise, an act
wondrous *(para. 5)*	amazing, astonishing, surprising
exposure *(para. 6)*	the act of being exposed or found out
orientation *(para. 8)*	awareness of and adjustment to one's situation or condition
deceit *(para. 10)*	act or practice of lying or misleading

Sam Nunn didn't need to hold Senate hearings to come up with his "don't ask, don't tell" solution for handling gays in the military. If he'd asked me, I could have told him this was exactly the policy some of my relatives suggested years ago when I informed them that I planned to tell my grandmother that I was gay. They said, "She's old, it'll kill her. You'll destroy her image of you. If she doesn't ask, why tell?" 1

"Don't ask, don't tell" made a lot of sense to these relatives because it sounded like an easy solution. For them, it was. If I didn't say anything to my grandmother, they wouldn't have to deal with her upset over the truth 2 about her grandson. But for me, "not telling" was an exhausting nightmare, because it meant withholding everything that could possibly give me away and living in fear of being found out. At the same time, I didn't want to cause Grandma pain by telling her I was gay, so I was easily persuaded to continue the charade.

If I hadn't been close to my grandmother, or saw her only once a year, 3 hiding the truth would have been relatively easy. But we'd had a special relationship since she cared for me as a child when my mother was ill, and we visited often, so lying to her was especially difficult.

I started hiding the truth from everyone in 1965, when I had my first 4 crush. That was in second grade and his name was Hugh. No one told me, but I knew I shouldn't tell anyone about it, not even Hugh. I don't know how I knew that liking another boy was something to hide, but I did, so I kept it a secret.

I fell in love for the first time when I was 17. It was a wondrous experience, but I didn't dare tell anyone, especially my family, because telling them about Bob would have given me away. I couldn't explain to them that for the first time in my life I felt like a normal human being.

By the time I was an adult, I'd stopped lying to my immediate family, 6 with the exception of my grandmother, and told them I was gay. I was a second-rate liar so I was lucky that Grandma was the only person in my life around whom I had to be something I wasn't. I can't imagine what it's like for gays and lesbians in the military to hide the truth from the men and women with whom they serve. The fear of exposure must be extraordinary, especially because exposure would mean the end of their careers. For me, the only risk was losing Grandma's love.

Hiding the truth from her grew ever more challenging in the years that 7 followed. I couldn't tell her about the man I then shared my life with. I couldn't talk about my friends who had AIDS because she would have wondered why I knew so many ill men. I couldn't tell her that I volunteered for a gay peer-counseling center. I couldn't talk to her about the political issues that most interested me because she would have wondered why I had such passionate feelings about gay rights. Eventually I couldn't even tell her about all of my work, because some of my writing was on gay issues. In the end, all we had left to talk about was the weather.

If being gay were only what I did behind closed doors, there would 8 have been plenty of my life left over to share with my grandmother. But my life as a gay man isn't something that takes place only in the privacy of my bedroom. It affects who my friends are, whom I choose to share my life with, the work I do, the organizations I belong to, the magazines I read, where I vacation and what I talk about. I know it's the same for heterosexuals because their sexual orientation affects everything, from a choice of senior-prom date and the finger on which they wear their wedding band to the birth announcements they send and every emotion they feel.

So the reality of the "don't ask, don't tell" solution for dealing with my grandmother and for dealing with gays in the military means having to lie about or hide almost every aspect of your life. It's not nearly as simple as just not saying, "I'm gay." 9

After years of "protecting" my grandmother I decided it was time to stop lying. In the worst case, I figured she might reject me, although that seemed unlikely. But whatever the outcome, I could not pretend anymore. Some might think that was selfish on my part, but I'd had enough of the "don't tell" policy, which had forced me into a life of deceit. I also hoped that by telling her the truth, we could build a relationship based on honesty, a possibility that was worth the risk. 10

The actual telling was far less terrifying than all the anticipation. While my grandmother cried plenty, my family was wrong, because the truth didn't kill her. In the five years since, Grandma and I have talked a lot about the realities of my life and the lives of my gay and lesbian friends. She's read many articles and a few books, including mine. She's surprised us by how quickly she's set aside her myths and misconceptions. 11

Grandma and I are far closer than we ever were. Last fall we even spent a week together in Paris for her birthday. And these days, we have plenty to talk about, including the gays in the military issue. 12

A few months ago, Grandma traveled with me to Lafayette College, Pa., where I was invited to give a speech on the history of the gay civil-rights movement. After my talk, several students took us to dinner. As I conversed with the young women across the table from me, I overheard my grandmother talking to the student sitting next to her. She told him he was right to tell his parents he was gay, that with time and his help they would adjust. She said, "Don't underestimate their ability to change." 13

I wish Sam Nunn had called my grandmother to testify before his Senate committee. He and the other senators, as well as Defense Secretary Les Aspin and the President, could do far worse than listen to her advice. 14

RESPONDING TO READING

Marcus claims that sexual orientation, whether gay or straight, affects "everything" in a person's life (para. 8). Explore this idea in your journal. Do you think sexual identity influences the choices we make (of friends, work, leisure activities, and so forth)?

GAINING WORD POWER

Marcus uses several words that begin with prefixes. A prefix is a syllable or syllables used at the beginning of a word to change or add to the meaning. For example, *in*complete means "not complete," *re*write means "to write again," *mis*use means "improper or incorrect use," *dis*approve means "to fail or refuse to approve," *mal*adjusted means "poorly or badly adjusted." Examine the following words that come from Marcus's essay, and explain how the prefix changes the meaning of the base word. Try to figure out the meaning on your own first; then look the words up in a dictionary.

*un*likely	*mis*conceptions	*under*estimate
*extra*ordinary	*with*holding	*hetero*sexuals

Now add the indicated prefix to the following words and explain the change in meaning that occurs. Use your dictionary to help you. Here are a couple of examples to get you started:

Add ir- to regular.
New word: irregular
New meaning: not regular

Add with- to draw.
New word: withdraw
New meaning: move or draw back, take back

1. Add non- to sense.
2. Add mis- to understood.
3. Add un- to reliable.
4. Add extra- to sensory.
5. Add dis- to agree.
6. Add under- to rated.
7. Add mal- to practice.
8. Add re- to cycle.

Now try using these eight words in sentences of your own.

CONSIDERING CONTENT

1. Why did the author's relatives want him to hide his sexual identity from his grandmother? Did they really think she would die if he told her?
2. What was the effect on Marcus of having to lie? Why was it exhausting? Why did he find it especially difficult to mislead his grandmother?
3. Marcus says he knew, even in the second grade, that liking another boy was something to hide. How do you suppose he knew that?
4. What does Marcus mean when he says that "for the first time in my life I felt like a normal human being" (para. 5)? How is he using the word *normal?*
5. What reason does Marcus give for finally deciding to tell his grandmother? What positive effect did he hope for? What effects did his revelation have?

6. Marcus says the "actual telling was far less terrifying than all the anticipation." Explain why.
7. What is Marcus's main purpose? Is it to share his personal experience or to comment on the military's "don't ask, don't tell" policy?

CONSIDERING METHOD

1. The title is a variation of the old saying "ignorance is bliss." What does the saying mean? Why does the author change the saying?
2. Why does Marcus include information about his first crush and the first time he fell in love (paras. 4–5)?
3. What details and examples does Marcus include to show the effects of keeping his secret from his grandmother?
4. How many times does Marcus compare his personal dilemma to the situation of gay people in the military? Why does he repeat this comparison?
5. Why does the author include the brief story about his trip to Lafayette College (para. 13)? What is the effect of quoting his grandmother?
6. How does the last paragraph echo the introduction? Would it have been more effective to close with the previous paragraph?

WRITING STEP BY STEP

Write an essay about a time when you were reluctant to reveal something to a family member or a very close friend because you feared a negative reaction. Perhaps it was something you had done, a choice you had made, or an opinion or belief that you felt strongly about.

A. Begin by describing what it is that you were afraid to reveal. Get your readers' attention by including plenty of specific details.
B. Give the reasons for your reluctance to reveal the truth. If other people advised you not to say anything, quote their advice directly, as Marcus does in his opening paragraph.
C. Explain why you wanted to tell this particular person and why you expected a negative response. What effects did you expect your revelation to have? Also describe how you felt about not being able to share your secret with this person.
D. Explain why you decided to reveal your secret, and describe what happened when you did. Was the response what you expected, or did the other person surprise you? Use dialogue to help recreate this scene.

E. Tell how things worked out. Are you still on good terms with this person? Give some supporting evidence, as Marcus does in paragraphs 11 through 13, to show how your relationship was affected by your revelation.

F. Conclude with some comments about how you feel now. Are you glad you revealed your secret? If you had to do it again, would you do the same thing?

OTHER WRITING IDEAS

1. Write an essay about an experience or incident from the past that had a strong effect on you. Perhaps it taught you an important lesson about yourself or changed the way you think about yourself. The experience doesn't have to be a negative one; you can choose an incident that had a positive effect.

2. Think of a prejudice or a belief that offends you. Explain why people think this way and why it offends you.

3. Write an essay about the effects of divorce on children. Gather ideas by talking to friends and classmates who are children of divorced parents.

EDITING SKILLS: DISTINGUISHING
BETWEEN HOMOPHONES

Look at these two sentences from Eric Marcus's essay:

I know it's the same for heterosexuals because their sexual orientation affects everything, from a choice of senior-prom date and the finger on which they *wear* their wedding band. . . .

A few months ago Grandma traveled with me to Lafayette College, Pa., *where* I was invited to give a speech. . . .

Why did Marcus use *wear* in the first sentence but *where* in the second? Words like *wear* and *where,* which have the same pronunciation but different meanings and different spellings, are called **homophones.** There are a lot of these sound-alike words in English, and they cause problems for many writers. The only way to handle homophones is to stay alert for them and double-check their every use when you proofread. It's not just a matter of learning how to spell the words correctly; you also have to match the spelling with the meaning. Keeping a list of the ones that give you trouble will increase your awareness and save you time when you edit. And remember: the spell checker on your computer won't help you with homophones.

EXERCISE

Each of the following words from Marcus's essay has a common homophone. Identify the homophone, and then write sentences that show the difference in meaning between the word Marcus used and its homophone.

1. weather (para. 7)
2. there (para. 8)
3. right (para. 13)
4. would (paras. 3, 5, 7, etc.)
5. knew (paras. 4, 7)
6. for (paras. 1, 2, 3, etc.)
7. week (para. 12)
8. In paragraph 7, Marcus uses the word *then,* and in paragraphs 11 and 12, he uses the word *than.* What is the difference between these two words? Although there is a slight variation in the way these words are pronounced, their sounds are similar enough to cause confusion. Write sentences that show the difference in meaning.

Compare your sentences with a classmate's. Then proofread the essay you have just written, looking for sound-alike words that you may have used incorrectly. If you have time, look back over previous essays for homophone errors; check to see that you're not still making the same ones.

Do you enjoy horror movies? Why do you like to watch them? How do you react when you view them? If you don't enjoy horror movies, can you explain why they do not appeal to you?

Why We Crave Horror Movies

STEPHEN KING

You know Stephen King as the master of terror, the author of a string of best-selling horror novels. And you have probably seen some of the movies made from his novels: *Carrie, Misery, Christine, Pet Sematary,* and *Firestarter* (among others). In the following essay, King offers an entertaining explanation of why people like being scared out of their wits.

TERMS TO RECOGNIZE

grimaces *(para. 1)*	twisted facial expressions
hysterical *(para. 1)*	emotionally uncontrolled
province *(para. 3)*	proper area or sphere
depleted *(para. 3)*	used up, drained, worn out
innately *(para. 4)*	naturally, essentially
reactionary *(para. 4)*	wanting to return to an earlier time
menaced *(para. 6)*	threatened, endangered
voyeur *(para. 6)*	a peeping Tom, someone who enjoys watching something private or forbidden
penchant *(para. 7)*	a strong fondness or inclination
psychic *(para. 7)*	mental, psychological
status quo *(para. 9)*	existing condition or state of affairs
sanctions *(para. 10)*	expressions of disapproval, punishments
anarchistic *(para. 11)*	disorderly, ignoring the rules
morbidity *(para. 12)*	an interest in gruesome and horrible things
subterranean *(para. 12)*	underground

1   think we're all mentally ill; those of us outside the asylums only hide it a little better—and maybe not all that much better, after all. We've all known people who talk to themselves, people who sometimes squinch their faces into horrible grimaces when they believe no one is watching,

people who have some hysterical fear—of snakes, the dark, the tight place, the long drop . . . and, of course, those final worms and grubs that are waiting so patiently underground.

When we pay our four or five bucks and seat ourselves at tenth-row   2
center in a theater showing a horror movie, we are daring the nightmare.

Why? Some of the reasons are simple and obvious. To show that we   3
can, that we are not afraid, that we can ride this roller coaster. Which is not
to say that a really good horror movie may not surprise a scream out of us
at some point, the way we may scream when the roller coaster twists
through a complete 360 or plows through a lake at the bottom of the drop.
And horror movies, like roller coasters, have always been the special
province of the young; by the time one turns 40 or 50, one's appetite for
double twists or 360-degree loops may be considerably depleted.

We also go to re-establish our feelings of essential normality; the horror   4
movie is innately conservative, even reactionary. Freda Jackson as the horrible melting woman in *Die, Monster, Die!* confirms for us that no matter how
far we may be removed from the beauty of a Robert Redford or a Diana
Ross, we are still light-years from true ugliness.

And we go to have fun.   5

Ah, but this is where the ground starts to slope away, isn't it? Because   6
this is a very peculiar sort of fun, indeed. The fun comes from seeing others
menaced—sometimes killed. One critic has suggested that if pro football
has become the voyeur's version of combat, then the horror film has
become the modern version of the public lynching.

It is true that the mythic, "fairy-tale" horror film intends to take away   7
the shades of gray. . . . It urges us to put away our more civilized and adult
penchant for analysis and to become children again, seeing things in pure
blacks and whites. It may be that horror movies provide psychic relief on
this level because this invitation to lapse into simplicity, irrationality and
even outright madness is extended so rarely. We are told we may allow our
emotions a free rein . . . or no rein at all.

If we are all insane, then sanity becomes a matter of degree. If your   8
insanity leads you to carve up women like Jack the Ripper or the Cleveland Torso Murderer, we clap you away in the funny farm (but neither of
those two amateur-night surgeons was ever caught, heh-heh-heh); if, on the
other hand, your insanity leads you only to talk to yourself when you're
under stress or to pick your nose on your morning bus, then you are left
alone to go about your business . . . though it is doubtful that you will ever
be invited to the best parties.

The potential lyncher is in almost all of us (excluding saints, past and   9
present; but then, most saints have been crazy in their own ways), and every

now and then, he has to be let loose to scream and roll around in the grass. Our emotions and our fears form their own body, and we recognize that it demands its own exercise to maintain proper muscle tone. Certain of these emotional muscles are accepted—even exalted—in civilized society; they are, of course, the emotions that tend to maintain the status quo of civilization itself. Love, friendship, loyalty, kindness—these are all the emotions that we applaud, emotions that have been immortalized in the couplets of Hallmark cards and in the verses (I don't dare call it poetry) of Leonard Nimoy.

When we exhibit these emotions, society showers us with positive rein- 10 forcement; we learn this even before we get out of diapers. When, as children, we hug our rotten little puke of a sister and give her a kiss, all the aunts and uncles smile and twit and cry, "Isn't he the sweetest little thing?" Such coveted treats as chocolate-covered graham crackers often follow. But if we deliberately slam the rotten little puke of a sister's fingers in the door, sanctions follow—angry remonstrance from parents, aunts and uncles; instead of a chocolate-covered graham cracker, a spanking.

But anticivilization emotions don't go away, and they demand periodic 11 exercise. We have such "sick" jokes as, "What's the difference between a truckload of bowling balls and a truckload of dead babies?" (You can't unload a truckload of bowling balls with a pitchfork . . . a joke, by the way, that I heard originally from a ten-year-old.) Such a joke may surprise a laugh or a grin out of us even as we recoil, a possibility that confirms the thesis: If we share a brotherhood of man, then we also share an insanity of man. None of which is intended as a defense of either the sick joke or insanity but merely as an explanation of why the best horror films, like the best fairy tales, manage to be reactionary, anarchistic, and revolutionary all at the same time.

The mythic horror movie, like the sick joke, has a dirty job to do. It 12 deliberately appeals to all that is worst in us. It is morbidity unchained, our most base instincts let free, our nastiest fantasies realized . . . and it all happens, fittingly enough, in the dark. For those reasons, good liberals often shy away from horror films. For myself, I like to see the most aggressive of them—*Dawn of the Dead,* for instance—as lifting a trap door in the civilized forebrain and throwing a basket of raw meat to the hungry alligators swimming around in that subterranean river beneath.

Why bother? Because it keeps them from getting out, man. It keeps 13 them down there and me up here. It was Lennon and McCartney who said that all you need is love, and I would agree with that.

As long as you keep the gators fed. 14

RESPONDING TO READING

Do you agree with King that we are all mentally ill and that our "anticivilization emotions don't go away"? Respond to these ideas in your journal.

GAINING WORD POWER

What does it mean to do "a complete 360"? (King uses the expression in para. 3.) You may know that 360 refers to the number of degrees in a circle and that the phrase means to go all the way around to where you started; to travel in a complete circle. One way of expressing the opposite idea is to say you did "an about-face," which is a military command for pivoting around to face in the opposite direction.

Both of these phrases—"a complete 360" and "an about-face"—are figurative expressions; they're supposed to put a picture in our minds by referring to an object (like a circle) or an action (like a military maneuver). Figurative language requires interpretation; we have to figure out the references and imagine the picture that the writer wants to put in our minds. Here are some more figurative phrases that Stephen King uses in his essay. Explain what they mean, and tell what you see in your mind's eye. If you're not sure of what King means, ask other people for their interpretations.

1. "those final worms and grubs that are waiting so patiently underground"
2. "tenth-row center"
3. "shades of gray"
4. "clap you away in the funny farm"
5. "the couplets of Hallmark cards"
6. "before we get out of diapers"
7. "lifting a trap door in the civilized forebrain and throwing a basket of raw meat to the hungry alligators swimming around in that subterranean river beneath"

CONSIDERING CONTENT

1. What does King mean when he says that we are all mentally ill? What is the nature of the "insanity" that we share?
2. What are the obvious reasons for enjoying horror movies? What are some of the not-so-obvious reasons?
3. King talks about "the mythic, 'fairy-tale' horror film." What does he mean? How are horror movies like fairy tales? Do you think this is a good comparison?
4. King refers to our "anticivilization emotions" that occasionally need exercise. What are these emotions? Why do they need to be exercised?

5. According to King, what "dirty job" do sick jokes and horror movies perform? Do you agree with this claim?

6. Do you think Stephen King is biased in his defense of horror movies? Do you think you would respond differently to this essay if it were written by someone you had never heard of?

CONSIDERING METHOD

1. King begins with a startling statement about insanity. What is the effect and point of this opening?

2. How does he maintain the insanity theme throughout the essay? Do you think this is an effective strategy?

3. At what point in the essay does King reveal that he will be dealing with causes?

4. Does King deal with immediate causes or long-term causes or both? In what order does he arrange the causes he discusses?

5. In paragraph 3, King compares watching horror movies to riding a roller coaster. This form of brief comparison is an analogy. What other analogies does King use in his essay? What purpose do they serve?

6. Identify comments or passages that you think are humorous. What does the humor contribute to this essay?

7. What is the function of the two one-sentence paragraphs (paras. 5 and 14)?

WRITING STEP BY STEP

Think of another form of entertainment that people seem to crave, and write an essay explaining why. You might write about soap operas, MTV, video games, action movies, talk shows, court TV, sports programs, jogging (or other exercise activities), bodybuilding, shopping, or the like.

A. Begin with a startling statement, as Stephen King does.

B. Give background about the subject by explaining your opening statement.

C. Discuss the obvious or immediate causes first. Identify at least three reasons and explain them.

D. Then examine the long-term or underlying causes. Show how these causes produce the craving that you are writing about.

E. Be sure to name specific programs, games, or other examples.

F. Use figurative language and analogies to help explain the causes. Even include a little humor the way King does, if you want to.

G. Write a conclusion in which you comment on the behavior you have analyzed. Make your comment an outgrowth of your discussion of underlying causes.

OTHER WRITING IDEAS

1. Interview a variety of people to find out why they like a certain type of entertainment (hospital shows, arcade games, stock car races, line dancing, rock concerts, ballet, situation comedies, or the like). Ask them to give you specific reasons. Then write an essay explaining why this form of entertainment is popular. Use several direct quotations from the people you interview to support your explanations.

2. Conduct an informal survey among your friends and relatives about their favorite junk food: what do they like about it? when do they eat it? how often? Using this information, do some freewriting about why you think people love this kind of food. Then gather your thoughts, and write an essay about either the causes or the effects of eating junk food.

3. Write an essay about the effects of watching too much TV.

EDITING SKILLS: CHECKING PRONOUN REFERENCE

Whenever you use pronouns (words like *he, she, it, his, her, their,* etc., that stand in for nouns), you must be sure that each has a clear antecedent (the noun that the pronoun stands for). If the antecedents aren't clear, your readers can get lost. Look at this sentence from Stephen King's essay:

> We've all known people *who* talk to *themselves,* people *who* sometimes squinch *their* faces into horrible grimaces when *they* believe no one is watching. . . .

The pronouns *themselves, who, their,* and *they* all clearly refer to the antecedent *people.*

Several pronouns are especially troublesome when they appear without specific antecedents: *this, which,* and *these.* King uses these words eleven times. Sometimes he places them right before the nouns they refer to—"this roller coaster," "this level," "this invitation," "these emotions"—so there is no misunderstanding about what they mean. But in other instances, he uses *this, these,* and *which* as free-standing pronouns. Find these other uses (in paras. 3, 6, 9, 10, and 11), and see if you can name the thing or idea to which these pronouns refer. Do you think King has used these pronouns clearly?

EXERCISE

The following sentences are vague because they contain pronouns without clear antecedents. Rewrite each sentence to make it clear.

Example: Clyde made Gary do his homework.
Revisions: Gary did his homework because Clyde made him.
            Gary did Clyde's homework because Clyde made him.

1. Hampton aced the history test because he made it so easy.
2. Carlo is working on the railroad in Tennessee, which depresses him.
3. Kesha dropped out of school after they took away fall break.
4. Our cat chased the ground squirrel until he got tired.
5. Although Juan's mother is a chemist, Juan hates it.
6. Rosa tried to support herself by painting and acting. This was a mistake.
7. Mel blamed his failure on his choice of occupations, which was unfortunate.
8. Washington wore a sombrero and sequined gloves to the prom. This was a big hit.

Now look at the essay you have just written. Pay particular attention to your use of pronouns. Make sure each has a clear antecedent.

PREPARING TO READ

Did your parents ever forbid you to do something that you went ahead and did anyway? What happened? How did you feel about it later?

Fifth Chinese Daughter

JADE SNOW WONG

Jade Snow Wong grew up in San Francisco, the daughter of immigrant parents who brought with them from China an ancient and rigid set of family traditions. The following excerpt from Wong's autobiography, *Fifth Chinese Daughter,* recounts the inevitable conflict between traditional parents and a young woman who is beginning to discover a different world beyond her home and neighborhood.

TERMS TO RECOGNIZE

oblige *(para. 2)*	accommodate, please
adamant *(para. 3)*	unyielding, inflexible
edict *(para. 3)*	command, rule
incurred *(para. 4)*	acquired, taken on
nepotism *(para. 7)*	favoritism shown to relatives
incredulous *(para. 12)*	unwilling to admit or accept what is heard; unbelieving
unfilial *(para. 12)*	disrespectful to parents
revered *(para. 12)*	honored, respected
innuendos *(para. 14)*	sly suggestions, indirect hints
devastated *(para. 15)*	crushed, overwhelmed
perplexed *(para. 16)*	puzzled, confused

by the time I was graduating from high school, my parents had done their best to produce an intelligent, obedient daughter, who would know more than the average Chinatown girl and should do better than average at a conventional job, her earnings brought home in repayment for their years of child support. Then, they hoped, she would marry a nice Chinese boy and make him a good wife, as well as an above-average mother for his children. Chinese custom used to decree that families should "introduce" chosen partners to each other's children. The groom's family should pay handsomely to the bride's family for rearing a well-bred

1

daughter. They should also pay all bills for a glorious wedding banquet for several hundred guests. Their daughter belonged to the groom's family and must henceforth seek permission from all persons in his home before returning to her parents for a visit.

But having been set upon a new path, I did not oblige my parents with the expected conventional ending. At fifteen, I had moved away from home to work for room and board and a salary of twenty dollars per month. Having found that I could subsist independently, I thought it regrettable to terminate my education. Upon graduating from high school at the age of sixteen, I asked my parents to assist me in college expenses. I pleaded with my father, for his years of encouraging me to be above mediocrity in both Chinese and American studies had made me wish for some undefined but brighter future. 2

My father was briefly adamant. He must conserve his resources for my oldest brother's medical training. Though I desired to continue on an above-average course, his material means were insufficient to support that ambition. He added that if I had the talent, I could provide for my own college education. When he had spoken, no discussion was expected. After this edict, no daughter questioned. 3

But this matter involved my whole future—it was not simply asking for permission to go to a night church meeting (forbidden also). Though for years I had accepted the authority of the one I honored most, his decision that night embittered me as nothing ever had. My oldest brother had so many privileges, had incurred unusual expenses for luxuries which were taken for granted as his birthright, yet these were part of a system I had accepted. Now I suddenly wondered at my father's interpretation of the Christian code: was it intended to discriminate against a girl after all, or was it simply convenient for my father's economics and cultural prejudice? Did a daughter have any right to expect more than a fate of obedience, according to the old Chinese standard? As long as I could remember, I had been told that a female followed three men during her lifetime: as a girl, her father; as a wife, her husband; as an old woman, her son. 4

My indignation mounted against that tradition and I decided then that my past could not determine my future. I knew that more education would prepare me for a different expectation than my other female schoolmates, few of whom were to complete a college degree. I, too, had my father's unshakable faith in the justice of God, and I shared his unconcern with popular opinion. 5

So I decided to enter junior college, now San Francisco's City College, because the fees were lowest. I lived at home and supported myself with an after-school job which required long hours of housework and cooking but paid me twenty dollars per month, of which I saved as much as possible. 6

The thrills derived from reading and learning, in ways ranging from chemistry experiments to English compositions, from considering new ideas of sociology to the logic of Latin, convinced me that I had made a correct choice. I was kept in a state of perpetual mental excitement by new Western subjects and concepts and did not mind long hours of work and study. I also made new friends, which led to another painful incident with my parents, who had heretofore discouraged even girlhood friendships.

The college subject which had most jolted me was sociology. The 7 instructor fired my mind with his interpretation of family relationships. As he explained to our class, it used to be an economic asset for American farming families to be large, since children were useful to perform agricultural chores. But this situation no longer applied and children should be regarded as individuals with their own rights. Unquestioning obedience should be replaced with parental understanding. So at sixteen, discontented as I was with my parents' apparent indifference to me, those words of my sociology professor gave voice to my sentiments. How old-fashioned was the dead-end attitude of my parents! How ignorant they were of modern thought and progress! The family unit had been China's strength for centuries, but it had also been her weakness, for corruption, nepotism, and greed were all justified in the name of the family's welfare. My new ideas festered; I longed to release them.

One afternoon on a Saturday, which was normally occupied with my 8 housework job, I was unexpectedly released by my employer, who was departing for a country weekend. It was a rare joy to have free time and I wanted to enjoy myself for a change. There had been a Chinese-American boy who shared some classes with me. Sometimes we had found each other walking to the same 8:00 A.M. class. He was not a special boyfriend, but I had enjoyed talking to him and had confided in him some of my problems. Impulsively, I telephoned him. I knew I must be breaking rules, and I felt shy and scared. At the same time, I was excited at this newly found forwardness, with nothing more purposeful than to suggest another walk together.

He understood my awkwardness and shared my anticipation. He asked 9 me to "dress up" for my first movie date. My clothes were limited but I changed to look more graceful in silk stockings and found a bright ribbon for my long black hair. Daddy watched, catching my mood, observing the dashing preparations. He asked me where I was going without his permission and with whom.

I refused to answer him. I thought of my rights! I thought he surely 10 would not try to understand. Thereupon Daddy thundered his displeasure and forbade my departure.

I found a new courage as I heard my voice announce calmly that I was   11
no longer a child, and if I could work my way through college, I would
choose my own friends. It was my right as a person.

My mother had heard the commotion and joined my father to face me;   12
both appeared shocked and incredulous. Daddy at once demanded the
source of this unfilial, non-Chinese theory. And when I quoted my college
professor, reminding him that he had always felt teachers should be revered,
my father denounced that professor as a foreigner who was disregarding the
superiority of our Chinese culture, with its sound family strength. My
father did not spare me; I was condemned as an ingrate for echoing dishon-
orable opinions which should only be temporary whims, yet nonetheless
inexcusable.

The scene was not yet over. I completed my proclamation to my father,   13
who had never allowed me to learn how to dance, by adding that I was
attending a movie, unchaperoned, with a boy I met at college.

My startled father was sure that my reputation would be subject to whis-   14
pered innuendos. I must be bent on disgracing the family name; I was ruining my future, for surely I would yield to temptation. My mother
underscored him by saying that I hadn't any notion of the problems
endured by parents of a young girl.

I would not give in. I reminded them that they and I were not in China,   15
that I wasn't going out with just anybody but someone I trusted! Daddy
gave a roar that no man could be trusted, but I devastated them in declaring that I wished the freedom to find my own answers.

Both parents were thoroughly angered, scolded me for being shameless,   16
and predicted that I would some day tell them I was wrong. But I dimly
perceived that they were conceding defeat and were perplexed at this
breakdown of their training. I was too old to beat and too bold to intimidate.

RESPONDING TO READING

Has college affected you in the same way that it affected Jade Snow
Wong? Write in your journal about the effects college has had on you;
compare your reactions to Wong's.

GAINING WORD POWER

Come up with definitions of your own for the italicized words in the
following sentences. Use the clues from the surrounding words and
sentences to help you. Then check your definition against a dictionary definition.

1. "Chinese custom used to *decree* that families should 'introduce' chosen partners to each other's children." (para. 1)
2. "Having found that I could *subsist* independently, I thought it regrettable to *terminate* my education." (para. 2)
3. "I pleaded with my father, for his years of encouraging me to be above *mediocrity* in both Chinese and American studies had made me wish for some undefined and brighter future." (para. 2)
4. "My *indignation* mounted against that tradition and I decided then that my past could not determine my future." (para. 5)
5. "I was kept in a state of *perpetual* mental excitement by new Western subjects and concepts and did not mind long hours of work and study." (para. 6)
6. "My new ideas *festered;* I longed to release them." (para. 7)
7. "He was not a special boyfriend, but I had enjoyed talking to him and had *confided* in him some of my problems. *Impulsively,* I telephoned him. I knew I must be breaking rules, and I felt shy and scared." (para. 8)
8. "I was too old to beat and too bold to *intimidate.*" (para. 16)

CONSIDERING CONTENT

1. What did you learn about Wong's parents and their traditional beliefs in the first paragraph?
2. What caused Wong to rebel against her parents? What situations and experiences contributed to her quest for independence?
3. Why was Wong sure that more education would prepare her for a different future from her classmates'? Did it?
4. Why did the sociology course affect Wong so strongly? What did she learn in that course that changed her views and fed her rebellion?
5. What action did Wong take to demonstrate her independence? Why did she choose this particular way of disobeying her parents? Do her actions seem risky and rebellious to you?
6. In what ways was Wong a lot like her father? Which of his beliefs and attitudes actually contributed to his daughter's rebellion?
7. Wong writes that her parents "were perplexed at this breakdown of their training" (para. 16). What didn't they understand? Did their cultural background cause their lack of understanding, or do all parents face this same problem?

CONSIDERING METHOD

1. Why is the first paragraph important? How does the information in this paragraph prepare you for Wong's actions?

2. What does Wong accomplish by mentioning her oldest brother? What is she trying to show?

3. What is the function of the questions in paragraph 4? Why does Wong express these ideas in questions instead of in statements? (See p. 127 for an explanation of rhetorical questions.)

4. How much time passes in this selection? How does Wong indicate the passage of time? Where does she move back in time? Why does she do so?

5. Find sentences or comments that reveal that Wong has positive feelings for her father. Why is it important to include these feelings?

6. Paragraph 8 opens with these words: "One afternoon on a Saturday . . ." What do these words signal? What mode of writing begins at this point?

7. Wong doesn't use direct quotations or quoted conversation. How does she report what she said to her parents and what they said to her? What is the effect of this indirect presentation?

8. How would you describe the tone of this selection? Does Wong sound angry, sad, upset, calm, confident, relieved, happy, or what?

WRITING STEP BY STEP

As we grow older, we sometimes change our minds about our parents. We begin to see things more from their point of view. Think of a piece of advice, a household rule, or a parental opinion that you used to hate but now understand. If you don't want to write about your parents, think of another adult, like a teacher or a coach, who set down rules or gave advice that you once rejected but now think appropriate. Write an essay in which you explain what caused you to change your mind.

A. Begin with a statement of your general point. You might say something like "I used to think my parents' advice was outdated and pointless, but a lot of it makes sense to me today" or "Now that I'm coaching pee-wee soccer, I follow some of the same rules I used to hate when I was a player."

B. Explain the particular rule, opinion, advice, or guideline you used to resist. Re-create specific incidents and arguments you used to have that illustrate your earlier response.

C. Analyze your change in attitude. Cite specific reasons or causes, and explain them.

D. If there was a key incident or turning point in your thinking, focus on that event and describe it in detail.

E. Conclude by revealing how you feel about this change in thinking. Does it mean that you've grown up or that you've sold out?

OTHER WRITING IDEAS

1. Explain why some jobs or professions seem to be done mainly by women (like child care, housework, nursing, and elementary school teaching). As you plan your paper, talk to some women who do these jobs or who are preparing to enter one of these professions, and ask their opinions. Also talk to some men, and ask them how they would feel about teaching grade school, being a nurse, cleaning houses, or taking care of children for a living.

2. Write an essay about why adolescents leave home. Or write an essay about the effects of their leaving home.

3. Talk to someone who comes from a cultural background different from yours. If you can, spend some time with this person's friends and family. Then, with your classmates as audience, write an essay explaining what you learned about this culture and how it affected your attitudes toward these people.

EDITING SKILLS: USING PARALLEL STRUCTURE

Look at these last two sentences from paragraph 3 in Wong's essay:

When he had spoken, no discussion was expected.

After his edict, no daughter questioned.

When you look at the sentences like this, with one on top of the other, you can see how they match up in size and form. This correspondence is called **parallelism,** or **parallel structure.** Parallel structure often occurs within a sentence, as the following sentences from Wong's essay show. (The parallel parts are in italics.)

As long as I could remember, I had been told that a female followed three men during her lifetime: *as a girl, her father; as a wife, her husband; as an old woman, her son.*

I was *too old to beat* and *too bold to intimidate.*

Writers use parallel structure to catch the reader's attention and, as Wong does, to compare or contrast important points. Parallel structures also add emphasis and variety to a sentence or paragraph.

EXERCISE

Copy two of the sentences quoted in the previous section; then write two or three sentences of your own that imitate Wong's use of parallel structure. Then examine the following sentences, and write your own sentences that imitate the parallel structures:

1. "This freedom, like all freedoms, has its dangers and its responsibilities." —James Baldwin

   Imitation: This new attendance policy, like all school policies, has its supporters and its critics.

2. "We must stop talking about the American dream and start listening to the dreams of Americans." —Reubin Askew

   Imitation: We must stop asking silly questions and start questioning silly policies.

Look over your own essay and revise two or three sentences, using parallel structure. Read the new sentences aloud. If they sound clear and effective, keep them in your essay.

PREPARING TO READ

Have you ever had a job where you were unappreciated? If so, write a paragraph in your journal telling how you felt about your employer. If you've never been unhappily employed, write a paragraph telling how you felt about an employer who valued your services and treated you well.

Working: Nobody Talks about the Common Person's Life

STEVE LOPEZ

Steve Lopez is a columnist for the *Philadelphia Inquirer*. The following article, syndicated by the Knight-Ridder/Tribune News Service, appeared in a number of newspapers around the country in August of 1996. Lopez tells about his father's employment experiences to support his criticism of the way working-class people are treated by the bosses of America. The very short paragraphs tell you that the piece was first printed in narrow columns.

TERMS TO RECOGNIZE

grievance *(para. 9)*	formal complaint of unfair treatment
ecstasy *(para. 11)*	intense pleasure, delight
CEOs *(para. 21)*	Chief Executive Officers
blather *(para. 30)*	foolish talk, nonsense

The older I get, the more I realize my attitudes about work come from my father.   1

Almost 70 and still working part-time, my father has survived a half-century of being laid off, fired, downsized, taken for granted and blamed for problems that weren't his doing.   2

Through it all, he has put on his pants each morning and found a way to earn a buck.   3

I've been thinking about this lately because of the presidential campaign and all the stories about the economy, job security and welfare.   4

I've been thinking about it because my father's experience reminds me how out of touch the average politician is with people who work for a living, or try to.   5

My father's parents ran a mom-and-pop grocery store in the small town 6
where he grew up, and he spent his childhood working in the store. My
mother did the same at her family's grocery store four blocks away.

Tony Lopez became a star athlete in high school; Grace Costanza Nuzzo 7
was a cheerleader. Fifty years later, they are still together.

When my older sister was born, my father drove a milk truck. But by 8
the time I came into the world, he had been fired for taking a day off he
had earned with overtime.

The Teamsters union stepped in, and my father eventually won his griev- 9
ance. But by then, the union had helped him find another job. Now he
drove a truck for Wonder Bread.

As a boy, I thought that was the next-best job to playing centerfield for 10
the Giants. The truck carried more than just bread. My father delivered
Hostess cakes, too.

Sometimes he'd come home for lunch and let me inspect his cargo, but 11
I couldn't touch and I couldn't eat. It was ecstasy and torture, and to this
day, I have a weakness for anything fresh and sweet.

When I was 10 or 11, my father's job was on the line. I didn't know all 12
the details then. I only knew, for the first time in my life, that nothing
could be trusted.

If a store wasn't moving bread and cake, the boss said it was my father's 13
fault. If an order got screwed up at the warehouse, it was his fault. They
were laying everything on him.

He was under enormous pressure and it walked in the door with him 14
each night filling his face with shadows, and we ate dinner in silence.

One morning he threw his back out and collapsed on the floor, but he 15
was afraid to miss a day of work.

He told my mother to run a hot shower, and he dragged himself into 16
it and ran water on his back and put on his clothes and went to work.

In the end, he lost the job. His boss's son wanted to drive a truck, it 17
turned out; and to clear the way, they fired the man with the least senior-
ity. They fired my father.

The Teamsters took up the grievance and my father won, again. But he 18
knew his bosses would make his life hell so he took another job, and
another, and another. Foster's muffins. Cloverleaf milk. Blue Seal bread.
Dolly Madison cakes.

In the late '60s he caught on with a candy and tobacco distributor. Six 19
years ago sitting on healthy profits, that company won a 28 percent salary
and benefits giveback from the union by spreading fear. They had just busted
another division, turned employees out and replaced them at lower salaries.

Modern Business 101. 20

These are the economics I know. The economics of greed at the top 21
and of hard work and lousy pay at the bottom. The economics of million-
dollar bonuses for CEOs who turn employees onto the streets.

The rich get richer, my father always says; the little guy gets it in the 22
neck, and the man in the middle pays.

In some ways, my father was lucky. He had to hustle in his time, but 23
unlike today's market, there were plenty of jobs for unskilled, uneducated
people. The unions were strong and although the pay didn't put you in a
Cadillac, you got by.

Go to college, he always told us. Go to college so you don't end up like 24
your old man. But for all his warnings, I ended up a lot like my father.

I have his contempt for anyone who expects a free pass and his compas- 25
sion for anyone who's trying to make it without one. Like him, I trust
nobody associated with money, politics or authority.

Week in and week out, some doofus in a suit and a smile stands up 26
and tells us the economy is in great shape, and it always raises a question
for me.

Do they ever get outside? 27

We have the highest child poverty rate in the industrial world, and the 28
bottom is falling out for people by the millions who came up the way my
family came up.

And as it gets harder down there, the talk from on high gets meaner. 29
They tell you that if you're not working today, you're a louse. Period.

Like my father, I tune out that blather the same way I tune out the 30
notion that the issue of our time is abortion, or terrorism, or taxes.

It is none of those. 31

The challenge of our time, as we head toward the election that takes us 32
into the next century, isn't even being discussed. No one is talking about
how to educate, train, and employ those who have fallen behind or never
even got started.

The issue is the fate of the common, ordinary working person, who has 33
been written out of the book of American politics.

RESPONDING TO READING

What do you think about the current trend to downsize the workforce
in order to improve corporate profits? Do you know anybody like Lopez's
father who has lost a job despite good work performance? Do you agree
with Lopez that this practice is wrong? Or do you think employers have
the right to get rid of anybody they choose to fire?

GAINING WORD POWER

Explain as thoroughly as you can what the following phrases mean in Lopez's essay.

1. mom-and-pop grocery store (para. 6)
2. on the line (para. 12)
3. filling his face with shadows (para. 14)
4. caught on with (para. 19)
5. busted another division (para. 19)
6. put you in a Cadillac (para. 23)
7. a free pass (para. 25)
8. some doofus in a suit (para. 26)
9. the bottom is falling out (para. 28)
10. the book of American politics (para. 33)

CONSIDERING CONTENT

1. Why does Lopez think that the average politician is "out of touch" with working people (para. 5)?
2. What were some of the reasons that Lopez's father repeatedly lost his job?
3. Why did Lopez, as a child, like having his father work for Wonder Bread?
4. Explain as completely as you can the meaning of "Modern Business 101" (para. 20).
5. What advice did Lopez's father always give his children (para. 24)? Do you think it's good advice?
6. What economic problems does Lopez point out in paragraphs 28 and 29? What does he see as the cause of these problems?
7. What does Lopez think is the "challenge of our time," a crucial need that "isn't even being discussed" (para. 32)? Why do you suppose politicians are not discussing this issue?

CONSIDERING METHOD

1. Does this article move from causes to effects or from effects to causes? What makes this structure more effective than the reverse?
2. Why does Lopez include the details about the early lives of his father and mother in paragraphs 6 and 7?
3. What is the purpose of the brief narrative in paragraphs 15 and 16?
4. Why is the phrase "Modern Business 101" set off as a complete paragraph (para. 20)?

5. Why do you think the word "Period" is punctuated as a complete sentence at the end of paragraph 29? What does it mean?

6. What is the author's *tone* (that is, Lopez's attitude toward what he's writing about)? Is it neutral or do you detect an element of resentment or anger? Locate specific details—words and sentences—that convey the tone.

WRITING STEP BY STEP

Think of an event that touched your life forcefully enough that you can describe its effects on you. You need to choose an event with causes you understand well enough to analyze or at least to speculate about. Then write an essay exploring your difficulty, whatever it was or is—a serious accident or illness, your parents' divorce, a date rape, high school drug addiction, an unwanted pregnancy, an incident involving racial prejudice or sexual harassment. (If your life has been blessedly free from trauma and upsets, select a topic from the first "Other Writing Ideas.")

A. Begin with the effects of this traumatic event on your life, the way Lopez describes the effects of his father's employment insecurity in the first half of his essay. Include specific details when you can (like the Hostess cakes, his father's bad back, the hot shower).

B. Make a transition similar to the one Lopez uses in the opening sentence of paragraph 23: "In some ways, my father was lucky."

C. Then discuss the causes, as you understand them, of your problem, the way Lopez presents the underlying economic causes of his father's off-and-on employment.

D. If you can come up with a solution to your problem, present that next, as Lopez does in paragraph 32, when he mentions that "No one is talking about how to educate, train, and employ those who have fallen behind or never even got started."

E. Conclude with a call for action, as Lopez does in his final sentence. By declaring that "the fate of the common, ordinary working person . . . has been written out of the book of American politics," he is, in effect, issuing a challenge to right-minded people to take note of this injustice and to see about correcting it.

OTHER WRITING IDEAS

1. Think of some habit you have or an activity you engage in that you would like to quit, like smoking cigarettes, being late all the time, eating junk food, watching soap operas, or reading *The National Enquirer*. Following the step-by-step instructions above,

write an account of how the activity affects you; then discuss the causes of the habit; finally, explain your plan to stop. Your concluding sentence will be your resolution to follow through in beating the habit.

2. Select a magazine advertisement and analyze the reasons for its appeal. Submit the ad (or a photocopy) along with your essay.

3. Brainstorm a list of causes for some problem you are facing, such as paying your bills, getting all your work done, dealing with a difficult friend or teacher, or sticking to your diet. Organize the list into immediate and long-term causes. Write an essay analyzing the causes of your problem and concluding with your solution.

EDITING SKILLS: ELIMINATING WORDINESS

A good writer would never write only short, simple sentences, but a good clean sentence is better than a wordy, cluttered one. Look at these spare sentences from Lopez's essay:

Fifty years later, they are still together.

They fired my father.

These are the economics I know.

Go to college, he always told us.

A less skillful writer might have used a lot more words to say the same thing, like this:

Through thick and thin, through hard times and good times, through better and worse, for half a century they have stayed married to each other.

With no thought that his self-esteem might be hurt or damaged or that his family might suffer hardship, they ended my father's term of employment.

These are the unfair and unjust economic realities operating in America as I have been able to observe them so far in my lifetime.

You can better yourselves financially and intellectually and improve your prospects in life by going to college, he repeatedly advised us.

There's nothing actually wrong with those sentences except what English teachers call *verbiage* and everybody else calls *wordiness*. Be careful not to say the same thing twice ("hurt or damaged," "unfair and unjust," "so far in my lifetime"). And avoid these common expressions:

WORDY	CONCISE
tall in height	tall
past history	history
blue in color	blue
advance forward	advance
expensive in price	expensive
consensus of opinion	consensus
continue to remain	remain
join together	join
few in number	few
positive benefits	benefits
at this point in time	at this time

Now go through your final draft one more time looking only for verbal clutter. Then, in the words of Mark Twain, "When in doubt, leave it out."

Student Essay Analyzing Causes

Soap Operas: Entertainment for Everyone

Amelia Doggett

I have watched soap operas for as long as I can   1
remember. Even now that I'm a full-time college
student with a part-time job, I still find time to
tape and watch *All My Children* and *General Hospital*.
It has been a tradition in my family since the dawn
of soaps. My mother is a cook, but she always makes
time for her soaps. Her mother, my grandmother, is a
housekeeper who schedules her breaks during her
favorite soaps. Even her mother, my great-grandmother,
still watches her soaps. She has found time for them
since they began on radio. While maintaining her
house, working in the fields, and raising eight
children, she never missed an important daytime
moment.

For over fifty years, people have been tuning in   2
for a daily dose of daytime drama. People all over
the world seem to love soap operas. There are
currently eleven daytime soaps on the air in the
United States. Men and women, young and old alike,
enjoy watching this form of entertainment for a
variety of reasons.

The prevailing stereotype of a typical soap   3
viewer is a housewife with nothing better to do than
sit in front of the television all day eating bon-
bons. That image, however, couldn't be further from
the truth. People from all walks of life watch
daytime dramas. Busy college students and career women
set their VCRs every day to catch their shows.
Working men watch them too. My Uncle Randy rushes
home from his job every day just to catch *All My
Children* on his lunch break. Age doesn't seem to be a
factor either. High school students gather in study
halls to discuss what's happening on their soaps.
Elderly people who have watched shows since their
beginning are still viewers. My two grandmas live
together, which unfortunately means they have to view
their shows together. They spend hours arguing about

what's going to happen next. As a matter of fact, none of the soap opera fans I know are housewives, have a lot of spare time, or eat bon-bons.

Beyond my family, millions of people faithfully tape and watch soap operas. One reason is for the temporary escape they provide. As my mother says, "No matter how lousy your life is at the moment, you know you can turn on the TV and see people whose lives are much, much worse." Soap opera characters are always in such turmoil that it's easy to forget your own problems while watching them, even if it is for only an hour or so a day. 4

Another reason people watch their soap operas so regularly is the attachment to the characters. Soap viewers share weddings, funerals, births, high moments, low moments, and all of the special little times in these characters' lives. Soap viewers invite these people into their homes every day and get to know the personalities, backgrounds, and intimate feelings of each character. Some viewers know the fictional people on their soaps better than they know some of their own family members. 5

Many people watch soap operas for the different kinds of entertainment they provide. On some days, soap operas take their characters on wild adventures full of action and intrigue. Other days are full of lighthearted, romantic plots, and sometimes soaps show the silly side of life, giving viewers a chance to laugh a little. Then there are the times a soap opera shows the harsher, heart-wrenching realities of life. Viewers are educated about the realities of AIDS, cancer, organ transplants, and drunk driving. On the best days, a soap opera manages to combine all of these forms of entertainment--action, humor, romance, and heartbreak. 6

Although sometimes the story lines test the limits of believability, for the most part soap operas are entertaining, educating shows. There are many valid reasons why people watch them, and there are all sorts of people who enjoy them. These folks aren't uneducated, unemployed slobs--they are ordinary people. 7

STRATEGIES FOR INFLUENCING OTHERS

Argument and Persuasion

"Thinking," said educator John Dewey, "is a problem-solving activity." It's a good thing, too, because we don't have to look very far to find problems to think about. People are suing one another, homelessness is increasing, health care is too expensive, children are taking guns to school, politicians are self-serving, sports have been tarnished by drugs and money, violence against women continues, and the VCR still doesn't work right. If you decide to write about a controversy or problem, you will have plenty of subjects to choose from.

THE POINT OF ARGUMENT AND PERSUASION

Your purpose in this type of writing is to encourage the readers to accept your point of view, solution, plan, or complaint as their own. Traditionally, the word **persuasion** refers to attempts to sway the readers' emotions, while the word **argument** refers to tactics that address the readers' logic. Most convincing writing today mixes the two types of appeal. A personal testimony from a paraplegic accident victim pleading with readers to use their seat belts persuades through emotional identification. A list of statistics concerning injury rates before and after seatbelt laws went into effect argues the point through rationality. A combination of the two tactics would probably be quite effective. In everyday language, *persuasion* means influence over the audience, whether emotional or rational.

THE PRINCIPLES OF ARGUMENT AND PERSUASION

Presenting a conventional persuasive essay involves five tasks.

1. *State the issue your essay will address, and put it in a context.* Why is it controversial or problematic? Why do people care about it? Why do people disagree about it?
2. *State your main point or thesis.* What point of view, solution, or stance do you wish the readers to adopt?
3. *Provide well-developed evidence on your own side of the issue.* You can develop your point through facts, statistics, examples, testimony of experts, and logical reasoning (cause and effect, analogy), just to name a few strategies. This is the longest part of a conventional argument, and each piece of evidence will probably take a paragraph or more to develop.
4. *Respond to opposing viewpoints.* This is called the **refutation** section. Especially when arguments against your own are widely known, you need to acknowledge them and deal with them, or your essay will have an obvious hole in it. You might minimize their importance, demonstrate that they are not logical or factual, or offer alternative ways of thinking about them.
5. *Close by reminding your reader of your main point and the strength of your evidence.* Many persuasive essays include a call to action, encouraging the reader to do something in support of your cause.

Writers often alter this conventional plan, especially tasks 3 and 4. For example, in this chapter, "The Case for Cloning" focuses on refutation, countering popular fears about cloning, one by one. "Why Prisons Don't Work" begins with refutation, followed by the evidence on the writer's side, instead of the other way around. "A Crime of Compassion" gives the most space to the moving personal story of an expert on the topic of euthanasia. You can tailor your essay to fit your topic, audience, purpose, and the nature of your evidence.

THE PITFALLS OF ARGUMENT AND PERSUASION

If you follow the plan outlined previously, you should be able to write a convincing essay. But there are some risks to be aware of in this kind of writing.

Taking on Too Much

Narrowing your topic is always a good idea, but it's especially important in argumentation. You won't be able to write a sensible essay on

"What's Wrong with the American Economy." Select a more manageable problem, like unemployment or unbridled greed. Even those problems are probably too broad to cover in a short essay. Always consider moving the issue closer to home. For example, if someone in your family has been unemployed, you are probably equipped to write about the psychological effects of unemployment on the individual. If you have found yourself in terrifying and unnecessary credit card debt, you can probably write persuasively about uncontrolled consumerism. In these cases, you have *credibility* to discuss the issue. Credibility is an important part of your appeal, and you will notice that each author in this chapter establishes the right to claim knowledge about his or her subject, either explicitly or implicitly.

Mistaking the Audience

The readers you most want to reach with a controversial essay are the ones in the middle—those who are undecided and might be swayed by your ideas. People with extreme opinions on either side are likely to be unmovable. Even with persuadable audiences, you must expect some resistance. Be sure your tone does not bolster this resistance by being insulting or condescending. The voice of sweet reason and a "we're in this together" attitude invite your readers to agree with you.

Logical Fallacies

Flaws in reasoning can undermine your cause and harm your credibility. Be sure that you are not guilty of these common logical fallacies:

1. *Overgeneralization.* Recently, a national survey found that the number of unmarried women among highly educated people was much larger than among the less educated. Articles on the alarming shortage of men willing to marry educated females abounded, and solutions to the difficulty were proposed. Actually, most of the single educated females had chosen their unmarried status. The problem was the false generalization that all unmarried women *wanted* husbands and were seeking them. The shortage of marriage-minded men was not proven.

2. *Either-or thinking.* Be sure that you don't present only two alternatives when more exist. For example, some writers in education want us to believe that either we set national standards for mathematical achievement, or our children will continue to fall behind other countries' children in math skills. The fallacy is that national standards are not the only route to high math achievement: smaller classes, better teaching conditions, early intervention policies, and parent involvement are just a few ideas left out

of the either-or reasoning. (In fact, the existence of national standards is not correlated with math achievement internationally.)

3. *False analogy.* Analogy is a compelling form of argument, but you must take care that the two cases you compare are really similar. If you argue that your college should imitate a successful general education program used at another university, you must be sure that the two institutions have similar students, faculty, goals, and organizational structures. Otherwise, adopting a plan that works for someone else could be disastrous. Recently, a U.S. congressman claimed that foreign dignitaries, while in our country, should say the Pledge of Allegiance because, similarly, we show respect at the Olympics when other countries' national anthems are played. The analogy falls apart when you consider what the Pledge of Allegiance actually *says.*

4. *Faulty claims about causation.* Remember that two things that occur closely in time or one after the other are not necessarily causally related. In our cities, ice cream sales and murder rates both increase in the summer; can we say that eating ice cream causes aggression? No, probably it's the heat that encourages both. We say "children who are hugged are more likely to be nice," and "children who are beaten are more likely to be unpleasant." But the causes and effects could be the other way around. Maybe nice children are hugged *because* they're nice, and unpleasant children get beaten *because* they're unpleasant.

WHAT TO LOOK FOR IN ARGUMENT AND PERSUASION

Here are some guidelines to follow as you study the selections in this chapter.

1. *Look for the specific issue being addressed.* Has the author narrowed the topic successfully?
2. *Examine the description of the issue.* Does the author assume that you will recognize the problem and its seriousness? Or does the writer present reasons and evidence to demonstrate that a problem exists and needs addressing?
3. *Observe the strategies.* Does the writer follow the conventional plan or alter it? Look for the use of examples, testimony, facts, statistics, and logical reasoning. How are possible objections dealt with? Check for the pitfalls listed in the previous section.
4. *Assess the proposed solution or point of view.* Does the author offer a concrete plan? Is the point of view reasonable and practical? Were you persuaded by the argument?

What problem are the people in this cartoon trying to avoid?

What's funny about the solution the one character has come up with?

What serious point does the cartoon make?

PREPARING TO READ

What solutions have you heard proposed for the nation's or your state's crime problem? Make a list with a classmate's help. Which solution do you agree with most?

Why Prisons Don't Work

WILBERT RIDEAU

Wilbert Rideau (b. 1942) has been in prison since 1961 for the murder of a bank teller. During eleven years on death row before the 1972 Supreme Court ban on execution, he learned to read and write well, although he was an eighth-grade dropout. He is the editor of the award-winning newspaper *The Angolite,* the only uncensored prison publication in this country. With Ron Wikberg, also a convicted murderer, he wrote *Life Sentences: Rage and Survival Behind Bars* in 1992. This book and his lectures, interviews, and columns have been influential in criminal justice circles.

TERMS TO RECOGNIZE

consigned *(para. 1)*	handed over
vies *(para. 2)*	competes
deter *(para. 3)*	restrain, hold back
incorrigible *(para. 3)*	irreformable, can't be saved or corrected
abhors *(para. 3)*	hates
adverse *(para. 7)*	harmful

i was among thirty-one murderers sent to the Louisiana State Penitentiary   1
in 1962 to be executed or imprisoned for life. We weren't much different from those we found here, or those who had preceded us. We were unskilled, impulsive, and uneducated misfits, mostly black, who had done dumb, impulsive things—failures, rejects from the larger society. Now a generation has come of age and gone since I've been here, and everything is much the same as I found it. The faces of the prisoners are different, but behind them are the same impulsive, uneducated, unskilled minds that made dumb, impulsive choices that got them into more trouble than they ever thought existed. The vast majority of us are consigned to suffer and die here so politicians can sell the illusion that permanently exiling people to prison will make society safe.

Getting tough has always been a "silver bullet," a quick fix for the crime   2
and violence that society fears. Each year in Louisiana—where excess is a
way of life—lawmakers have tried to outdo each other in legislating
harsher mandatory penalties and in reducing avenues of release. The only
thing to do with criminals, they say, is get tougher. They have. In the
process, the purpose of prison began to change. The state boasts one of
the highest lockup rates in the country, imposes the most severe penalties
in the nation, and vies to execute more criminals per capita than anywhere
else. This state is so tough that last year, when prison authorities here
wanted to punish an inmate in solitary confinement for an infraction, the
most they could inflict on him was to deprive him of his underwear. It
was all he had left.

If getting tough resulted in public safety, Louisiana citizens would be   3
the safest in the nation. They're not. Louisiana has the highest murder rate
among states. Prison, like the police and the courts, has a minimal impact
on crime because it is a response after the fact, a mop-up operation. It
doesn't work. The idea of punishing the few to deter the many is coun-
terfeit because potential criminals either think they're not going to get
caught or they're so emotionally desperate or psychologically distressed that
they don't care about the consequences of their actions. The threatened
punishment, regardless of its severity, is never a factor in the equation. But
society, like the incorrigible criminal it abhors, is unable to learn from its
mistakes.

Prison has a role in public safety, but it is not a cure-all. Its value is   4
limited, and its use should also be limited to what it does best: isolating
young criminals long enough to give them a chance to grow up and get
a grip on their impulses. It is a traumatic experience, certainly, but it should
be only a temporary one, not a way of life. Prisoners kept too long tend
to embrace the criminal culture, its distorted values and beliefs; they have
little choice—prison is their life. There are some prisoners who cannot be
returned to society—serial killers, serial rapists, professional hit men, and the
like—but the monsters who need to die in prison are rare exceptions in
the criminal landscape.

Crime is a young man's game. Most of the nation's random violence is   5
committed by young urban terrorists. But because of long, mandatory
sentences, most prisoners here are much older, having spent fifteen, twenty,
thirty, or more years behind bars, long past necessity. Rather than pay for
new prisons, society would be well served by releasing some of its older
prisoners who pose no threat and using the money to catch young street
thugs. Warden John Whitley agrees that many older prisoners here could
be freed tomorrow with little or no danger to society. Release, however,
is governed by law or by politicians, not by penal professionals. Even

murderers, those most feared by society, pose little risk. Historically, for example, the domestic staff at Louisiana's Governor's mansion has been made up of murderers, hand-picked to work among the chief-of-state and his family. Penologists have long known that murder is almost always a once-in-a-lifetime act. The most dangerous criminal is the one who has not yet killed but has a history of escalating offenses. He's the one to watch.

Rehabilitation can work. Everyone changes in time. The trick is to influence the direction that change takes. The problem with prisons is that they don't do more to rehabilitate those confined in them. The convict who enters prison illiterate will probably leave the same way. Most convicts want to be better than they are, but education is not a priority. This prison houses 4,600 men and offers academic training to 240, vocational training to a like number. Perhaps it doesn't matter. About 90 percent of the men here may never leave this prison alive. 6

The only effective way to curb crime is for society to work to *prevent* the criminal act in the first place, to come between the perpetrator and crime. Our youngsters must be taught to respect the humanity of others and to handle disputes without violence. It is essential to educate and equip them with the skills to pursue their life ambitions in a meaningful way. As a community, we must address the adverse life circumstances that spawn criminality. These things are not quick, and they're not easy, but they're effective. Politicians think that's too hard a sell. They want to be on record for doing something now, something they can point to at reelection time. So the drumbeat goes on for more police, more prisons, more of the same failed policies. 7

Ever see a dog chase its tail? 8

RESPONDING TO READING

Rideau gives some suggestions in paragraph 7 about a better way to prevent crime. What specific actions or policies can you suggest that would fit in with this better way?

GAINING WORD POWER

Look up the following words in a college dictionary. Then write a sentence of your own for each word.

1. impulsive (para. 1)
2. mandatory (para. 2)
3. potential (para. 3)
4. infraction (para. 2)
5. traumatic (para. 4)

6. distorted (para. 4)
7. escalating (para. 5)
8. rehabilitate (para. 6)
9. spawn (para. 7)

CONSIDERING CONTENT

1. From paragraph 1, how do you think Rideau explains criminal behavior? What are its sources?
2. After reading paragraph 1, can you state the thesis of the essay? Is it directly stated or implied?
3. What is the politicians' role in the prison system? Where in the essay does Rideau emphasize this role?
4. When is prison an appropriate punishment, according to Rideau? What length of terms for what types of crimes are suitable?
5. What are some reasons why prisons don't work?
6. If you were going to find out more about young versus old prisoners, where might you look for information?

CONSIDERING METHOD

1. How does the writer establish his credibility on this topic?
2. Explain the logical reasoning employed in paragraphs 2 and 3.
3. List the types of evidence used to support the points in paragraph 5.
4. What is Rideau's refutation for the deterrence argument? Find and discuss at least two more places where Rideau refutes the points or reasoning of his opponents.
5. In your own words, write the main point of each paragraph. Compare the structure of this argument with the conventional structure presented in the opening of this chapter.
6. Underline several instances of unusually short sentences. Can you explain the writer's use of these brief sentences?

WRITING STEP BY STEP

Each of us is aware of some system that doesn't (or didn't) work. Think about fads like miracle weight-loss plans; customs like dating, spanking, and marriage; university or school rules or requirements; local government policies like curfews; or even national laws like prohibition. Surely there is somewhere in society that you perceive inadequacy in addressing a real problem. Write an essay based on Rideau's example in which you explain what doesn't work and why.

A. Be sure to establish your credibility for writing about this topic. If your credentials aren't based on personal experience, maybe they are based on some other expertise.
B. Write a paragraph telling why the current situation exists. What is the system you're criticizing supposed to do?
C. Write one paragraph explaining that the problem is real but the present system doesn't address it effectively.

D. Devote two or three paragraphs to evidence for your own claim that the system doesn't work. Each paragraph should develop one point on your side of the matter. Use at least two different types of evidence (facts, statistics, testimony of experts, examples, logical reasoning, personal experience).

E. Some or all of the evidence paragraphs described previously may be based on refuting claims of the opposite side, as in Rideau's paragraph 4.

F. In your closing paragraph, suggest a better approach for efforts to deal with the problem or situation. You don't have to go into detail (Rideau doesn't), but you do need to indicate why you consider this approach more workable.

OTHER WRITING IDEAS

1. Sometimes people cause problems for others without realizing it. Is there something you do that creates a problem for someone else? Describe your behavior and explain how it's a problem. Then say what you're going to do about it.

2. Write about a habit (smoking, procrastinating, overeating, or being late, for example) that you broke. To get started, meet with a group of classmates and friends to share stories about bad habits and how to break them. When you write your essay, present the habit as a problem, describe its seriousness, and explain your solution.

3. Sometimes people turn a minor difficulty into a major catastrophe. Write a humorous essay in which you take a trivial concern and treat it as a serious problem. Ask your friends and classmates for ideas. When you write your essay, use enough exaggeration to let your readers know that you're not serious.

EDITING SKILLS: SUBJECT-VERB AGREEMENT

Look at the verbs in the following sentences from Wilbert Rideau's essay:

The state <u>boasts</u> one of the highest lockup rates in the country, <u>imposes</u> the most severe penalties in the nation, and <u>vies</u> to execute more criminals per capita than anywhere else.

So the drumbeat <u>goes</u> on for more police, more prisons, more of the same failed policies.

The convict who <u>enters</u> prison illiterate will probably leave the same way.

The verbs that we have highlighted are in the present tense; they express actions that are happening at the present time or that happen all the time.

We also use the present tense to state facts or general truths. You will notice that the verbs end in -*s*. That's because the subject of each verb is singular (state, drumbeat, convict). When the subject of a present-tense verb is *he*, *she*, or *it*—or a noun that could be replaced by *he, she,* or *it*—we put an *s* on the end.

This ending is an exception. Present-tense verbs with other subjects do not require the -*s* ending:

> Most convicts <u>want</u> to be better than they are.
> The only thing to do with criminals, they <u>say</u>, is get tougher.
> I <u>agree</u> with your opinion.
> You <u>deny</u> that getting tough is a silver bullet.

Because we don't always put an ending on a present-tense verb, some people forget to add it. That causes an error in subject-verb agreement. And sometimes it is difficult to tell what the subject of the verb really is, as in this sentence:

> <u>Prison</u>, like the police and the courts, <u>produces</u> little change in the crime rate.

The subject of the verb <u>produces</u> is <u>prison</u>, but the words in between might lead a writer to think that <u>the police and the courts</u> is the subject—and to mistakenly leave the -*s* ending off. Now take a look at this example:

> Even murderers, those most feared by society, <u>pose</u> little risk.

Can you figure out why there is no -*s* on the verb <u>pose</u>? That's because the subject is <u>murderers,</u> a word that does not mean *he, she,* or *it.* When trying to figure out the subject-verb agreement, you just have to forget about the words that come between <u>murderers</u> and <u>pose</u>.

EXERCISE

In each of the following sentences, underline the subject and then circle the verb that agrees with it. Example:

A <u>verb</u> in the present tense take/(takes) an -*s* ending when its subject is he, she, or it—or a noun that means he, she, or it.

1. An anthropologist study/studies buildings, tools, and other artifacts of ancient cultures.

2. Anthropologists always look/looks for signs of social change.
3. A box of fruit arrive/arrives at the house every month.
4. An adult student who has children find/finds little time for party-ing.
5. Low scores on the Scholastic Aptitude Test discourage/discourages students from applying to some colleges.
6. It give/gives me great pleasure to introduce tonight's speaker.
7. The first baseman, along with most of his teammates, refuse/refuses to sign autographs after the game.
8. Bonsai trees require/requires careful pruning.
9. Many movies of the past year contain/contains scenes of violence.

Now check over the essay you have just written. Look at all the verbs, especially those in the present tense. Did you use the -*s* ending on the appropriate verbs? Edit your writing carefully for subject–verb agreement.

PREPARING TO READ

Would you like to have a clone of yourself to raise as a child? Would you prefer it to a child of yours and your spouse? To an adopted child? Why did you answer the way you did?

In 1997, the first successful cloning of animals was accomplished, starting with the sheep Dolly. This long-awaited event created a huge controversy, bringing up questions of the meaning of individuality and life. Most people, of course, made the leap from the cloning of animals to the cloning of humans. Here we present three points of view on the issue.

Of Headless Mice . . . and Men: The Ultimate Cloning Horror

CHARLES KRAUTHAMMER

Charles Krauthammer (b. 1950) has enjoyed a varied career beginning with a college major in political science, then attending medical school to become a psychiatrist, and combining his fields of interest as a successful writer. He won a Pulitzer Prize in 1987 for his commentary in political and social columns in publications such as *The New Republic* and the *Washington Post*. The column we reprint here first appeared in *Time* in 1998.

TERMS TO RECOGNIZE

titters *(para. 1)*	light laughter
acquiesce *(para. 8)*	agree, consent, go along with
bioethical *(para. 8)*	concerning the morality of biological science
facsimile *(para. 10)*	copy
narcissism *(para. 12)*	self-absorption resulting in neglect of others' needs
draconian *(para. 14)*	severe

Last year Dolly the cloned sheep was received with wonder, titters and some vague apprehension. Last week the announcement by a Chicago physicist that he is assembling a team to produce the first human clone occasioned yet another wave of Brave New World anxiety. But the scariest news of all—and largely overlooked—comes from two obscure labs, at the University of Texas and at the University of Bath. During the past four years, one group created headless mice; the other, headless tadpoles.

For sheer Frankenstein wattage, the purposeful creation of these animal monsters has no equal. Take the mice. Researchers found the gene that tells the embryo to produce the head. They deleted it. They did this in a thousand mice embryos, four of which were born. I use the term loosely. Having no way to breathe, the mice died instantly. 2

Why then create them? The Texas researchers want to learn how genes determine embryo development. But you don't have to be a genius to see the true utility of manufacturing headless creatures: for their organs—fully formed, perfectly useful, ripe for plundering. 3

Why should you be panicked? Because humans are next. "It would almost certainly be possible to produce human bodies without a forebrain," Princeton biologist Lee Silver told the *London Sunday Times*. "These human bodies without any semblance of consciousness would not be considered persons, and thus it would be perfectly legal to keep them 'alive' as a future source of organs." 4

"Alive." Never have a pair of quotation marks loomed so ominously. Take the mouse-frog technology, apply it to humans, combine it with cloning, and you are become a god: with a single cell taken from, say, your finger, you produce a headless replica of yourself, a mutant twin, arguably lifeless, that becomes your own personal, precisely tissue-matched organ farm. 5

There are, of course, technical hurdles along the way. Suppressing the equivalent "head" gene in man. Incubating tiny infant organs to grow into larger ones that adults could use. And creating artificial wombs (as per Aldous Huxley), given that it might be difficult to recruit sane women to carry headless fetuses to their birth/death. 6

It won't be long, however, before these technical barriers are breached. The ethical barriers are already cracking. Lewis Wolpert, professor of biology at University College, London, finds producing headless humans "personally distasteful" but, given the shortage of organs, does not think distaste is sufficient reason not to go ahead with something that would save lives. And Professor Silver not only sees "nothing wrong, philosophically or rationally," with producing headless humans for organ harvesting; he wants to convince a skeptical public that it is perfectly O.K. 7

When prominent scientists are prepared to acquiesce in—or indeed encourage—the deliberate creation of deformed and dying quasi-human life, you know we are facing a bioethical abyss. Human beings are ends, not means. There is no grosser corruption of biotechnology than creating a human mutant and disemboweling it at our pleasure for spare parts. 8

The prospect of headless human clones should put the whole debate about "normal" cloning in a new light. Normal cloning is less a treatment for infertility than a treatment for vanity. It is a way to produce an exact genetic replica of yourself that will walk the earth years after you're gone. 9

But there is a problem with a clone. It is not really you. It is but a twin, 10
a perfect John Doe Jr., but still a junior. With its own independent
consciousness, it is, alas, just a facsimile of you.

The headless clone solves the facsimile problem. It is a gateway to the 11
ultimate vanity: immortality. If you create a real clone, you cannot transfer
your consciousness into it to truly live on. But if you create a headless
clone of just your body, you have created a ready source of replacement
parts to keep you—your consciousness—going indefinitely.

Which is why one form of cloning will inevitably lead to the other. 12
Cloning is the technology of narcissism, and nothing satisfies narcissism
like immortality. Headlessness will be cloning's crowning achievement.

The time to put a stop to this is now. Dolly moved President Clinton 13
to create a commission that recommended a temporary ban on human
cloning. But with physicist Richard Seed threatening to clone humans, and
with headless animals already here, we are past the time for toothless
commissions and meaningless bans.

Clinton banned federal funding of human-cloning research, of which 14
there is none anyway. He then proposed a five-year ban on cloning. This
is not enough. Congress should ban human cloning now. Totally. And
regarding one particular form, it should be draconian: the deliberate
creation of headless humans must be made a crime, indeed a capital crime.
If we flinch in the face of this high-tech barbarity, we'll deserve to live in
the hell it heralds.

Will Cloning End Human Evolution?

MICHAEL MAUTNER

Michael Mautner is a research professor of chemistry at the University
of Canterbury in New Zealand. His writings reflect concern for the human
side of technological advances. The 1997 article published here is his third
contribution to *The Futurist* magazine.

TERMS TO RECOGNIZE

despots *(para. 3)*	oppressive rulers
susceptible *(para. 3)*	open or unresistant to some influence or disease
mutations *(para. 5)*	basic changes in biological and genetic make-up
propagate *(para. 11)*	to cause to continue or increase by sexual reproduction
communal *(para. 14)*	democratic, in common

Cloning is not only less fun than sex, it would freeze evolution and destroy our chances for survival in the future. 1

The recent cloning of the first mammal brings the prospects of human cloning closer to reality. Now the public should ponder the implications. Among these, the most important is the effect on our future evolution. 2

Cloning will be attractive because of some medical uses. Genetic replicas of geniuses might also benefit society. On the other hand, ruthless and egocentric despots may replicate themselves millions of times over. Cloning on a large scale would also reduce biological diversity, and the entire human species could be wiped out by some new epidemic to which a genetically uniform population was susceptible. 3

Beyond these important but obvious results, cloning raises problems that go to the core of human existence and purpose. One important fact to recognize is that cloning is asexual reproduction. It therefore bypasses both the biological benefits of normal reproduction and the emotional, psychological, and social aspects that surround it: courtship, love, marriage, family structure. Even more importantly, if cloning became the main mode of reproduction, human evolution would stop in its tracks. 4

In sexual reproduction, some of the genetic material from each parent undergoes mutations that can lead to entirely new biological properties. Vast numbers of individual combinations become possible, and the requirements of survival—and choices of partners by the opposite sex—then gradually select which features will be passed on to the following generations. 5

Cloning will, in contrast, reproduce the same genetic makeup of an existing individual. There is no room for new traits to arise by mutation and no room for desirable features to compete and win by an appeal to the judgment of the opposite sex. The result: Human evolution is halted. 6

Is it necessary for the human species to evolve further? Absolutely! We are certainly far from achieving perfection. We are prone to diseases, and the capacity of our intelligence is limited. Most importantly, human survival will depend on our ability to adapt to environments beyond Earth—that is, in the rich new worlds of outer space. 7

Some people question whether we can save ourselves from man-made 8
environmental disasters on Earth, whose resources are already pressured by
human population growth. And limiting the population to one planet puts
us at risk of extinction from all-out nuclear or biological warfare, climate
change, and catastrophic meteorite impacts.

Humanity could vastly expand its chances for survival by moving into 9
space, where we would encounter worlds with diverse environments. To live
in space, we will have to increase our tolerance to radiation, to extremes
of heat and cold, and to vacuum. We will also need more intelligence to
construct habitats. Our social skills will need to advance so that billions of
humans can work together in the grand projects that will be needed.

If we are to expand into space, we surely cannot freeze human evolu- 10
tion. The natural (and possibly designed) mechanisms of evolution must
therefore be allowed to continue.

Socially, the relations between the sexes underlie most aspects of human 11
behavior. The rituals of dating, mating, and marriage and the family structures that surround sexual reproduction are the most basic emotional and
social factors that make our lives human. Without the satisfactions of love
and sex, of dating and of families, will cloned generations even care to
propagate further?

Cloning therefore raises fundamental questions about the human future: 12
Have we arrived yet at perfection? Where should we aim future human
evolution? What is the ultimate human purpose? The prospect of human
cloning means that these once-philosophical questions have become urgent
practical issues.

As living beings, our primary human purpose is to safeguard, propagate, 13
and advance life. This objective must guide our ethical judgments, including those on cloning.

Our best guide to this purpose is the love of life common to most 14
humans, which is therefore reflected in our communal judgment. All individuals who sustain the present and build the future should have the right
to participate equally in these basic decisions. Our shared future may be best
secured by the practice of debating and voting on such biotechnology issues
in an informed "biodemocracy."

The Case for Cloning

J. MADELEINE NASH

J. Madeleine Nash (b. 1943) has been a researcher and Chicago correspondent for *Time* magazine. She contributed to the book *Schools Where Parents Make a Difference,* edited by Don Davies, in 1976. The article reprinted here appeared in *Time* in 1998.

TERMS TO RECOGNIZE

Tay-Sachs disease *(para. 2)*	a fatal hereditary disorder associated with mental retardation
maverick *(para. 3)*	nonconformist, renegade
moratorium *(para. 3)*	suspension, halt
endocrinology *(para. 5)*	the study of the endocrine system (hormones)
coddled *(para. 6)*	cooked gently
augment *(para. 8)*	enhance, strengthen

An elderly man develops macular degeneration, a disease that destroys vision. To bolster his failing eyesight, he receives a transplant of healthy retinal tissue—cloned from his own cells and cultivated in a lab dish. 1

A baby girl is born free of the gene that causes Tay-Sachs disease, even though both her parents are carriers. The reason? In the embryonic cell from which she was cloned, the flawed gene was replaced with normal DNA. 2

These futuristic scenarios are not now part of the debate over human cloning, but they should be. Spurred by the fear that maverick physicist Richard Seed, or someone like him, will open a cloning clinic, lawmakers are rushing to enact broad restrictions against human cloning. To date, 19 European nations have signed an anticloning treaty. The Clinton Administration backs a proposal that would impose a five-year moratorium. House majority leader Dick Armey has thrown his weight behind a bill that would ban human cloning permanently, and at least 18 states are contemplating legislative action of their own. "This is the right thing to do, at the right time, for the sake of human dignity," said Armey last week. "How can you put a statute of limitations on right and wrong?" 3

But hasty legislation could easily be too restrictive. Last year, for instance, Florida considered a law that would have barred the cloning of human DNA, a routine procedure in biomedical research. California passed badly 4 worded legislation that temporarily bans not just human cloning but also a procedure that shows promise as a new treatment for infertility.

Most lawmakers are focused on a nightmarish vision in which billion- 5 aires and celebrities flood the world with genetic copies of themselves. But scientists say it's unlikely that anyone is going to be churning out limited editions of Michael Jordan or Madeleine Albright. "Oh, it can be done," says Dr. Mark Sauer, chief of reproductive endocrinology at Columbia University's College of Physicians and Surgeons. "It's just that the best people, who could do it, aren't going to be doing it."

Cloning individual human cells, however, is another matter. Biologists are 6 already talking about harnessing for medical purposes the technique that produced the sheep called Dolly. They might, for example, obtain healthy cells from a patient with leukemia or a burn victim and then transfer the nucleus of each cell into an unfertilized egg from which the nucleus has been removed. Coddled in culture dishes, these embryonic clones—each genetically identical to the patient from which the nuclei came—would begin to divide.

The cells would not have to grow into a fetus, however. The addition 7 of powerful growth factors could ensure that the clones develop only into specialized cells and tissue. For the leukemia patient, for example, the cloned cells could provide an infusion of fresh bone marrow, and for the burn victim, grafts of brand-new skin. Unlike cells from an unrelated donor, these cloned cells would incur no danger of rejection; patients would be spared the need to take powerful drugs to suppress the immune system. "Given its potential benefit," says Dr. Robert Winston, a fertility expert at London's Hammersmith Hospital, "I would argue that it would be unethical not to continue this line of research."

There are dangers, but not the ones everyone's talking about, accord- 8 ing to Princeton University molecular biologist Lee Silver, author of *Remaking Eden*. Silver believes that cloning is the technology that will finally make it possible to apply genetic engineering to humans. First, parents will want to banish inherited diseases like Tay-Sachs. Then they will try to eliminate predispositions to alcoholism and obesity. In the end, says Silver, they will attempt to augment normal traits like intelligence and athletic prowess.

Cloning could be vital to that process. At present, introducing genes into 9 chromosomes is very much a hit-or-miss proposition. Scientists might achieve the result they intend once in 20 times, making the procedure far too risky to perform on a human embryo. Through cloning, however, scientists could make 20 copies of the embryo they wished to modify, greatly boosting their chance of success.

Perhaps now would be a good time to ask ourselves which we fear   10
more: that cloning will produce multiple copies of crazed despots, as in the
film *The Boys from Brazil;* or that it will lead to the society portrayed in
Gattaca, the recent science-fiction thriller in which genetic enhancement
of a privileged few creates a rigid caste structure. By acting sensibly, we
might avoid both traps.

_____

RESPONDING TO READING

How much control do you feel you have, as an individual, over scientific
decisions like the extent of cloning? Would you like to do anything about it?

GAINING WORD POWER

While today almost everyone uses the word *clone,* it has not been a part
of popular vocabulary for that long. What other words have come into
common usage through technological advances? Make a list of four or five
terms people use today that probably people in your parents' day did not
use (or did not use in the same way). The computer era has brought many
new terms (or new meanings) into common use: RAM, interface, software. See whether today's meaning of each word on your list is in your
dictionary. Find a dictionary more than ten years old, and see whether the
word and meaning are in there.

CONSIDERING CONTENT

1. What different types or uses of cloning are discussed in the three essays?
2. Which essay did you find most persuasive, and why?
3. What points of view toward "human nature," or what can be
   expected of people, are endorsed in the three articles?
4. What is the problem with legislation against cloning, according to
   Nash? What are some other problems with this method of controlling scientific research?
5. Aldous Huxley's *Brave New World* is referred to in two of the essays.
   What is this novel about? Why does it come up in discussions of
   the role of science in future society?

CONSIDERING METHOD

1. In one sentence each, using your own words, summarize the main
   argument of each of the three essays.
2. Make a list of loaded—highly connotative—language used in each
   article. Which author uses the most emotionally laden words? What
   effect did this usage have on you as a reader?

3. What types of evidence are used by each author?

4. Look for logical fallacies in each essay. Are there overgeneralizations? Either-or thinking? Jumping to conclusions? Did you notice flaws in logic while you were reading the first time?

5. Which arguments does Nash attempt to refute in her pro-cloning article? What strategy does she use to refute them?

6. Compare the way Lee Silver is presented in the Krauthammer and the Nash articles. How does the difference in presentation matter?

WRITING STEP BY STEP

You will write an essay praising or denouncing another scientific advance—for example, some new use of computer technology, the genetic alteration of food sources, or space colonization. Use J. Madeleine Nash's essay as a sample.

A. Be sure that you can establish credibility to discuss the topic. Perhaps you have studied it more extensively than most people or have followed the news stories more closely.

B. Begin by setting forth some "futuristic scenarios" involving the scientific advance.

C. Follow the scenarios by explaining the terms of the debate concerning the advance. What are the two sides doing? Why?

D. Think of two or three separate points of disagreement on the advance, especially on how it will be used in the future.

E. Develop each of your points into a separate paragraph. You will begin with a statement of what people fear about the advance. If you are on the "pro" side, you will develop by trying to ease these fears. If you are on the "con" side, you will develop by showing how these fears are well founded.

F. Whichever side you take, give some consideration to the strong points that the other side has going for it. Refute these points by minimizing their importance, questioning their factuality, or offering a different point of view on them. Put your refutation in one or two paragraphs.

G. Close by suggesting how society can avoid the potential bad effects of this scientific advance.

OTHER WRITING IDEAS

1. When it became possible to attach erasers to the ends of pencils, some social critics objected, claiming that the ease of erasure would lead to careless writing. Look up the printed commentaries on some

other innovation in history—the automobile, train, microwave, organ donation, or space exploration, for example. Write an essay comparing and contrasting what was predicted at first with what actually happened.

2. Invent a technological advance, and write an essay in which you attempt to sell it to a suspicious or unfriendly audience.

3. Choose some small or harmless new invention or method from your own time period, and write a humorous essay making frightful predictions about its effect on society.

EDITING SKILLS: COLONS

Copy the following passages from the articles in this section exactly.

But you don't have to be a genius to see the true utility of manufacturing headless creatures: for their organs—fully formed, perfectly useful, ripe for plundering.

It is a gateway to the ultimate vanity: immortality.

It therefore bypasses both the biological benefits of normal reproduction and the emotional, psychological, and social aspects that surround it: courtship, love, marriage, family structure.

And regarding one particular form, it should be draconian: the deliberate creation of headless humans must be made a crime, indeed a capital crime.

If you copied correctly, you put a colon (:) in each passage. Reread what you copied, and see whether you can come up with a rule about the use of the colon.

If you looked closely, you noticed that a colon comes after a complete sentence. Go back and reread the first portion of each example. The colon then introduces a quotation, a list, or an explanation—something that specifies or expands on the sentence before the colon. If you think of the colon as a verbal equals sign (=), you get the main relationship it suggests between the two parts.

EXERCISE

Complete the following passages that include colons.

1. Sami has already bought her party supplies: _____
_____.

2. Beau's next statement gave away his secret plans: _____
   _____.

3. Marcus acted very strangely toward Doreen: _____
   _____.

4. _____: a paperback detective
   novel, a historical romance, and a Far Side cartoon book.

5. _____: Austin only cried a little
   while.

Now edit the essay you just wrote, looking for places where you could have used a colon instead of a period or a semicolon. After consulting with your instructor, change the punctuation mark to a colon.

PREPARING TO READ

Do you think our society pays too much attention to athletes and athletics? Do you play a sport? If so, what do you think your chances are of becoming a professional?

Send Your Children to the Libraries

ARTHUR ASHE

Arthur Ashe was the first black player to win a major men's tennis tournament: the U.S. Open in 1968 and the Wimbledon championship in 1975. Ashe survived heart surgery in 1979 and announced his retirement from competition in 1980, although he continued to serve as the nonplaying captain of the U.S. Davis Cup team. He became infected with the AIDS virus, probably through a blood transfusion that he received during his second bypass operation in 1983; he died of complications from AIDS in 1993. In this letter, published in the *New York Times* in 1977, Ashe argues that the lure of professional sports is actually harmful to black children.

TERMS TO RECOGNIZE

pretentious *(para. 2)*	falsely superior
expends *(para. 3)*	spends, uses up
dubious *(para. 3)*	doubtful, questionable
emulate *(para. 4)*	follow, copy
attributing *(para. 7)*	assigning, crediting
viable *(para. 9)*	possible, workable
channel *(para. 12)*	direct
Wimbledon *(para. 18)*	suburb of London and site of the world-famous tennis tournament
Forest Hills *(para. 18)*	location of the U.S. Open tennis tournament in 1968

Since my sophomore year at University of California, Los Angeles, I have become convinced that we blacks spend too much time on the playing fields and too little time in the libraries.   1

Please don't think of this attitude as being pretentious just because I am a black, single, professional athlete.   2

I don't have children, but I can make observations. I strongly believe the   3
black culture expends too much time, energy and effort raising, praising and
teasing our black children as to the dubious glories of professional sports.

All children need models to emulate—parents, relatives or friends. But   4
when the child starts school, the influence of the parent is shared by teachers and classmates, by the lure of books, movies, ministers and newspapers,
but most of all by television.

Which televised events have the greatest number of viewers? Sports—   5
the Olympics, Super Bowl, Masters, World Series, pro basketball playoffs,
Forest Hills. ABC-TV even has sports on Monday night prime time from
April to December.

So your child gets a massive dose of O. J. Simpson, Kareem Abdul-Jabbar,   6
Muhammad Ali, Reggie Jackson, Dr. J. and Lee Elder and other pro athletes.
And it is only natural that your child will dream of being a pro athlete himself.

But consider these facts: For the major professional sports of hockey,   7
football, basketball, baseball, golf, tennis and boxing, there are roughly only
3,170 major league positions available (attributing 200 positions to golf, 200
to tennis and 100 to boxing). And the annual turnover is small.

We blacks are a subculture of about 28 million. Of the 13½ million   8
men, 5–6 million are under twenty years of age, so your son has less than
one chance in a thousand of becoming a pro. Less than one in a thousand.
Would you bet your son's future on something with odds of 999 to 1
against you? I wouldn't.

Unless a child is exceptionally gifted, you should know by the time he   9
enters high school whether he has a future as an athlete. But what is more
important is what happens if he doesn't graduate or doesn't land a college
scholarship and doesn't have a viable alternative job career. Our high school
dropout rate is several times the national average, which contributes to our
unemployment rate of roughly twice the national average.

And how do you fight the figures in the newspapers every day? Ali has   10
earned more than $30 million boxing, O. J. just signed for $2½ million,
Dr. J. for almost $3 million, Reggie Jackson for $2.8 million, Nate Archibald
for $400,000 a year. All that money, recognition, attention, free cars, girls,
jobs in the off-season—no wonder there is Pop Warner football, Little
League baseball, National Junior League tennis, hockey practice at 5 A.M.
and pickup basketball games in any center city at any hour.

There must be some way to assure that the 999 who try but don't make   11
it to pro sports don't wind up on the street corners or in the unemployment
lines. Unfortunately, our most widely recognized role models are athletes and
entertainers—"runnin' " and "jumpin' " and "singin' " and "dancin' " While
we are 60 percent of the National Basketball Association, we are less than 4

percent of the doctors and lawyers. While we are about 35 percent of major league baseball, we are less than 2 percent of the engineers. While we are about 40 percent of the National Football League, we are less than 11 percent of construction workers such as carpenters and bricklayers.

Our greatest heroes of the century have been athletes—Jack Johnson, Joe 12 Louis and Muhammad Ali. Racial and economic discrimination forced us to channel our energies into athletics and entertainment. These were the ways out of the ghetto, the ways to that Cadillac, those alligator shoes, that cashmere sport coat.

Somehow, parents must instill a desire for learning alongside the desire 13 to be Walt Frazier. Why not start by sending black professional athletes to high schools to explain the facts of life?

I have often addressed high school audiences and my message is always 14 the same. For every hour you spend on the athletic field, spend two in the library. Even if you make it as a pro athlete, your career will be over by the time you are thirty-five. So you will need that diploma.

Have these pro athletes explain what happens if you break a leg, get a 15 sore arm, have one bad year or don't make the cut for five or six tournaments. Explain to them the star system, wherein for every O. J. earning millions there are six or seven others making $15,000 or $20,000 or $30,000 a year.

But don't just have Walt Frazier or O. J. or Abdul-Jabbar address your 16 class. Invite a benchwarmer or a guy who didn't make it. Ask him if he sleeps every night. Ask him whether he was graduated. Ask him what he would do if he became disabled tomorrow. Ask him where his old high school athletic buddies are.

We have been on the same roads—sports and entertainment—too long. 17 We need to pull over, fill up at the library and speed away to Congress and the Supreme Court, the unions and the business world. We need more Barbara Jordans, Andrew Youngs, union cardholders, Nikki Giovannis and Earl Graveses. Don't worry: We will still be able to sing and dance and run and jump better than anybody else.

I'll never forget how proud my grandmother was when I graduated 18 from UCLA in 1966. Never mind the Davis Cup in 1968, 1969, and 1970. Never mind the Wimbledon title, Forest Hills, etc. To this day, she still doesn't know what those names mean.

What mattered to her was that of her more than thirty children and 19 grandchildren, I was the first to be graduated from college, and a famous college at that. Somehow, that made up for all those floors she scrubbed all those years.

RESPONDING TO READING

Do you think the athletes at your school receive special treatment? Do they spend too much time on their sports and too little time on their studies? In your journal, express your opinion about the place of athletics in colleges and universities.

GAINING WORD POWER

Explain in your own words the meaning of the following phrases. Use clues from surrounding sentences to help you.

1. the lure of books and movies (para. 4)
2. a massive dose (para. 6)
3. the black subculture (para. 8)
4. an exceptionally gifted child (para. 9)
5. pickup basketball games (para. 10)
6. economic discrimination (para. 12)
7. instill a desire for learning (para. 13)
8. make the cut (para. 15)
9. the star system (para. 15)

CONSIDERING CONTENT

1. What problem is Ashe concerned about? What solution does he propose?
2. Ashe is clearly addressing the parents of black sons. Are his opinions relevant to other races or to parents of girls? Why or why not?
3. In paragraph 12, Ashe says that "economic discrimination" has forced blacks into sports and entertainment. What does he mean? Do you agree?
4. According to Ashe, why do black athletes need a diploma? Do these reasons apply to other races and to nonathletes?
5. Who are Barbara Jordan, Andrew Young, Nikki Giovanni, and Earl Graves? Why does Ashe say "we need more" of these people?
6. In paragraph 17, Ashe says that blacks have been "on the same roads—sports and entertainment—too long." Does he want blacks to avoid these careers?
7. This letter was written in 1977, more than twenty years ago. Are Ashe's views still relevant?

CONSIDERING METHOD

1. Ashe states the problem in his first sentence. Where does he restate it? Why does he restate the problem several times?

2. What is the point of paragraphs 2 and 3? What criticisms is Ashe anticipating in these paragraphs?
3. In his letter, Ashe uses a lot of statistics. How convincing are they?
4. What other kinds of evidence does Ashe use to support his main points?
5. How does Ashe make it clear that he is part of the audience he's addressing? Why does he want his readers to know that he is not an outsider?
6. Notice Ashe's frequent use of parallel structure, items in a series, and intentional repetition. Find several examples of each. What effect is Ashe trying to achieve with these elements?
7. Explain the metaphor that Ashe uses in paragraph 17.
8. Why does Ashe conclude with comments about his grandmother? Is this an effective ending?
9. What stereotypes about blacks does Ashe refer to? Why does he use the word *black* and not *African American?*

WRITING STEP BY STEP

Write a letter to a newspaper in which you encourage fellow students or fellow citizens to join you in solving some problem that affects you all. Choose a problem close to home—something on campus or in your community that you want fixed, improved, regulated, legalized, banned, or reorganized.

A. Begin, as Ashe does, with a clear and direct statement of the problem.
B. Explain your interest or involvement in the situation. Make it clear to your readers that you are not an outsider: use the pronouns *we, us, our,* and *ours.*
C. Describe the problem and, if necessary, explain why you think it needs a solution. Your readers may not realize how serious the problem is or how much it affects them.
D. Use actual examples and, if possible, give statistics to support your claims.
E. Emphasize your points and keep your readers' attention by using parallel structure, items in series, and intentional repetition.
F. State your solution, and explain how it will work.
G. If appropriate, show why other solutions won't work and why your proposal is the best one.
H. Conclude with a personal anecdote or comment, like Ashe's story about his grandmother's pride.

OTHER WRITING IDEAS

1. Is there some rule change that would make your favorite sport safer, fairer, or more interesting to watch? Using a problem-solution approach, write a letter to a sports magazine (like *Sports Illustrated*) or to an athletic organization (like the NCAA), and present your proposal for changing the rules.

2. Write a letter to the Consumer Protection Agency about some problem you have experienced as a consumer. Identify the problem, explain why it needs to be solved, and present your solution.

3. Think of a problem in your life that's bothering you: lack of money, lack of friends, the wrong kind of friends, too much work, too little time. Make sure it is some problem you genuinely need to solve. Work through the techniques described in the introduction to this chapter. Then write a report or a letter to yourself, suggesting at least two reasonable ways to improve the situation.

EDITING SKILLS: AVOIDING SEXIST LANGUAGE

In the opening sentence of paragraph 9, Arthur Ashe writes, "Unless a *child* is exceptionally gifted, you should know by the time *he* enters high school whether *he* has a future as an athlete" (our italics). When this letter was published in 1977, it was acceptable to use masculine pronouns to refer to virtually all living beings as if they were male. And, of course, Ashe is thinking of *sons* as becoming professional athletes—even though he later mentions that we need more "Barbara Jordans" and "Nikki Giovannis" (para. 17).

These days you need to avoid using masculine pronouns to refer to people of both sexes. If Ashe were still alive today, he probably would not write, "And it is only natural that your *child* will dream of being a pro athlete *himself*" (para. 6). More likely he would cast that sentence in the plural this way: "And it is only natural that your *children* will dream of being pro athletes *themselves.*" Both sexes are included in all plural pronouns. People don't think either male or female when they read *we, us, our, you, your, they, them, their, ourselves, yourselves, themselves.* So, if you simply write in the plural, the problem disappears.

Occasionally you can revise a sentence to eliminate the pronoun, like this:

(sexist)   A tennis player must practice daily to stay at the top of *his* form.

(revised)   A tennis player must practice daily to stay in top form.

Or, if you find yourself once in a while needing to write a singular sentence for some good reason, it's quite all right to use both male and female pronouns, like this:

Everyone on board must wear a lifejacket for *his or her* own safety.

Just don't do it this way too often, or your writing will get annoyingly cluttered.

EXERCISE

Since your readers may be bothered by sexist pronouns, you should write in the plural most of the time. For practice, rewrite the following sentences in the plural to get rid of the italicized masculine pronouns.

1. An Olympic swimmer needs to work out daily to perform at *his* best.
2. But a championship bridge player can take a week off without ruining *his* game.
3. A professional athlete needs to watch *his* diet, as well as exercise *his* body.
4. A chess player is constantly exercising *his* mind, but *he* can eat whatever *he* pleases.
5. Even an amateur golfer gets plenty of exercise when *he* plays eighteen holes, unless *he* rides in a cart.

Now go back over the essay you just wrote and check the personal pronouns. Did you use any (like *he, his, him* or *she, her, hers*) that unfairly or inaccurately exclude the other sex? Make any necessary changes—such as using *he or she* or rewriting in the plural to allow *they, their,* or *them.*

PREPARING TO READ

If you were dying, slowly and painfully, from an incurable disease, what would you want the hospital staff to do? Should they let you die, or prolong your life (and your pain)?

A Crime of Compassion

BARBARA HUTTMANN

Barbara Huttmann is the associate director of nursing for Children's Hospital in San Francisco. She has written two books about the rights of patients: *The Patient's Advocate* and *Code Blue: A Nurse's True-Life Story*. In the following essay, which originally appeared on the "My Turn" page of *Newsweek* magazine in 1983, Huttmann tells about her decision to let a suffering patient die.

TERMS TO RECOGNIZE

resuscitated *(para. 3)*	revived, brought back to life
haggard *(para. 5)*	worn out
IV solutions *(para. 6)*	liquids given by injection (IV stands for intravenous—"in the vein")
irrigate *(para. 7)*	wash out, flush
lucid *(para. 10)*	aware, clear-minded
impotence *(para. 10)*	powerlessness
imperative *(para. 11)*	command, directive
riddled *(para. 13)*	pierced with numerous holes
pallor *(para. 15)*	paleness, lack of color

"**m**urderer," a man shouted. "God help patients who get *you* for a nurse." 1

"What gives you the right to play God?" another one asked. 2

It was the Phil Donahue show where the guest is a fatted calf and the audience a 220-strong flock of vultures hungering to pick at the bones. I had told them about Mac, one of my favorite cancer patients. "We resuscitated him 52 times in just one month. I refused to resuscitate him again. I simply sat there and held his hand while he died." 3

There wasn't time to explain that Mac was a young, witty, macho cop who walked into the hospital with 32 pounds of attack equipment, looking 4 as if he could single-handedly protect the whole city, if not the entire state. "Can't get rid of this cough," he said. Otherwise, he felt great.

Before the day was over, tests confirmed that he had lung cancer. And 5 before the year was over, I loved him, his wife, Maura, and their three kids as if they were my own. All the nurses loved him. And we all battled his disease for six months without ever giving death a second thought. Six months isn't such a long time in the whole scheme of things, but it was long enough to see him lose his youth, his wit, his macho, his hair, his bowel and bladder control, his sense of taste and smell, and his ability to do the slightest thing for himself. It was also long enough to watch Maura's transformation from a young woman into a haggard, beaten old lady.

When Mac had wasted away to a 60-pound skeleton kept alive by liquid 6 food we poured down a tube, IV solutions we dripped into his veins, and oxygen we piped to a mask on his face, he begged us: "Mercy . . . for God's sake, please just let me go."

The first time he stopped breathing, the nurse pushed the button that 7 calls a "code blue" throughout the hospital and sends a team rushing to resuscitate the patient. Each time he stopped breathing, sometimes two or three times in one day, the code team came again. The doctors and technicians worked their miracles and walked away. The nurses stayed to wipe the saliva that drooled from his mouth, irrigate the big craters of bedsores that covered his hips, suction the lung fluids that threatened to drown him, clean the feces that burned his skin like lye, pour the liquid food down the tube attached to his stomach, put pillows between his knees to ease the bone-on-bone pain, turn him every hour to keep the bedsores from getting worse, and change his gown and linen every two hours to keep him from being soaked in perspiration.

At night I went home and tried to scrub away the smell of decaying flesh 8 that seemed woven into the fabric of my uniform. It was in my hair, the upholstery of my car—there was no washing it away. And every night I prayed that Mac would die, that his agonized eyes would never again plead with me to let him die.

Every morning I asked his doctor for a "no-code" order. Without that 9 order, we had to resuscitate every patient who stopped breathing. His doctor was one of several who believe we must extend life as long as we have the means and knowledge to do it. To not do it is to be liable for negligence, at least in the eyes of many people, including some nurses. I thought about what it would be like to stand before a judge, accused of murder, if Mac stopped breathing and I didn't call a code.

And after the fifty-second code, when Mac was still lucid enough to beg 10 for death again, and Maura was crumbled in my arms again, and when no amount of pain medication stilled his moaning and agony, I wondered about a spiritual judge. Was all this misery and suffering supposed to be building character or infusing us all with the sense of humility that comes from impotence?

Had we, the whole medical community, become so arrogant that we 11 believed in the illusion of salvation through science? Had we become so self-righteous that we thought meddling in God's work was our duty, our moral imperative and our legal obligation? Did we really believe that we had the right to force "life" on a suffering man who had begged for the right to die?

Such questions haunted me more than ever early one morning when 12 Maura went home to change her clothes and I was bathing Mac. He had been still for so long, I thought he at last had the blessed relief of coma. Then he opened his eyes and moaned, "Pain . . . no more . . . Barbara . . . do something . . . God, let me go."

The desperation in his eyes and voice riddled me with guilt. "I'll stop," 13 I told him as I injected the pain medication.

I sat on the bed and held Mac's hands in mine. He pressed his bony 14 fingers against my hand and muttered, "Thanks." Then there was one soft sigh and I felt his hands go cold in mine. "Mac?" I whispered, as I waited for his chest to rise and fall again.

A clutch of panic banded my chest, drew my finger to the code button, 15 urged me to do something, anything . . . but sit there alone with death. I kept one finger on the button, without pressing it, as a waxen pallor slowly transformed his face from person to empty shell. Nothing I've ever done in my 47 years has taken so much effort as it took *not* to press that code button.

Eventually, when I was as sure as I could be that the code team would 16 fail to bring him back, I entered the legal twilight zone and pushed the button. The team tried. And while they were trying, Maura walked into the room and shrieked, "No . . . don't let them do this to him . . . for God's sake . . . please, no more."

Cradling her in my arms was like cradling myself, Mac, and all those 17 patients and nurses who had been in this place before, who do the best they can in a death-denying society.

So a TV audience accused me of murder. Perhaps I am guilty. If a 18 doctor had written a no-code order, which is the only *legal* alternative, would he have felt any less guilty? Until there is legislation making it a criminal act to code a patient who has requested the right to die, we will all of us risk the same fate as Mac. For whatever reason, we developed the means to prolong life, and now we are forced to use it. We do not have the right to die.

RESPONDING TO READING

Huttmann says, "We do not have the right to die." Should we have this right? In your journal, write down your thoughts and feelings about "the right to die."

GAINING WORD POWER

Writers sometimes make passing references to familiar or significant people, places, objects, or events from history, the Bible, and literature. These references are called **allusions;** they help a writer to set the tone or heighten the meaning without going into a long explanation. Explain the following phrases from Barbara Huttmann's essay. Use a dictionary or other reference works to help you.

1. The "fatted calf" (para. 3) refers to the biblical parable of the Prodigal Son. If you don't remember what happens to the fatted calf, look up the parable (Luke 15:11–32), and explain why Huttmann makes this reference.
2. The "twilight zone" (para. 16) was the name of an old TV program. Do you know the show? What quality of that show is Huttmann calling on in this reference? Can you see how it fits her point?
3. "Code blue" is a medical term. You can probably figure out its general meaning from the essay. But why is it a "code," and why is the code "blue" (instead of some other color)?
4. What is the legal definition of "liable" (para. 9)? Do you think Huttmann used the word because of its legal associations?
5. The title of the essay is a variation of the phrase "crime of passion." Do you know what a crime of passion is? How does the meaning of this phrase relate to Huttmann's title?

CONSIDERING CONTENT

1. How does this selection qualify as a problem-solution essay? What problem is Huttmann presenting? What is her solution?
2. Explain what a "no-code" order is. Why wouldn't Mac's doctor issue one?
3. Huttmann says that Mac's doctor believes "we must extend life as long as we have the means and knowledge to do it." Is that what you believe? What does Huttmann believe?
4. What does the author mean by "a spiritual judge"?
5. Explain the question that ends paragraph 10.
6. Huttmann was accused of "playing God" for letting Mac die. How does she turn the accusation around in paragraph 11? According to Huttmann, who is playing God?

7. Did Huttmann commit a crime? Explain your answer.
8. Do we live in a "death-denying society," as the author claims (para. 17)? What do you think she means by this phrase?
9. Do you think Huttmann feels guilty? Why did she publicly reveal what happened?

CONSIDERING METHOD

1. Why does Huttmann begin by quoting audience members of the Phil Donahue show? Why does she return to the TV audience again in her last paragraph?
2. Why does Huttmann describe Mac on the day he entered the hospital (para. 4)? How does she use a contrast to that description in the next paragraph?
3. What contrast between doctors and nurses does the writer present in paragraph 7? How does this contrast relate to the difference of opinion about the "no-code" order (para. 9)?
4. Why does Huttmann go into so much detail about what the nurses did for Mac (paras. 6 and 7)?
5. How does Huttmann attempt to enlist sympathy for Mac's situation and for hers? Identify specific details that appeal to the readers' emotions.
6. Paragraph 11 is made up entirely of questions. Why does the author use this method of presenting these ideas?
7. What purpose do the quotations from Mac and Maura serve (paras. 6, 12, 14, and 16)?
8. Explain the irony in Huttmann's next-to-last sentence. (Irony is the use of language to express an unexpected outcome or to suggest that something is not what it seems to be.)

WRITING STEP BY STEP

Write an essay about a time when you had to make a difficult choice, one that involved a conflict of values. Perhaps a good friend asked you to give her financial and moral support for getting an abortion, and you're opposed to abortion. Or maybe your parents got divorced, and you had to choose which one to live with. Perhaps the decision involved having a beloved pet put to death, standing up for an unpopular opinion, or revealing the dishonesty of someone you liked and admired.

A. Write the essay as a first-person account.
B. Begin with a narrative of the events leading up to the moment of decision. Make the narrative come to life with quotations and concrete details.

C. Tell about making the decision. How did you solve your dilemma? Did you have to compromise?

D. Narrate in detail the sequence of events that followed your decision. Explain how you felt at the time.

E. Discuss the consequences of your decision. How did it affect you? How did it affect others? Did people support you?

F. In your conclusion, express your current feelings about the decision and its consequences. Did things turn out all right? Do you regret your decision? If you had to do it again, would you make the same choice?

OTHER WRITING IDEAS

1. Many topics of public concern are controversial because there are strong arguments on both sides of the issue. Select an important social issue, one that you're familiar with and have mixed feelings about. Write an essay entitled "My Uncertainty about _____" or "My Doubts about _____."

2. Write about a time when you performed an act of kindness or helped someone solve a problem.

3. Write an essay about the problems of being in the minority: of being a smoker in an antismoking society, of being left-handed in a world made for right-handers, of being a nondriver in a society dependent on automobiles—or something similar. Talk to other members of the minority to get more information for your essay.

EDITING SKILLS: USING SHORT SENTENCES FOR EMPHASIS

Experienced writers vary their sentences, both in structure and in length. If you look at Barbara Huttmann's sentences, you will see that most of them are at least ten words long and many are more than twenty. But sometimes she throws in a very short sentence for effect:

> There wasn't time to explain that Mac was a young, witty, macho cop who walked into the hospital with thirty-two pounds of attack equipment, looking as if he could single-handedly protect the whole city, if not the entire state [41 words]. "Can't get rid of this cough," he said [8 words]. Otherwise, he felt great [4 words].

Huttmann uses another four-word sentence in the last paragraph—"Perhaps I am guilty"—and a six-word sentence in the third paragraph: "I refused to resuscitate him again." These sentences express very important points;

they grab our attention by being noticeably different from the longer sentences around them. The other unusually short sentence in Huttmann's essay is the last one. It contains eight one-syllable words, which drive the final point home: "We do not have the right to die."

As you can see, Huttmann doesn't use short sentences very often, but when she does, she creates a strong effect. Examine the sentences in your essay. Can you find a place to use a short sentence for emphasis? Try to end a paragraph with a short statement. Also take a look at your conclusion; that's another good place to sum up the main point in a short sentence. If you can't think of a new sentence, try shortening one that you've already written.

Student Essay Using Argument

Too Bad It's Just an Ad

Amanda Davis

As I watch sexy advertisements on television, or
gaze upon them while flipping through one of my
favorite magazines, the same thought usually occurs to
me: Why can't I be like one of those people? Why
can't I graciously surrender to a man's desires
without fear of rape or retribution? Why can't I
engage in sex without worrying about pregnancy or
disease? Why can't anyone? Luckily, the answer is
much clearer than the atmosphere, but only if one
thinks straight. Sex is a very alluring tool, and
marketers everywhere know it. The challenge for all
consumers and viewers is to see past the glamour and
sensuality and realize that such advertising is not
serving our best interests.

No big secret: teenagers today are sexually
active. So it comes as no surprise that our nation
has been burdened with unwanted pregnancies, a
whirlwind of sexually transmitted diseases, and an
outbreak of sexual violence. Sure, advertising that
implies sexuality is not entirely to blame, but its
contribution is obvious. For example, in an
advertisement for Sand and Sable perfume, a ruggedly
handsome man and a voluptuously beautiful woman
embrace each other by the ocean, as he delicately
kisses her neck. She, of course, is lost in a wave of
passion, as the caption goes on to read, "Who needs
the sable?" No one, right? Just like a contraceptive
isn't needed, either, or a moment of reflection about
consequences. What's all fine when sex is insinuated
in advertising is not dandy here in the real world.
In the real world babies are born every day with no
healthy place to go, thousands are dying from
diseases stemming from unprotected sex, and men are
forcing women into sex they believe they owe. What
people in this world really do need is sexual
education and moral judgment to go along with it. In
the real world, sand just won't suffice.

As I continue to flip through my magazine, a very   3
seductive, exquisite ad captures my interest. Again, a
lovely woman is the center of desire, but this time
she is scantily dressed in only lacy lingerie. The ad
reads, "*Longing* perfume . . . makes a man remember," as
an attractive man gazes into the beautiful waves of
the ocean. "Remember what?" I ask myself. For some
odd reason, I don't think that the ad suggests that a
man remembers a family day at the beach or a
stimulating discussion that drove him wild. In this
advertising world of fantasy, the thing a man
remembers is an evening filled with lust and sexual
ecstasy. Is there anything else?

I should consider myself fortunate because very   4
seldom do I fall victim to ads like these. The
problem is, many do develop false expectations of
what impulsive sex is all about. In a nation that is
slipping further and further into corruption, it seems
clear that the producers of advertisements could take
responsibility for the messages they aim so
enticingly. And we could try not to provide such easy
targets.

Chapter 11

FURTHER READINGS

This chapter provides you with additional reading selections. Although some of these readings are developed by one controlling strategy, most of them illustrate combinations of various strategies. As you read, use the following questions to analyze how a writer combines strategies:

- What are the purpose and thesis of the essay? Who is the intended audience?
- Which strategy controls or dominates the essay?
- How does this strategy help readers to understand the essay's thesis and purpose?
- What other strategies appear in the essay?
- What do these strategies contribute to the readers' understanding of the essay's thesis and purpose?

Also keep in mind our suggestions for being an active reader: preview the selection, make predictions, pay attention to conventions, mark the text, use the dictionary, make inferences and associations, and summarize your reactions on paper. After reading the selection actively, you can then follow the process you've used in earlier chapters: first, reflect on the content; then analyze the writer's techniques; and, finally, write something of your own that relates to the reading. When possible, discuss the readings with your classmates and consult with them about your written responses.

Coming to America, to Clean

A N A   M A R I A   C O R O N A

I grew up in a *pueblito* in Sinaloa, in the countryside not far from Rosa-   1
morada. I was happy enough, but my friends always talked about getting
married or leaving town and going someplace more exciting. My friends
told me I was too pretty to stay there, that I should go where I would be
appreciated by real men, have a fine life. Even my uncle told me I should
go out into the world, not stay there. "Like a flower in the dust," he said.
But how was I to make my way?

There was one way. Go to the border and find work as a maid in a   2
foreign household. Every year some of the girls would catch the bus to
Tijuana or Ciudad Juarez and try to get jobs on the other side of the fron-
tier. Some came back to visit with nice clothes and money. Some never
came back.

My cousin Blanca was the one who first made the decision to go to   3
Tijuana. She was pretty wild, but even she wouldn't travel alone, so she
asked me to go with her. Her argument was that if we didn't leave when
we were young, we would be trapped. Our families wanted us to stay,
because they didn't want to lose us as workers and producers of more
workers. She said, "If we are going to clean house, we might as well get
paid for it." I thought about it and realized she was right. I begged my uncle
to loan me money to go to Tijuana. I had a little money of my own, and
we could stay with Blanca's aunt in Tijuana. He gave me the money but
made me promise not to tell my mother he had given it to me. I left without saying good-bye to her; I just left a letter. Blanca and I caught a ride
to Rosamorada and bought tickets to Tijuana. We were two very excited
girls, giggling but scared half to death. I'll never forget stepping off the bus
into that huge station full of men looking us over and *coyotes* offering us
rides to Los Angeles. I was very excited and glad that I had come.

Blanca found us both jobs in homes in San Diego in less than a month—   4
with the help of our aunt and a thousand of her friends, of course. That's
how it works: it's all word of mouth. Young girls move on or get married
or make enough money to go back home, so they give word to their

friends and the news passes around. There's a huge network of relatives, friends, inquiries, lost phone messages, old women carrying tales. Once Blanca and I had jobs, we had to find a way to get across the border to claim them.

Our future *patrones* were not willing to smuggle us across in their cars, which would have been the safest way for us. We would have to report to work through our own efforts.   5

We had heard the usual terrible stories of difficult crossings through dangerous terrain, of people being betrayed and sold, of people being robbed and raped and killed. But we were lucky. We met an excellent *coyote* named Javier, who said he could take us across as easily as we could cross a street downtown. He wanted $300 apiece, which my uncle said was a high price but fair enough if Javi was as good as he said. Blanca's aunt loaned her the fee and mine would be paid by my *patrones* when Javi delivered me. In return, I would work the first month for them without pay. This had all been arranged through the network of calls and whispers and customs.   6

On the night we were to go, I was terrified. If Blanca hadn't been going with me, I wouldn't have left the house. We met Javi at La Dichosa, a large open-air taco stand in lower Libertad. I was nervous and scared, and couldn't eat a thing. There were eight of us—five men in their twenties and another girl, the fiancée of one of the men. We waited in La Dichosa, everyone nervous, until after midnight. Finally a big red-and-black taxi came, and we all got in.   7

At first we seemed to be just driving around. Nobody was talking except Javi and the taxi driver. We were driving without head lights and we stopped several times while Javi and the driver stared across into the dark and said things that made no sense to me. Then we entered a short alley that led to a fence. I looked at it, wondering if I could climb it. Javi got out, walked over to the fence, and just opened it up like a door.   8

The fence had been neatly cut and hooked on nails so that the cuts could not be seen from the other side. Javi motioned us out of the taxi and through the opening in the fence. He told us, very casually, to walk behind him and keep quiet. But if he said "Drop," we were to fall flat on the ground, and if he said "Back," we should run back to the fence, where the taxi driver would be waiting to open it for us. But there was no need. We walked across the weeds like we were strolling through a park. When we reached the highway a van pulled over, Javi opened the door, and we jumped in and drove off. Javi smiled at me and said, "See? You could have worn your high heels." I realized that we were in the United States, and that I was an outlaw.   9

When we got to the parking lot where I was to meet my new *patrones,*   10
Javi walked me over to a huge blue Cadillac. The people in the car looked
like good people to me, a middle-aged couple that you could tell had been
married a long time by the way they sat.

Javi took money from the man, counted it, then told me, "Get in, go   11
with them. They just bought you for a month, a year, who knows how
long." I got in the backseat of the Cadillac, and the lady turned around and
smiled at me. She said, *"Bienvenidos."* She kept on talking to me, but I
couldn't understand her. I felt like I'd jumped off a bridge and was washing down the river. It was two weeks before Christmas. I had just turned
sixteen.

Salvation

LANGSTON HUGHES

i was saved from sin when I was going on thirteen. But not really saved. 1
It happened like this. There was a big revival at my Auntie Reed's church. Every night for weeks there had been much preaching, singing, praying, and shouting, and some very hardened sinners had been brought to Christ, and the membership of the church had grown by leaps and bounds. Then just before the revival ended, they held a special meeting for children, "to bring the young lambs to the fold." My aunt spoke of it for days ahead. That night I was escorted to the front row and placed on the mourners' bench with all the other young sinners, who had not yet been brought to Jesus.

My aunt told me that when you were saved you saw a light, and some- 2
thing happened to you inside! And Jesus came into your life! And God was with you from then on! She said you could see and hear and feel Jesus in your soul. I believed her. I had heard a great many old people say the same thing and it seemed to me they ought to know. So I sat there calmly in the hot crowded church, waiting for Jesus to come to me.

The preacher preached a wonderful rhythmical sermon, all moans and 3
shouts and lonely cries and dire pictures of hell, and then he sang a song about the ninety and nine safe in the fold, but one little lamb was left in the cold. Then he said, "Won't you come? Won't you come to Jesus? Young lambs, won't you come?" And he held out his arms to all us young sinners there on the mourners' bench. And the little girls cried. And some of them jumped up and went to Jesus right away. But most of us just sat there.

A great many old people came and knelt around us and prayed, old 4
women with jet-black faces and braided hair, old men with work-gnarled hands. And the church sang a song about the lower lights are burning, some poor sinners to be saved. And the whole building rocked with prayer and song.

Still I kept waiting to see Jesus. 5

Finally all the young people had gone to the altar and were saved, but 6
one boy and me. He was a rounder's son named Westley. Westley and I were surrounded by sisters and deacons praying. It was very hot in the

church, and getting late now. Finally Westley said to me in a whisper: "Goddamn! I'm tired o' sitting here. Let's get up and be saved." So he got up and was saved.

Then I was left all alone on the mourners' bench. My aunt came and 7 knelt at my knees and cried, while prayers and songs swirled all around me in the little church. The whole congregation prayed for me alone, in a mighty wail of moans and voices. And I kept waiting serenely for Jesus, waiting, waiting—but he didn't come. I wanted to see him, but nothing happened to me. Nothing! I wanted something to happen to me, but nothing happened.

I heard the songs and the minister saying: "Why don't you come? My 8 dear child, why don't you come to Jesus? Jesus is waiting for you. He wants you. Why don't you come? Sister Reed, what is this child's name?"

"Langston," my aunt sobbed. 9

"Langston, why don't you come? Why don't you come and be saved? 10 Oh, Lamb of God! Why don't you come?"

Now it was really getting late. I began to be ashamed of myself, hold- 11 ing everything up so long. I began to wonder what God thought about Westley, who certainly hadn't seen Jesus either, but who was now sitting proudly on the platform, swinging his knickerbockered legs and grinning down at me, surrounded by deacons and old women on their knees pray- ing. God had not struck Westley dead for taking his name in vain or for lying in the temple. So I decided that maybe to save further trouble, I'd better lie, too, and say that Jesus had come, and get up and be saved.

So I got up. 12

Suddenly the whole room broke into a sea of shouting, as they saw me 13 rise. Waves of rejoicing swept the place. Women leaped into the air. My aunt threw her arms around me. The minister took me by the hand and led me to the platform.

When things quieted down, in a hushed silence, punctuated by a few 14 ecstatic "Amens," all the new young lambs were blessed in the name of God. Then joyous singing filled the room.

That night, for the last time in my life but one—for I was a big boy 15 twelve years old—I cried. I cried, in bed alone, and couldn't stop. I buried my head under the quilts, but my aunt heard me. She woke up and told my uncle I was crying because the Holy Ghost had come into my life, and because I had seen Jesus. But I was really crying because I couldn't bear to tell her that I had lied, that I had deceived everybody in the church, and I hadn't seen Jesus, and that now I didn't believe there was a Jesus any more, since he didn't come to help me.

'I Know What I Can Do'

S H E R Y L   F L A T O W

"It was the most exciting moment of my entire life," said Curtis Pride,   1
an outfielder in the Montreal Expos organization. "It was the middle
of a pennant race, and there I was, pinch hitting with runners on first and
second base against the Philadelphia Phillies. I hit the first pitch I saw for
a two-run double. I got my first standing ovation. I was overwhelmed. As
I stood on second base and saw all those people cheering, I reflected back
on life, on how I'd come a long way."

Curtis Pride is deaf. He was born with a 95 percent hearing loss. In his   2
left ear he wears a hearing aid that amplifies sound and enables him to hear
voices, though not clearly. But Pride has never allowed his lack of hearing
to deter him from pursuing his dreams. In September 1993, after eight years
in the minor leagues, he made it to Montreal. On Sept. 17, in only his
second at-bat, he got his first major-league hit. It helped spark the second-
place Expos to a come-from-behind victory over the first-place Phillies.

"My parents encouraged me that I could do anything," Pride said. "But   3
I'm also very confident. I know what I'm capable of doing."

How did Pride develop such unshakable confidence? How did the will   4
to succeed evolve into success? Those were the things I set out to discover
when I interviewed Curtis and his parents at the family home in Silver
Spring, Maryland.

Pride, 25, is gracious, good-humored and completely at ease in talking   5
about his deafness. He is a superb lip-reader, and his speech, though not
entirely fluid, is clear. (Last season, he appeared on a radio call-in show in
Montreal. The host lip-synched the questions, and Pride responded without missing a beat.)

Curtis is the only son of Sallie and John Pride, who also have two   6
daughters. The household is further enlivened by a little girl named Leonda,
whom the Prides are adopting. They are a warm, handsome and determined family. "I knew for a long time that Curt had a special talent," said
his father. "I intended to make sure Curt saw it too, that he believed in
himself."

Curtis was found to be deaf at 6 months. The Prides immediately   7
enrolled him in a special program at the hospital, which he attended once
a week for three years, and after that in a free program offered by the public
school system in Montgomery County, Maryland. The couple also began
to educate themselves on how to create an environment for their son that
would enable him to succeed academically and socially. "We read a lot," said
Sallie. "We talked a lot, especially to other parents with deaf children. That
was really helpful. They tell you the truth."

Sallie, a registered nurse, decided to stay at home with her son. John is   8
a specialist in disabilities with the U.S. Department of Health and Human
Services. "I got into disability work as a byproduct of Curt being born
deaf," he said.

One of the early and most crucial decisions Sallie and John made was   9
to have Curtis not learn sign language. "When you introduce kids to sign
language, they tend to rely on it, and it hinders their oral growth," John
explained. "We wanted Curt to rely on oral communication."

Curtis was fitted with a hearing aid as a baby. He worked with a speech   10
therapist from infancy through high school. His parents also helped teach
him to say words and, later, sentences. "There were days my mom would
hold up a ball," he recalled, "and she would say the word 'ball' over and over.
I would read her lips, and I could sort of 'hear' what it sounded like. I'd
put those two things together until I could say the word."

Curtis looks back at his first few years in school as the most difficult time   11
of his life. "Kids were always making fun of me," he said, "of the way I
talked, of the funny thing in my ear. I had a hard time dealing with it. I
used to come home angry, and I would cry all the time."

"By the second or third grade, he realized that he had fallen way behind   12
other children in spoken language," said John. "It became apparent to him
that he was not going to catch up. That's when he had to come to terms
with his deafness."

"My parents would reassure me, but they wouldn't let me feel sorry for   13
myself," said Curtis. "They helped me understand that this was the way I
was born, and there was nothing I could do about it. So I had to get on
with my life." Both Curtis and his parents agreed that this happened in the
fourth grade.

It helped tremendously that he was already a gifted athlete, excelling in   14
soccer, basketball, baseball, football, and other sports. "People wanted me on
their team," said Curtis.

Soon, no one was making fun of him. "I never heard any kid make a   15
cruel remark," said John, who took turns with Sallie accompanying their
son to practice sessions to make sure Curtis understood whatever instructions he was given. "The coaches would not have tolerated any nonsense.

Later on, when he began playing against different kids, his reputation was such that if someone had resorted to making remarks about him, that person would have been ridiculed by his teammates."

Curtis also became a top-notch student. Prior to entering the seventh 16 grade, he decided he wanted to be mainstreamed—against the recommendations of the auditory staff of his county. "I wanted to be more independent," he said. "It was a challenge for me. I would be the only deaf person in the whole school." Still, he conceded, "I was nervous and shy. I wondered how people would treat me."

But the kids and the teachers were supportive. And though his parents 17 always made sure the teachers knew what he needed, Sallie said, "Curt had an inner drive to succeed. He motivated himself. We never said, 'Now; Curt, you've got to practice, you've got to do your homework.' He did it on his own."

Curtis graduated from John F. Kennedy High School with a 3.6 aver- 18 age. He starred in three sports and earned *Parade* all-American honors as a striker for the soccer team. "I've worked hard at everything I've done," he said, "whether it's classwork or sports. I want to be the best at everything I do."

After high school, Pride was drafted by the New York Mets. He also had 19 the opportunity to attend the College of William and Mary on a basketball scholarship. "My parents and I agreed it was important for me to get an education," he said. "There's no guarantee of making it in professional sports. So I worked out an agreement with the Mets that allowed me to go to college full-time and play in the minor leagues in the summers." Following his graduation in 1990 with a degree in finance, Pride turned his undivided attention to baseball.

Pride was in the Mets organization for seven years but batted just .251. 20 "While I was in college, my playing time was limited," he said. "That hurt my development a lot. But I have no regrets." Pride became a minor-league free agent at the end of the 1992 season, and he signed with the Expos that December. "I needed to get a fresh start," he said.

Pride approaches the game much the same as a hearing person. He even 21 joked that his deafness can be an advantage at bat. "The crowd noise won't get to me," he said. "I'm able to maintain my full concentration." When he plays center field, he said, "We have one simple rule: Any time I call for the ball, it's automatically mine. If someone else calls for it, he'll wave me off with a glove."

The key for Pride, always, is to keep his eyes on the ball. As a result, he 22 said, he is probably more visually astute than most ballplayers. Prior to the 1993 season, he worked at length with a sports vision trainer, in order to fine-tune his visual skills even further.

Despite getting four hits in nine at-bats with the Expos last fall, Pride   23
is now with the Ottawa Lynx, a Montreal farm team. Regardless of how
his career turns out, he's already a hero to many people. Pride firmly
believes in giving back to others, and these are not just words: Following
the '92 season, he worked as an instructional aide in a special-education
class. "I helped the children with their schoolwork and tried to build their
confidence," said Pride. "I shared my experiences with them. It gave me
great satisfaction to see them do well in school, to see them feel good
about themselves."

Pride said he wants to inspire as many people as he can—and not just   24
those with disabilities. "I want inner-city children to know they have no
excuse for not being successful," said Pride. "They see people like me, and
they see that I overcame a handicap. I never let my deafness hold me back.
I never feel sorry for myself. Never. I know I have a disability. I've accepted
it. I can't worry about it. I want to make the most of my life. And I am."

Thank You

A L E X   H A L E Y

•t was 1943, during World War II, and I was a young U.S. coastguardsman, 1
1serial number 212-548, a number we never seem to forget. My ship, the
USS *Murzim,* had been under way for several days. Most of her holds
contained thousands of cartons of canned or dried foods. The other holds
were loaded with five-hundred-pound bombs packed delicately in padded
racks. Our destination was a big base on the Island of Tulagi in the South
Pacific.

I was one of the *Murzim's* several cooks and, quite the same as for folk 2
ashore, this Thanksgiving morning had seen us busily preparing a traditional dinner featuring roast turkey.

Well, as any cook knows, it's a lot of hard work to cook and serve a big 3
meal, and clean up and put everything away. But finally around sundown,
with our whole galley crew just bushed, we finished at last and were free
to go flop into our bunks in the fo'c'sle.

But I decided first to go out on the *Murzim's* afterdeck for a breath of 4
open air. I made my way out there, breathing in great, deep draughts while
walking slowly about, still wearing my white cook's hat and the long apron,
my feet sensing the big ship's vibrations from the deep-set, turbine diesels
and my ears hearing that slightly hissing sound the sea makes in resisting
the skin of a ship.

I got to thinking about Thanksgiving. In reflex, my thoughts registered 5
the historic imagery of the Pilgrims, Indians, wild turkeys, pumpkins, corn
on the cob and the rest.

Yet my mind seemed to be questing for something else—some way that 6
I could personally apply to the waning Thanksgiving. It must have taken
me a half hour to sense that maybe some key to an answer could result from
reversing the word "Thanksgiving"—at least that suggested a verbal direction, "Giving thanks."

Giving thanks—as in praying, thanking God, I thought. Yes, of course. 7
Certainly.

Yet my mind continued nagging me. Fine. But something else. 8

After awhile, like a dawn's brightening, a further answer did come—that 9
there were *people* to thank, people who had done so much for me that I
could never possibly repay them. The embarrassing truth was I'd always just
accepted what they'd done, taken all of it for granted. Not one time had I
ever bothered to express to any of them so much as a simple, sincere
"Thank you."

At least seven people had been particularly and indelibly helpful to me. 10
I realized, with a gulp, that about half of them had since died—so they were
forever beyond any possible expression of gratitude from me. The more I
thought about it, the more ashamed I became. Then I pictured the three
who were still alive and, within minutes, I was down in the fo'c'sle.

Sitting at a mess table with writing paper and memories of things each 11
had done, I tried composing genuine statements of heartfelt appreciation
and gratitude to my dad, Simon A. Haley, a professor at the old AMNC
(Agricultural Mechanical Normal College) in Pine Bluff, Ark., now a
branch of the University of Arkansas; to my grandma, Cynthia Palmer, back
in our little home town of Henning, Tenn.; and to the Rev. Lonual Nelson,
my grammar school principal, retired and living in Ripley, six miles north
of Henning.

I couldn't even be certain if they would recall some of their acts of years 12
past, acts that I vividly remembered and saw now as having given me vital
training, or inspiration, or directions, if not all of these desirables rolled into
one.

The texts of my letters began something like, "Here, this Thanksgiving 13
at sea, I find my thoughts upon how much you have done for me, but I
have never stopped and said to you how much I feel the need to thank
you—." And briefly I recalled for each of them specific acts performed in
my behalf.

For instance, something uppermost about my father was how he had 14
impressed upon me from boyhood to love books and reading. In fact, this
graduated into a family habit of after-dinner quizzes at the table about
books read most recently and new words learned. My love of books never
diminished and later led me toward writing books myself. So many times
I have felt a sadness when exposed to modern children so immersed in the
electronic media that they have little to no awareness of the wondrous
world to be discovered in books.

I reminded the Reverend Nelson how each morning he would open our 15
little country town's grammar school with a prayer over his assembled
students. I told him that whatever positive things I had done since had
been influenced at least in part by his morning school prayers.

In the letter to my grandmother, I reminded her of a dozen ways she 16
used to teach me how to tell the truth, to be thrifty, to share, and to be

forgiving and considerate of others. (My reminders included how she'd make me pull switches from a peach tree for my needed lesson.) I thanked her for the years of eating her good cooking, the equal of which I had not found since. (By now, though, I've reflected that these peerless dishes are most gloriously flavored with a pinch of nostalgia.) Finally I thanked her simply for having sprinkled my life with stardust.

Before I slept, my three letters went into our ship's office mail sack. They got mailed when we reached Tulagi Island.

We unloaded cargo, reloaded with something else, then again we put to sea in the routine familiar to us, and as the days became weeks, my little personal experience receded. Sometimes, when we were at sea, a mail ship would rendezvous and bring us mail from home, which, of course, we accorded topmost priority.

Every time the ship's loudspeaker rasped, "Attention! Mail call!" two-hundred-odd shipmates came pounding up on deck and clustered about the raised hatch atop which two yeomen, standing by those precious bulging gray sacks, were alternately pulling out fistfuls of letters and barking successive names of sailors who were, in turn, hollering "Here! Here!" amid the jostling.

One "mail call" brought me responses from Grandma, Dad, and the Reverend Nelson—and my reading of their letters left me not only astounded, but more humbled than before.

Rather than saying they would forgive that I hadn't previously thanked them, instead, for Pete's sake, they were thanking *me*—for having remembered, for having considered they had done anything so exceptional.

Always the college professor, my dad had carefully avoided anything he considered too sentimental, so I knew how moved he was to write me that, after having helped educate many young people, he now felt that his best results included his own son.

The Reverend Nelson wrote that his decades as a "simple, old-fashioned principal" had ended with grammar schools undergoing such swift changes that he had retired in self-doubt. "I heard more of what I had done wrong than what I did right," he said, adding that my letter had brought him welcome reassurance that his career had been appreciated.

A glance at Grandma's familiar handwriting brought back in a flash memories of standing alongside her white wicker rocking chair, watching her "settin' down" some letter to relatives. Frequently touching her pencil's tip to pursed lips, character by character, each between a short, soft grunt, Grandma would slowly accomplish one word, then the next, so that a finished page would consume hours. I wept over the page representing my Grandma's recent hours invested in expressing her loving gratefulness to *me*—whom she used to diaper!

Much later, retired from the Coast Guard and trying to make a living 25
as a writer, I never forgot how those three "thank you" letters gave me an
insight into something nigh mystical in human beings, most of whom go
about yearning in secret for more of their fellows to express appreciation
for their efforts.

I discovered in time that, even in the business world, probably no two 26
words are more valued than "thank you," especially among people at stores,
airlines, utilities, and others that directly serve the public.

Late one night, I was one of a half-dozen passengers who straggled weary 27
and grumbling off a plane that had been forced to land at the huge
Dallas/Fort Worth Airport. Suddenly, a buoyant, cheerful, red-jacketed
airline man waved us away from the regular waiting room seats, saying,
"You sure look bushed. I know a big empty office where you can stretch
out while you wait." And we surely did. When the weather improved
enough for us to leave, "Gene Erickson" was in my notebook and, back
home, I wrote the president of that airline describing his sensitivity and his
courtesy. And I received a thank you!

I travel a good deal on lecture tours and I urge students especially to 28
tell their parents, grandparents, and other living elders simply "thank you"
for all they have done to make possible the lives they now enjoy. Many
students have told me they found themselves moved by the response. It is
not really surprising, if one only reflects how it must feel to be thanked
after you have given for years.

Now, approaching Thanksgiving of 1982, I have asked myself what will 29
I wish for all who are reading this, for our nation, indeed for our whole
world—since, quoting a good and wise friend of mine, "In the end we are
mightily and merely people, each with similar needs." First, I wish for us,
of course, the simple common sense to achieve world peace, that being
paramount for the very survival of our kind.

And there is something else I wish—so strongly that I have had this line 30
printed across the bottom of all my stationery: *"Find the good—and praise it."*

Computercide: A Reality in Our New Age of Frustration

ELLEN GOODMAN

the story came over the AP wire in one pristine paragraph. There it was, the Zeitgeist honed down to a solitary police blotter entry: 1

"A man was coaxed out of his home in Issaquah, Wash., by police officers after he pulled a gun and shot several times at his personal computer, apparently in frustration." 2

Who could resist a tale of computercide? Who among us who had ever booted up, crashed or freaked out could have done anything but exhale a resounding "YESSS!" for the man who pumped lead into his hard drive. "Apparently in frustration." 3

I for one taped this onto my personal computer as a cautionary tale. You might even call it a warning shot across the bow—or in this case, the mouse—directed at the computer gods that lie within: Don't you interface the wrong way with me, pal. 4

Now I do not usually applaud domestic violence. Nor can I imagine shooting a gun at hard or software. After all, there are so many other weapons available. As Dan Gookin, the author of *Word for Dummies,* writes, "I'm a firm believer in baseball bat therapy for computers." Bats will do the trick. 5

But no jury of his peers will ever convict this Issaquah man of premeditated computercide. Not when there is a plea of justified computercide or even self-defense. 6

Jury of his peers? This is a moment in history when millions of his peers are engaged in simultaneous sink-or-swimming. We are at the low end of the learning curve. And more than occasionally reaching the end of our cyberrope. 7

As you may have guessed, I am one of this miserable multitude. This summer I "upgraded" my computer to several levels above my head. I've now opened a new bleak Window on life. Opening Windows 97 is like opening windows in 1976 in the movie *Network* when everyone yelled into the air, "I'm mad as hell, and I'm not going to take it anymore." 8

Of course, there are some people who find this learning process easy. 9
These people are (1) below 25 years old, (2) employed residents of Seattle,
or (3) linguists who recently learned Urdu from teachers whose native
language is Mandarin.

New software is simple for those who understand at first reading the 10
meaning of instructions such as: "To Show Files with Hidden or System
Attributes Click the View Menu and then check the Show Hidden/System
Files check box." That handy tip can be located under something called
"Help."

It is equally simple for the guru who comes to solve your problem, takes 11
over your chair, and demonstrates the right moves at a triple-RAM speed
you can neither follow nor duplicate.

The rest of us, however, are experiencing what Avram Miller, the vice 12
president of Intel, describes with astounding understatement as the "pain
of ownership issues." We went looking for a tool, not a toy. We regard
bells and whistles as hassles. We are feeling computercidal. "Apparently in
frustration."

I was promised that within days I would be "calibrating your joystick" 13
and getting it on with the "new Hardware wizard."

In fact, I am slogging it out with the mouse and the file manager. I still 14
don't know what or where my joystick is, but I swear (frequently) that it's
overrated.

Like millions of people, I have been convinced to invest—waste?— 15
untold hours—days? weeks?—in order to become more productive.

I am struggling to learn a new way to do what I used to do the old way 16
so that I can once again work with everybody else who is also learning a
new way in order to work with me.

Soon, no doubt, I will have to learn a newer way. 17

This is progress. This is what is called "user-friendly." And this is one of 18
the great pickup lines of the late 20th century.

User-friendly? A friend does not require absolutely literal instructions. 19
A friend does not destroy your self-esteem. A friend, most assuredly, does
not lose three chapters of a book. And then say it's your own fault.

As for user-hostile, well, the very week that the man from Issaquah was 20
dragged off by the police for a mental health check, there was a report
about the public health dangers of aggressive drivers behind the wheel.

But that's nothing compared to the public health dangers of frustrated 21
drivers at the keyboard.

No, I don't think that computer killing will become the random 22
violence of the next decade. But just in case, I'm going to pin another sign
on my PC: "Before you shoot, back up."

The Discus Thrower

R I C H A R D   S E L Z E R

I spy on my patients. Ought not a doctor to observe his patients by any 1
means and from any stance, that he might the more fully assemble
evidence? So I stand in the doorways of hospital rooms and gaze. Oh, it is
not all that furtive an act. Those in bed need only look up to discover me.
But they never do.

From the doorway of Room 542 the man in the bed seems deeply 2
tanned. Blue eyes and close-cropped white hair give him the appearance
of vigor and good health. But I know that his skin is not brown from the
sun. It is rusted, rather, in the last stage of containing the vile repose within.
And the blue eyes are frosted, looking inward like the windows of a snowbound cottage. This man is blind. This man is also legless—the right leg
missing from midthigh down, the left from just below the knee. It gives him
the look of a bonsai, roots and branches pruned into the dwarfed facsimile of a great tree.

Propped on pillows, he cups his right thigh in both hands. Now and then 3
he shakes his head as though acknowledging the intensity of his suffering.
In all of this he makes no sound. Is he mute as well as blind?

The room in which he dwells is empty of all possessions—no get-well 4
cards, small, private caches of food, day-old flowers, slippers, all the usual
kick-shaws of the sickroom. There is only the bed, a chair, a nightstand, and
a tray on wheels that can be swung across his lap for meals.

"What time is it?" he asks. 5
"Three o'clock." 6
"Morning or afternoon?" 7
"Afternoon." 8
He is silent. There is nothing else he wants to know. 9
"How are you?" I say. 10
"Who is it?" he asks. 11
"It's the doctor. How do you feel?" 12
He does not answer right away. 13
"Feel?" he says. 14

"I hope you feel better," I say. 15

I press the button at the side of the bed. 16

"Down you go," I say. 17

"Yes, down," he says. 18

He falls back upon the bed awkwardly. His stumps, unweighted by legs 19
and feet, rise in the air, presenting themselves. I unwrap the bandages from
the stumps, and begin to cut away the black scabs and the dead, glazed fat
with scissors and forceps. A shard of white bone comes loose. I pick it away.
I wash the wounds with disinfectant and redress the stumps. All this while,
he does not speak. What is he thinking behind those lids that do not blink?
Is he remembering a time when he was whole? Does he dream of feet?
Of when his body was not a rotting log?

He lies solid and inert. In spite of everything, he remains impressive, as 20
though he were a sailor standing athwart a slanting deck.

"Anything more I can do for you?" I ask. 21

For a long moment he is silent. 22

"Yes," he says at last and without the least irony. "You can bring me a 23
pair of shoes."

In the corridor, the head nurse is waiting for me. 24

"We have to do something about him," she says. "Every morning he 25
orders scrambled eggs for breakfast, and, instead of eating them, he picks
up the plate and throws it against the wall."

"Throws his plate?" 26

"Nasty. That's what he is. No wonder his family doesn't come to visit. 27
They probably can't stand him any more than we can."

She is waiting for me to do something. 28

"Well?" 29

"We'll see," I say. 30

The next morning I am waiting in the corridor when the kitchen deliv- 31
ers his breakfast. I watch the aide place the tray on the stand and swing it
across his lap. She presses the button to raise the head of the bed. Then she
leaves.

In time the man reaches to find the rim of the tray, then on to find the 32
dome of the covered dish. He lifts off the cover and places it on the stand.
He fingers across the plate until he probes the eggs. He lifts the plate in
both hands, sets it on the palm of his right hand, centers it, balances it. He
hefts it up and down slightly, getting the feel of it. Abruptly he draws back
his right arm as far as he can.

There is the crack of the plate breaking against the wall at the foot of his 33
bed and the small wet sound of the scrambled eggs dropping to the floor.

And then he laughs. It is a sound you have never heard. It is something 34
new under the sun. It could cure cancer.

Out in the corridor, the eyes of the head nurse narrow.   35

"Laughed, did he?"   36

She writes something down on her clipboard.   37

A second aide arrives, brings a second breakfast tray, puts it on the night-   38
stand, out of his reach. She looks over at me shaking her head and making
her mouth go. I see that we are to be accomplices.

"I've got to feed you," she says to the man.   39

"Oh, no you don't," the man says.   40

"Oh, yes I do," the aide says, "after the way you just did. Nurse says so."   41

"Get me my shoes," the man says.   42

"Here's oatmeal," the aide says. "Open." And she touches the spoon to   43
his lower lip.

"I ordered scrambled eggs," says the man.   44

"That's right," the aide says.   45

I step forward.   46

"Is there anything I can do?" I say.   47

"Who are you?" the man asks.   48

In the evening I go once more to that ward to make my rounds. The   49
head nurse reports to me that Room 542 is deceased. She has discovered
this quite by accident, she says. No, there had been no sound. Nothing. It's
a blessing, she says.

I go into his room, a spy looking for secrets. He is still there in his bed.   50
His face is relaxed, grave, dignified. After a while, I turn to leave. My gaze
sweeps the wall at the foot of the bed, and I see the place where it has been
repeatedly washed, where the wall looks very clean and very white.

On Natural Death

L E W I S   T H O M A S

there are so many new books about dying that there are now special $\quad$ 1
shelves set aside for them in bookshops, along with the health-diet and
home-repair paperbacks and the sex manuals. Some of them are so packed
with detailed information and step-by-step instructions for performing the
function that you'd think this was a new sort of skill which all of us are
now required to learn. The strongest impression the casual reader gets, leaf-
ing through, is that proper dying has become an extraordinary, even an
exotic experience, something only the specially trained get to do.

Also, you could be led to believe that we are the only creatures capable $\quad$ 2
of the awareness of death, that when all the rest of nature is being cycled
through dying, one generation after another, it is a different kind of process,
done automatically and trivially, more "natural," as we say.

An elm in our backyard caught the blight this summer and dropped $\quad$ 3
stone dead, leafless, almost overnight. One weekend it was a normal-looking
elm, maybe a little bare in spots but nothing alarming, and the next weekend it was gone, passed over, departed, taken. Taken is right, for the tree
surgeon came by yesterday with his crew of young helpers and their cherry
picker, and took it down branch by branch and carted it off in the back of
a red truck, everyone singing.

The dying of a field mouse, at the jaws of an amiable household cat, is $\quad$ 4
a spectacle I have beheld many times. It used to make me wince. Early in
life, I gave up throwing sticks at the cat to make him drop the mouse,
because the dropped mouse regularly went ahead and died anyway, but I
always shouted unaffections at the cat to let him know the sort of animal
he had become. Nature, I thought, was an abomination.

Recently, I've done some thinking about that mouse, and I wonder if $\quad$ 5
his dying is necessarily all that different from the passing of our elm. The
main difference, if there is one, would be in the matter of pain. I do not
believe that an elm tree has pain receptors, and even so, the blight seems
to me a relatively painless way to go even if there were nerve endings in
a tree, which there are not. But the mouse dangling tail-down from the

teeth of a gray cat is something else again, with pain beyond bearing, you'd think, all over his small body.

There are now some plausible reasons for thinking it is not like that at all, and you can make up an entirely different story about the mouse and his dying if you like. At the instant of being trapped and penetrated by teeth, peptide hormones are released by cells in the hypothalamus and the pituitary gland; instantly these substances, called endorphins, are attached to the surfaces of other cells responsible for pain perception; the hormones have the pharmacologic properties of opium; there is no pain. Thus it is that the mouse seems always to dangle so languidly from the jaws, lies there so quietly when dropped, dies of his injuries without a struggle. If a mouse could shrug, he'd shrug.

I do not know if this is true or not, nor do I know how to prove it if it is true. Maybe if you could get in there quickly enough and administer naloxone, a specific morphine antagonist, you could turn off the endorphins and observe the restoration of pain, but this is not something I would care to do or see. I think I will leave it there, as a good guess about the dying of a cat-chewed mouse, perhaps about dying in general.

Montaigne had a hunch about dying, based on his own close call in a riding accident. He was so badly injured as to be believed dead by his companions, and was carried home with lamentations, "all bloody, stained all over with the blood I had thrown up." He remembers the entire episode, despite having been "dead, for two full hours," with wonderment:

> It seemed to me that my life was hanging only by the tip of my lips. I closed my eyes in order, it seemed to me, to help push it out, and took pleasure in growing languid and letting myself go. It was an idea that was only floating on the surface of my soul, as delicate and feeble as all the rest, but in truth not only free from distress but mingled with that sweet feeling that people have who have let themselves slide into sleep. I believe that this is the same state in which people find themselves whom we see fainting in the agony of death, and I maintain that we pity them without cause. . . . In order to get used to the idea of death, I find there is nothing like coming close to it.

Later, in another essay, Montaigne returns to it:

> If you know not how to die, never trouble yourself; Nature will in a moment fully and sufficiently instruct you; she will exactly do that business for you; take you no care for it.

The worst accident I've ever seen was on Okinawa, in the early days of the invasion, when a jeep ran into a troop carrier and was crushed nearly flat. Inside were two young MPs, trapped in bent steel, both mortally hurt, with only their heads and shoulders visible. We had a conversation while people with the right tools were prying them free. Sorry about the accident, they said. No, they said, they felt fine. Is everyone else okay, one of them said. Well, the other one said, no hurry now. And then they died.

Pain is useful for avoidance, for getting away when there's time to get 10 away, but when it is end game, and no way back, pain is likely to be turned off, and the mechanisms for this are wonderfully precise and quick. If I had to design an ecosystem in which creatures had to live off each other and in which dying was an indispensable part of living, I could not think of a better way to manage.

GLOSSARY

Abstract words: language that refers to ideas, conditions, and qualities that cannot be observed directly through the five senses. Words such as *beauty, love, joy, wealth, cruelty, power,* and *justice* are abstract. In his essay (p. 109), Isaac Asimov explores the abstract term "intelligence," offering a series of concrete examples and incidents to make the meaning clearer. *Also see* Concrete words.

Active reading: the process of getting involved with the reading material. An active reader surveys the text, makes predictions, writes questions and responses in the margins, rereads difficult passages, and spends time afterward summarizing and reflecting.

Allusion: a passing reference to a familiar person, place, or object in history, myth, or literature. Writers use allusions to enrich or illuminate their ideas. For instance, in her essay on cultural heritage, Barbara Ehrenreich mentions the "flight from Egypt" (p. 122), an allusion to the biblical story of the Israelites' deliverance from slavery in Egypt and their search for the Promised Land. And when Suzanne Britt mentions "Never-Never Land" (p. 183), she alludes to the imaginary land in *Peter Pan.*

Analogy: a comparison that uses a familiar or concrete item to explain an abstract or unfamiliar concept. For example, a geologist may compare the structure of the earth's crust to the layers of an onion, or a biologist may explain the anatomy of the eye by comparing it to a camera.

Anecdote: a brief story about an amusing or interesting event, usually told to illustrate an idea or support a point. Writers also use anecdotes to begin essays, as Barbara Huttmann does in "A Crime of Compassion" (p. 307) or Caroline Miller does in "Civil Rites" (p. 89).

Antonym: a word that has the opposite meaning of another word. For example, *wet* is an antonym of *dry; coarse* is an antonym of *smooth; cowardly* is an antonym of *brave.*

Argument: a type of writing in which the author tries to influence the reader's thinking on a controversial topic. See the introduction to Chapter 10.

Audience: the readers for whom a piece of writing is intended. Many essays are aimed at a general audience, but a writer can focus on a specific group of readers. For example, Arthur Ashe directs his essay "Send Your Children to the Libraries" (p. 300) to the parents of young African-American males, while Richard Gray, Jr., is addressing pet owners in "Flea Facts" (p. 224).

Block pattern: an organizational pattern used in comparison-and-contrast writing. In this method, a writer presents, in a block, all the important points about the first item to be compared and then presents, in another block, the corresponding points about the second item to be compared.

Brainstorming: a method for generating ideas for writing. In brainstorming, a writer jots down a list of as many details and ideas on a topic as possible without stopping to evaluate or organize them.

Causes: the reasons or explanations for why something happens. Causes can be *immediate* or *remote.* See the introduction to Chapter 9.

Chronological order: the arrangement of events according to time—that is, in the sequence in which they happened.

Classification: the process of sorting items or ideas into meaningful groups or categories. See the introduction to Chapter 6.

Cliché: a phrase or expression that has lost its originality or force through overuse. To illustrate, novelist and teacher Janet Burroway writes: "Clichés are *the last word* in bad writing, and it's *a crying shame* to see all you *bright young things* spoiling your *deathless prose* with phrases *as old as the hills.* You must *keep your nose to the grindstone,* because the *sweet smell of success* only comes to those who *march to the tune of a different drummer.*"

Coherence: the logical flow of ideas in a piece of writing. A writer achieves coherence by having a clear thesis and by making sure that all the supporting details relate to that thesis. *Also see* Unity.

Colloquial language: conversational words and expressions that are sometimes used in writing to add color and authenticity. Dave Barry (p. 115) and Mike Royko (p. 40) use colloquial language to good effect in their writing. *Also see* Informal writing.

Comparison and contrast: a pattern of writing in which an author points out the similarities and differences between two or more subjects. See the introduction to Chapter 7.

Conclusion: the sentences and paragraphs that bring an essay to its close. In the conclusion, a writer may restate the thesis, sum up important ideas, emphasize the topic's significance, make a generalization, offer a solution to a problem, or encourage the reader to take some action. Whatever the strategy, a conclusion should end the essay in a firm and definite way.

Concrete words: language that refers to real objects that can be seen, heard, tasted, touched, or smelled. Words like *tree, desk, car, orange, Chicago, Roseanne,* or *jogging* are concrete. Concrete examples make abstractions easier to understand, as in "Contentment is a well-fed cat asleep in the sun." *Also see* Abstract words.

Connotation and denotation: terms used to describe the different kinds of meaning that words convey. **Denotation** refers to the most specific or direct meaning of a word—the dictionary definition. **Connotations** are the feelings or associations that attach themselves to words. For example, *assertive* and *pushy* share a similar denotation—both mean "strong" or "forceful." But their differing connotations suggest different attitudes: an assertive person is admirable; a pushy person is offensive.

Controlling idea: *See* Thesis.

Conventions: customs or generally accepted practices. The conventions of writing an essay require a title, a subject, a thesis, a pattern of organization, transitions, and paragraph breaks.

Definition: a method of explaining a word or term so that the reader understands what the writer means. Writers use a variety of methods for defining words and terms; see the introduction to Chapter 5.

Denotation: *See* Connotation and denotation.

Dependent clause: a group of words that contains a subject and verb but does not stand alone as a sentence. For example, *until the game ended* is a dependent clause; its complete meaning depends on being attached to an independent clause: *Few fans stayed until the game ended. Also see* Independent clause.

Derivation: the historical origin and development of a word. For instance, the English word *verbiage* (meaning "too many words") comes from the French word *verbier* meaning "to chatter." *Also see* Root.

Description: writing that uses sensory details to create a word picture for the reader. See the introduction to Chapter 3.

Details: specific pieces of information (examples, incidents, dates, statistics, descriptions, and the like) that explain and support the general ideas in a piece of writing.

Development: the techniques and materials that a writer uses to expand and build on a general idea or topic.

Dialogue: speech or conversation recorded in writing. Dialogue, which is commonly found in narrative writing, reveals character and adds life and authenticity to an essay.

Diction: choice of words in writing or speaking.

Division: the process of breaking a large subject into its components or parts. Division is often used in combination with classification. See the introduction to Chapter 6.

Editing: the final stage of the writing process during which the writer focuses on correcting and improving the details of punctuation, spelling, word choice, and format.

Effects: the results or outcomes of certain events. Effects can be *immediate* or *long term*. Writers often combine causes and effects in explaining why something happens. See the introduction to Chapter 9.

Ellipsis: an omission of words that is signaled by three equally spaced dots.

Emphasis: the placement of words and ideas in key positions to give them stress and importance. A writer can emphasize a word or idea by putting it at the beginning or end of a paragraph or essay. Emphasis can also be achieved by using repetition and figurative language to call attention to an idea or term.

Essay: a short prose work on a limited topic. Essays can take many forms, but they usually focus on a central theme or thesis and often convey the writer's personal ideas about the topic.

Evidence: *See* Supporting material.

Example: a specific case or instance used to illustrate or explain a general concept. See the introduction to Chapter 4.

Fable: a brief narrative that teaches a lesson or truth.

Figurative language: words that create images or convey symbolic meaning beyond the literal level. Richard Selzer, for example, uses figurative language to portray the dramatic, often agonizing experiences of a practicing surgeon: "And the blue eyes are frosted, looking inward like the windows of a snowbound cottage" (see "The Discus Thrower," p. 332).

Figures of speech: deliberate departures from the ordinary, literal use of words in order to provide fresh perceptions and create lasting impressions. *See* Metaphor, Paradox, Personification, *and* Simile.

First person: the use of *I, me, we,* and *us* in speech and writing to express a personal view or present a firsthand report. *Also see* Point of view.

Focus: the narrowing of a topic to a specific aspect or set of features.

Freewriting: a procedure for exploring a topic that involves writing without stopping for a set period of time.

Generalization: a broad assertion or conclusion based on specific observations. The value of a generalization is determined by the number and quality of the specific instances.

Generic nouns: the name of a class of people, like *doctor, teacher, student, player, citizen, juror, consumer, reader, author,* and so forth. The use of such nouns in the singular to designate a whole class or group causes problems with pronoun selection. For example, a sentence like "Each applicant is responsible for scheduling his own interview" seems to ignore or exclude female applicants. This same point can be expressed without relying on the masculine pronoun (*his*): "Each applicant is responsible for scheduling his or her own interview," or "Applicants are responsible for scheduling their own interviews."

Homophone: a word that sounds the same as another but is different in spelling and meaning. *Knew* and *new* are homophones of each other.

Illustration: the use of examples, or a single long example, to support or explain an idea. See the introduction to Chapter 4.

Imagery: descriptions that appeal to our senses of sight, smell, sound, touch, or taste. Imagery adds interest and clarifies meaning.

Imperative sentence: a sentence that gives a command or a direction. Imperative sentences usually begin with a verb; they are often used in writing about a process: "Snap the knee up to the chest as close as possible"; "Leave enough space after the complimentary close to sign your name"; "Don't forget to proofread your final copy."

Independent clause: a group of words that contains a subject and verb and can stand alone as a sentence.

Inference: a conclusion drawn by a reader from the hints and suggestions provided by the writer. Writers sometimes express ideas indirectly rather than stating them outright; readers must use their own experience and knowledge to read between the lines and make inferences to gather the full meaning of a selection.

Informal writing: the familiar, everyday level of usage, which includes contractions and perhaps slang but requires standard grammar and punctuation.

Interrupter: a word or phrase that interrupts the normal flow of a sentence without changing the basic meaning. Interrupters are usually set off from the rest of the sentence with commas: "Magnum Oil Company, *our best client,* canceled its account." "Being lucky, *it seems to me,* is better than being smart."

Introduction: the beginning or opening of an essay, which usually presents the topic, arouses interest, and prepares the reader for the development of the thesis.

Irony: the use of words to express the opposite of what is stated. Writers use irony to expose unpleasant truths or to poke fun at human weakness.

Jargon: the specialized or technical language of a trade, profession, or similar group. To readers outside the group, however, jargon is nonsensical and meaningless.

Journalistic style: the kind of writing found in newspapers and popular magazines. It normally employs informal diction with relatively simple sentences and unusually short paragraphs. Many of the selections in this book first appeared as columns and articles in magazines or newspapers.

Logical order: arrangement of points and ideas according to some reasonable principle or scheme (e.g., from least important to most important).

Main idea: *See* Thesis.

Metaphor: a figure of speech in which a word or phrase that ordinarily refers to one thing is applied to something else, thus making an implied comparison. For example, Mark Twain writes of "the language of this water" and says the river "turned to blood" ("Two Views of the Mississippi," pp. 175–76). Similarly, Judith Ortiz Cofer refers to Mamá's room as "the heart of the house" (p. 55), and Scott Russell Sanders writes about "the narrow, ironclad days of fathers" and "what a prison a house could be" (p. 191).

A **dead metaphor** is an implied comparison that has become so familiar that we accept it as literal: the arm of a chair, the leg of a table.

Modes: *See* Patterns of organization.

Narration: writing that recounts an event or series of interrelated events; presentation of a story in order to illustrate an idea or make a point. See the introduction to Chapter 3.

Objective and subjective: terms that refer to the way a writer handles a subject. Objective writing presents the facts without including the writer's own feelings and attitudes. Subjective writing, on the other hand, reveals the author's personal opinions and emotions.

Onomatopoeia: the use of words that suggest or echo the sounds they are describing—*hiss, plop,* or *sizzle,* for example.

Order: the sequence in which the information or ideas in an essay are presented. *Also see* Chronological order *and* Logical order.

Paradox: a seeming contradiction that may nonetheless be true. For example, "Less is more" or "The simplest writing is usually the hardest to do."

Paragraph: a series of two or more related sentences. Paragraphs are units of meaning; they signal a division or shift in thought. In newspapers and magazines, paragraph divisions occur more frequently, primarily to break up the narrow columns of print and make the articles easier to read.

Parallelism: the presentation of two or more equally important ideas in similar grammatical form. In his essay "Send Your Children to the Libraries" (p. 300), Arthur Ashe emphasizes his thesis by using parallel structure: "I have become convinced that we blacks spend *too much time on the playing fields* and *too little time in the libraries.*" He also uses parallelism to make other points forceful and memorable: "Somehow, parents must instill *a desire for learning* alongside *the desire to be Walt Frazier*"; "*While we are about 35 percent of* major league baseball, *we are less than 2 percent of* the engineers. *While we are 40 percent of* the National Football League, *we are less than 11 percent of* construction workers such as carpenters and bricklayers."

Patterns of organization: strategies for presenting and developing ideas in writing. Some of these patterns relate to basic ways of thinking (classification, cause and effect, argumentation), whereas others reflect the most common means for presenting material (narration, comparison-contrast, process) or developing ideas (example and illustration, definition, description) in writing.

Person: *See* Point of view.

Personification: a figure of speech in which an inanimate object or an abstract concept is given human qualities. For example, "Hunger sat shivering on the road"; "Flowers danced on the lawn." In "Two Views of the Mississippi" (p. 175), Mark Twain refers to the "river's face" and describes the river as a subtle and dangerous enemy.

Persuasion: writing that attempts to move readers to action or to influence them to agree with a position or belief.

Point-by-point pattern: an organizational pattern used in comparison-and-contrast writing. In this method (also called the *alternating method*), the writer moves back and forth between the two subjects, focusing on particular features of each in turn: the first point or feature of subject *A* is followed by the first point or feature of subject *B*, and so on.

Point of view: the angle or perspective from which a story or topic is presented. Personal essays often take a first-person (or "I") point of view and sometimes address the reader as "you" (second person). The more formal third person ("he," "she," "it," "one," "they") is used to create distance and suggest objectivity.

Prefix: a syllable or syllables used at the beginning of a word to change or add to the meaning. For example, prefixes change *mature* to **im***mature* and **pre***mature;* and *form* can be expanded to **in***form,* **re***form,* **per***form,* **de***form,* **trans***form,* **uni***form,* and **mis***inform. See also* Root *and* Suffix.

Previewing: the first step in active reading in which the reader prepares to read by looking the text over and making preliminary judgments and predictions about what to expect.

Prewriting: the process that writers use to prepare for the actual writing stage by gathering information, considering audience and purpose, developing a provisional thesis, and mapping out a tentative plan.

Problem-solution: a strategy for analyzing and writing about a topic by identifying a problem within the topic and offering a solution or solutions. See the introduction to Chapter 10.

Process writing: a pattern in which the author explains the step-by-step procedure for doing something. See the introduction to Chapter 8.

Proper noun: a noun that names a single particular person, place, or historical event, and is written with a capital letter: Carlo, Warsaw, Mexico, Garfield, the Holocaust.

Purpose: the writer's reasons for writing; what the writer wants to accomplish in an essay.

Refutation: in argumentation, the process of acknowledging and responding to opposing views. See the introduction to Chapter 10.

Revision: the stage in the writing process during which the author makes changes in focus, organization, development, style, and mechanics to make the writing more effective.

Rhetorical question: a question that a writer or speaker asks to emphasize or introduce a point and usually goes on to answer. Barbara Ehrenreich uses a number of rhetorical questions in her essay "Cultural Baggage" (p. 121).

Root: the stem or base of a word; the element that carries the primary meaning of a word. The Latin word *videre,* meaning "to see," is the root of such English words as *video, vista, vision, visionary,* and *revision. See also* Derivation.

Satire: writing that uses wit and irony to attack and expose human folly, weakness, and stupidity. Dave Barry (p. 115) and Kathleen Fury (p. 136) use satire to question human behavior and criticize contemporary values.

Sentence: *See* Independent clause.

Sexist language: words and phrases that stereotype or ignore members of either sex. For example, the sentence "A doctor must finish his residency before he can begin to practice" suggests that only men are doctors. Writing in the plural will avoid this exclusion: "Doctors must finish their residencies before they can begin to practice." Terms like *mailman, stewardess, manpower,* and *mothering* are also sexist; try to use gender-neutral terms instead: *mail carrier, flight attendant, workforce, parenting.*

Simile: a figure of speech in which two essentially unlike things are compared, usually in a phrase introduced by *like* or *as.* For example, in "More Room" (p. 54) Judith Ortiz Cofer says the house is *"like* a chambered nautilus" and that "it rested on its perch *like* a great blue bird, more *like* a nesting hen. . . ."

Slang: the informal language of a given group or locale, often characterized by racy, colorful expressions and short-lived usage.

Standard English: the language written or spoken by most educated people.

Structure: the general plan, framework, or pattern of a piece of writing.

Style: individuality of expression, achieved in writing through selection and arrangement of words, sentences, and punctuation.

Subject: what a piece of writing is about.

Subjective: *See* Objective and subjective.

Subordination: the process of expressing less important ideas in dependent clauses and combining them with independent clauses. For example, the independent statement, "Tim heard a noise" can be subordinated and combined with "Tim began to run" by using the subordinator *when:* "Tim began to run *when he heard a noise.*"

Suffix: a syllable or syllables added to the end of a word to change or affect the meaning. For example, suffixes change *love* to *loved, lover, lovable, loveless, loving,* and *lovely. See also* Prefix *and* Root.

Supporting material: facts, figures, details, examples, reasoning, expert testimony, personal experiences, and the like, which are used to develop and explain the general ideas in a piece of writing.

Symbol: a concrete or material object that suggests or represents an abstract idea, quality, or concept. The lion is a symbol of courage; a voyage or journey can symbolize life; water suggests spirituality; dryness stands for the absence of spirituality. In Richard Selzer's "The Discus Thrower" (p. 332), the stumps of the patient's amputated legs can be seen as symbols of human helplessness and immobility.

Synonym: a word that means the same or nearly the same as another word. *Sad* is a synonym of *unhappy. See also* Antonym.

Thesis: the main point or proposition that a writer develops and supports in an essay. The thesis is often stated early, normally in the first paragraph, to give the reader a clear indication of the essay's main idea.

Third person: the point of view in which a writer uses *he, she, it, one,* and *they* to give the reader a less-limited and more seemingly objective account than a first-person view would provide. *See also* Point of view.

Title: the heading a writer gives to an article or essay. The title usually catches the reader's attention and indicates what the selection is about.

Tone: the attitude that a writer conveys toward the subject matter. Tone can be serious or humorous, critical or sympathetic, affectionate or hostile, sarcastic or soothing, passionate or detached—or any of numerous other attitudes.

Topic sentence: the sentence in which the main idea of a paragraph is stated. Writers often state the topic sentence first and develop the rest of the paragraph in support of this main idea. Sometimes a writer will build up to the topic sentence and place it at the end of a paragraph.

Transitions: words and expressions such as *for example, on the other hand, next,* or *to illustrate* that help the reader to see the connections between points and ideas.

Unity: the fitting together of all elements in a piece of writing; sticking to the point. *Also see* Coherence.

Usage: the accepted manner of using language.

Voice: the expression of a writer's personality in his or her writing; an author's distinctive style or manner of writing.

Wordiness: the use of roundabout expressions and unnecessary words, such as "majoring in the field of journalism" instead of "majoring in journalism"; or "these socks, which are made of wool" instead of "these wool socks"; or "in this day and age" instead of "today"; or "at this point in time" instead of "now."

Writing process: the series of steps that most writers follow in producing a piece of writing. The five major stages in the writing process are finding a subject (prewriting), focusing on a main idea and mapping out an approach (planning), preparing a rough draft (writing), reworking and improving the draft (revising), and correcting errors (editing).

CREDITS

Arthur Ashe, "Send Your Children to the Libraries" from *The New York Times* (February 6, 1977). Copyright © 1977 by The New York Times Company. Reprinted with the permission of The New York Times.

Isaac Asimov, "What Is Intelligence Anyway?" Copyright © by Isaac Asimov. Reprinted with the permission of the Estate of Isaac Asimov, c/o Ralph M. Vicinanza, Ltd.

Russell Baker, "Learning to Write" from *Growing Up*. Copyright © 1982 by Russell Baker. Reprinted with the permission of NTC/Contemporary Publishing Group.

Dave Barry, "When It Comes to Chewing the Fat, We're Obsessive." Reprinted with the permission of the author.

Suzanne Britt, "Neat People vs. Sloppy People" from *Show and Tell*. Copyright © 1983 by Suzanne Britt. Reprinted with the permission of the author.

Paul Chance, "I'm OK; You're a Bit Dull" from *Psychology Today* (July/August 1988). Copyright © 1988 Sussex Publishers, Inc. Reprinted with the permission of Psychology Today Magazine.

Judith Ortiz Cofer, "More Room" from *Silent Dancing: A Partial Remembrance of a Puerto Rican Childhood*. Copyright © 1990 by Judith Ortiz Cofer. Reprinted with the permission of Arte Publico Press/University of Houston.

Ana Maria Corona, "Coming to America, to Clean" from *Harper's Magazine* (April 1993). Reprinted by permission.

Ronald Dahl, "Burned Out and Bored" from *Newsweek* (December 18, 1997). Copyright © 1997 by Newsweek, Inc. Reprinted with the permission of Newsweek. All rights reserved.

Barbara Ehrenreich, "Cultural Baggage" from *The Snarling Citizen: Essays*. Copyright © 1992 by Barbara Ehrenreich. Reprinted with the permission of Farrar, Straus & Giroux, Inc.

David Elkind, "Types of Stress for Young People" from *All Grown Up and No Place to Go*. Copyright © 1988 by David Elkind. Reprinted with the permission of Addison-Wesley Longman.

Sheryl Flatow, "I Know What I Can Do" from *Parade* (August 7, 1994). Copyright © 1994 by Sheryl Flatow. Reprinted with the permission of the author.

Kathleen Fury, "It's Only a Paper World" from *Working Woman* (August 1986). Copyright © 1986 by Kathleen Fury. Reprinted with the permission of the author.

Daniel Golden, "How to Make Your Dendrites Grow and Grow" from *Life* (July 1994). Copyright © 1994 by Time, Inc. Reprinted with the permission of Time Life Syndication.

Ellen Goodman, "Computercide: A Reality in Our New Age of Frustration" from *The Boston Globe* (July 31, 1997). Copyright © 1997 by The Boston Newspaper Co./Washington Post Writers Group. Reprinted with the permission of The Washington Post Writers Group.

Richard Gray, Jr., "Flea Facts" from *Cats* (June 1994). Copyright © 1994 by Richard Gray, Jr. Reprinted with the permission of the author.

Alex Haley, "Thank You" from *Parade* (November 21, 1982). Copyright © 1982 by Alex Haley. Reprinted with the permission of the Estate of Alex Haley.

William Least Heat-Moon, "Wind" from *Prairyerth: Portraits from Chase County, Kansas*. Copyright © 1991 by William Least Heat-Moon. Reprinted with the permission of Houghton Mifflin Company. All rights reserved.

Langston Hughes, "Salvation" from *The Big Sea*. Copyright © 1940 by Langston Hughes, renewed © 1968 by Arna Bontemps and George Houston Bass. Reprinted with the permission of Hill and Wang, a division of Farrar, Straus & Giroux, Inc.

Barbara Huttmann, "A Crime of Compassion" from *Newsweek* (August 8, 1983). Copyright © 1983 by Barbara Huttmann. Reprinted with the permission of the author.

Garrison Keillor, "How to Write a Personal Letter" from *We Are Still Married*. Copyright © 1989 by Garrison Keillor. Reprinted with the permission of the Ellen Levine Literary Agency.

Stephen King, "Why We Crave Horror Movies" from *Playboy* (1982). Copyright © 1982 by Stephen King. Reprinted with the permission of Arthur B. Greene. All rights reserved.

Charles Krauthammer, "Of Headless Mice . . . and Men: The Ultimate Cloning Horror: Human Organ Farms" from *Time* (January 19, 1998). Copyright © 1998 by Time, Inc. Reprinted with the permission of Time Life Syndication.

Charles Kuralt, "Down with Forests" from *Dateline America*. Copyright © 1979 by CBS, Inc. Reprinted with the permission of Harcourt Brace and Company.

INDEX